Jonathan Edwards

Christian Love as manifested in the Heart and Life

Jonathan Edwards

Christian Love as manifested in the Heart and Life

ISBN/EAN: 9783743330832

Manufactured in Europe, USA, Canada, Australia, Japa

Cover: Foto ©Lupo / pixelio.de

Manufactured and distributed by brebook publishing software (www.brebook.com)

Jonathan Edwards

Christian Love as manifested in the Heart and Life

CHRISTIAN LOVE,

AS MANIFESTED IN THE HEART AND LIFE.

BY

JONATHAN EDWARDS,

SOMETIME PASTOR OF THE CHURCH AT NORTHAMPTON, MASSACHUSETTS,
AND PRESIDENT OF THE COLLEGE OF NEW JERSEY.

EDITED FROM THE ORIGINAL MANUSCRIPT

BY THE REV. TRYON EDWARDS, D. D.

SIXTH AMERICAN EDITION.

PHILADELPHIA:
PRESBYTERIAN BOARD OF PUBLICATION,
1334 CHESTNUT STREET.

INTRODUCTION.

PERHAPS no person ever lived, who more habitually and carefully committed his thoughts, on almost every subject, to writing, than the elder President Edwards. His ordinary studies were pursued, pen in hand, and with his note-books before him; and he not only often stopped, in his daily rides, by the way side, but frequently rose even at midnight, to commit to paper any important thought that occurred to him.

As the result of this habit, his manuscripts are perhaps as thoroughly the record of the intellectual life of their author, as those of almost any individual who has a name in either the theological or literary world. These manuscripts are also very numerous. The seventeenth century was an age of voluminous authorship. The works of Bishop Hall amount to ten volumes octavo; Lightfoot's to thirteen; Jeremy Taylor's, to fifteen; Dr. Goodwin's, to twenty; Owen's, to twenty-eight; while Baxter's would extend to some sixty volumes, or from thirty to forty thousand closely printed octavo pages. The writings of Edwards, if all that he wrote were published, would be more voluminous than the works of any of these writers, if possibly the last two be excepted. A large part of his unpublished manuscripts have been carefully preserved and kept together; and some years since, were committed to the editor of this work, as sole permanent trustee, by all the then surviving grandchildren of their author.

Included in these manuscripts are various papers, of interest and value, that have never been given to the public, among which are the Lectures contained in this volume. These Lectures were first preached by Mr. Edwards in 1738, in a series of sermons to the people of his charge in Northampton, and were apparently designed by himself for publication; for they were written out in full, and soon after they were completed he began his discourses on the "History of Redemption," which, it is known, he intended should be published. After his death they were selected for publication by Dr. Hopkins and Dr. Bellamy; and were, in part, copied out and prepared for the press, when, for some reason, their preparation was interrupted, so that now, for the first time, they are given to the public.

The subject of these Lectures is eminently practical and important. LOVE is the first outgoing of the renewed soul to God; "We *love* him because he first loved us." It is the true evidence of a saving work of grace in the soul; "The fruit of the Spirit is *love*." It lies at the very foundation of Christian character; we are "rooted and grounded in *love*." It is the path in which all the true children of God are found; they "walk in *love:*" the bond of their mutual union; their hearts are "knit together in *love:*" their protection in the spiritual warfare; they are to put on "the breast-plate of *love:*" the fulness and completeness of their Christian character; they are "made perfect in *love:*" the spirit through which they may fulfil all the divine acquirements; for "*love* is the fulfilling of law:" and that by which they may become like their Father in heaven, and fitted for his presence; for "God is love," and *Heaven is a world of* LOVE.

As to the character of the Lectures, it is sufficient in a word to say, that they are marked throughout, by that strong and clear thought, those broad and comprehensive views of truth, that thorough knowledge of human nature, and that accurate and familiar acquaintance with the Scriptures, which characterize the works of their distinguished author. It is believed they will at once take rank with his well-known works on the "Will," the "Affections," and "Redemption," and be deemed as valuable in their *practical* bearings, as the first is in its *metaphysical*, the second in its *experimental*, or the third in its *historical*. Of these Lectures, as of all his works, it may be said, as Johnson said to Boswell when asked by the latter, "What works of Baxter's he should read?" "Read all, for they are all excellent."

T. E.

PREFACE

TO THE SIXTH AMERICAN EDITION.

THIS work, under the title of "CHARITY AND ITS FRUITS," or "CHRISTIAN LOVE, AS MANIFESTED IN THE HEART AND LIFE," was first published, from the original manuscripts, in 1851. It was republished in England in 1852. After that, several editions were issued in this country, when the work was purchased by a Christian gentleman of wealth and culture, with the express view of printing it for distribution as a means of doing good. He had himself been so impressed with its great value as a treatise on the Christian spirit and life that he intended to issue edition after edition, at his own expense, for gratuitous circulation in every part of the land. On second thought, however, he liberally presented the stereotype plates to the PRESBYTERIAN BOARD OF PUBLICATION, so arranging with them as to be able to carry out his design, while, at the same time, the work, in their hands, might have a more extended circulation, and thus be the means of greater good.

From the day of its first publication, the work has received the highest testimonials to its value from numbers of those best qualified to judge. One of our ablest writers says: "This new work from the great mind and heart of Edwards needs from me no word of commendation. I find in it the same exhaustive analysis, the same earnest spirituality, and the same wonderful familiarity with the Bible and the human heart, which distinguish his great work on the 'Affections.' How true to the high standard of gospel truth! How full of the richest practical lessons! How affectionately severe to the reader's soul!" And John Angell James once said to an American clergyman, "Had I seen this noble work of Edwards before I published on the same subject, I should hardly have allowed my work ('Christian Charity Explained') to go to the press. It is admirable—every word of it!" One Christian gentleman, a man of thought and culture, writes, "I keep 'CHARITY AND ITS FRUITS' on my table, next to my Bible;" while another, a minister of ripe experience and extensive reading, says, "I hardly know a book that has interested or profited me more. I find, on looking over my copy, that I have marked with my pencil, as striking or instructive, more passages than there are pages to the book!"

Similar testimonies, from various sources, might easily be multiplied. But the work will best speak for itself. Published, as it now is, by the PRESBYTERIAN BOARD OF PUBLICATION, as one of its standard works, it is earnestly commended to the divine blessing, and to the prayerful study of the reader.

OCTOBER, 1872.

CONTENTS.

LECTURE I.
ALL TRUE GRACE IN THE HEART, SUMMED UP IN CHARITY, OR LOVE 1

LECTURE II.
CHARITY, OR LOVE, MORE EXCELLENT THAN THE EXTRAORDINARY GIFTS OF THE SPIRIT . . 38

LECTURE III.
ALL THAT CAN BE DONE OR SUFFERED, IN VAIN WITHOUT CHARITY OR LOVE 73

LECTURE IV.
CHARITY MEEK IN BEARING EVIL AND INJURIES . 96

LECTURE V.
CHARITY CHEERFUL AND FREE IN DOING GOOD . 139

LECTURE VI.

THE SPIRIT OF CHARITY, THE OPPOSITE OF AN ENVIOUS SPIRIT 161

LECTURE VII.

THE SPIRIT OF CHARITY, AN HUMBLE SPIRIT . . 185

LECTURE VIII.

THE SPIRIT OF CHARITY, THE OPPOSITE OF A SELFISH SPIRIT 226

LECTURE IX.

THE SPIRIT OF CHARITY, THE OPPOSITE OF AN ANGRY OR WRATHFUL SPIRIT 268

LECTURE X.

THE SPIRIT OF CHARITY, THE OPPOSITE OF A CENSORIOUS SPIRIT 294

LECTURE XI.

ALL TRUE GRACE IN THE HEART TENDS TO HOLY PRACTICE IN THE LIFE 318

LECTURE XII.

CHARITY WILLING TO UNDERGO ALL SUFFERINGS FOR CHRIST 361

LECTURE XIII.

ALL THE CHRISTIAN GRACES CONNECTED AND MUTUALLY DEPENDENT 386

LECTURE XIV.

CHARITY, OR TRUE GRACE, NOT TO BE OVERTHROWN BY OPPOSITION 410

LECTURE XV.

THE HOLY SPIRIT FOREVER TO BE COMMUNICATED TO THE SAINTS, IN CHARITY OR LOVE . . . 439

LECTURE XVI.

HEAVEN A WORLD OF CHARITY OR LOVE . . 463

LECTURE I.

CHARITY, OR LOVE THE SUM OF ALL VIRTUE.

"Though I speak with the tongues of men and of angels, and have not charity, I am become as sounding brass, or a tinkling cymbal. And though I have the gift of prophesy, and understand all mysteries, and all knowledge; and though I have all faith, so that I could remove mountains, and have not charity, I am nothing. And though I bestow all my goods to feed the poor, and though I give my body to be burned, and have not charity, it profiteth me nothing."—1 CORINTHIANS xiii. 1-3.

IN these words we observe—*First*, that some thing is spoken of as of special importance, and as peculiarly essential in Christians, which the Apostle calls CHARITY. And this charity, we find, is abundantly insisted on in the New Testament by Christ, and his apostles,—more insisted on, indeed, than any other virtue.

But, then, the word "charity," as used in the New Testament, is of much more extensive signification, than as it is used generally in common discourse. What persons very often mean by "charity," in their ordinary conversation, is a disposition to hope and think the best of others, and to put a good construction on their words and behavior; and sometimes the word is used for a disposition to give to the poor. But these things are only certain particular branches, or fruits of that great virtue of charity which is so much insisted on throughout the New Testament. The word properly signifies *love*, or *that disposition or affection whereby one is dear to another;* and the original ("agape"), which is here translated "*charity*," might better have been rendered "*love*," for that is the proper English of it: so that by charity in the New Testament, is meant the very same thing as Christian love; and though it be more frequently used for love to men, yet sometimes it is used to signify not only love to men, but love to God. So it is manifestly used by the Apostle in this epistle, as he explains himself in chapter viii. 1—"Knowledge puffeth up, but charity edifieth," &c. Here the comparison is between knowledge and charity—and the preference is given to charity, because knowledge puffeth up, but charity edifieth. And then, in the next two verses, it is more particularly explained how knowledge usually puffs up, and why charity edifieth; so that what is called *charity* in the first verse, is called *loving God* in the third, for the very same thing is evidently spoken of in the two places. And doubtless the apostle means the same thing by charity in this thirteenth chapter, that he does in the eighth; for he is here comparing the same two things together that he was there, viz.: knowledge and charity. "Though I have all knowledge and have not charity, I am nothing;" and again, "charity never faileth, but —knowledge, it shall vanish away." So that by charity here, we are doubtless to understand *Christian love* in its full extent, and whether it be exercised toward God, or our fellow-creatures.

And this charity is here spoken of, as that which is, in a distinguishing manner, the great and essential thing: which will appear more fully when we observe, *Secondly*, what things are mentioned as being in vain without it, viz.: the most excellent things that ever belong to natural men; the most excellent privileges, and the most excellent performances. *First*, the most excellent privileges, such as preaching with tongues, the gift of prophecy, understanding all mysteries, faith to remove mountains, &c.; and *Secondly*, the most excellent performances, such as giving all one's goods to feed the poor, and the body to be burned, &c. Greater things than these, no natural man ever had or did, and they are the kind of things in which men are exceedingly prone to trust; and yet the apostle declares that if we have them all, and have not charity, we are nothing. The doctrine taught, then, is this:

THAT ALL THE VIRTUE THAT IS SAVING, AND THAT DISTINGUISHES TRUE CHRISTIANS FROM OTHERS, IS SUMMED UP IN CHRISTIAN LOVE. This appears from the words of the text, because so many other things are mentioned that natural men may have, and the things mentioned are of the highest kind it is possible they should have, both of privilege and performance, and yet it is said they all avail nothing without this, whereas if any of them were saving, they would avail something without it.

And by the apostle's mentioning so many and so high things, and then saying of them all that they profited nothing without charity, we may justly conclude, that there is nothing at all that avails anything without it. Let a man have what he will, and do what he will, it signifies nothing without charity, which surely implies that charity is the great thing, and that everything which has not charity in some way contained or implied in it is nothing, and that this charity is the life and soul of all religion, without which all things that wear the name of virtues are empty and vain.

In speaking to this doctrine, I would first notice the nature of this divine love, and then show the truth of the doctrine respecting it. And

I. *I would speak of the nature of a truly Christian love.* And here I would observe

1. *That all true Christian love is one and the same in its principle.* It may be various in its forms and objects, and may be exercised either toward God or men, but it is the same principle in the heart that is the foundation of every exercise of a truly Christian love, whatever may be its object. It is not with the holy love in the heart of the Christian, as it is with the love of other men. Their love toward different objects, may be from different principles and motives, and with different views; but a truly Christian love is different

from this. It is one as to its principle, whatever the object about which it is exercised; it is from the same spring or fountain in the heart, though it may flow out in different channels and diverse directions, and therefore it is all fitly comprehended in the one name of *charity,* as in the text. That this Christian love is one, whatever the objects toward which it may flow forth, appears by the following things :—

First, It is all *from the same Spirit* influencing the heart. It is from the breathing of the same Spirit that true Christian love arises, both toward God and man. The Spirit of God is a Spirit of love, and when the former enters the soul, love also enters with it. God is love, and he that has God dwelling in him by his Spirit, will have love dwelling in him also. The nature of the Holy Spirit is love; and it is by communicating himself, in his own nature, to the saints, that their hearts are filled with divine charity. Hence we find that the saints are partakers of the divine nature, and Christian love is called the "love of the Spirit," Romans xv. 30, and "love in the Spirit," Col. i. 8, and the very bowels of love and mercy seem to signify the same thing with the fellowship of the Spirit, Phil. ii. 1. It is that Spirit, too, that infuses love to God, Rom. v. 5; and it is by the indwelling of that Spirit, that the soul abides in love to God and man, 1 John, xiv. 12, 13; and iii. 23, 24. And,

Second, Christian love both to God and man, is *wrought in the heart by the same work of the Spirit.* There are not two works of the Spirit of God, one to infuse a spirit of love to God, and the other to infuse a spirit of love to men, but in producing one, the Spirit produces the other also. In the work of conversion, the Holy Spirit renews the heart by giving it a divine temper; Eph. iv. 23, and it is one and the same divine temper thus wrought in the heart, that flows out in love both to God and man. And,

Third, When God and man are loved with a truly Christian love, they are both loved *from the same motives.* When God is loved aright, he is loved for his excellency, and the beauty of his nature, especially the holiness of his nature; and it is from the same motive that the saints are loved, for holiness' sake. And all things that are loved with a truly holy love, are loved from the same respect to God. Love to God is the foundation of gracious love to men; and men are loved, either because they are in some respect like God in the possession of his nature and spiritual image, or because of the relation they stand in to him as his children or creatures—as those who are blessed of him, or to whom his mercy is offered, or in some other way from regard to him. Only remarking that though Christian love be one in its principle, yet it is distinguished and variously denominated in two ways, with respect to its objects, and the kinds of its exercise, as for example, its degrees, &c. I now proceed,

II. *To show the truth of the doctrine, that all virtue that is saving or distinguishing of true Christians, is summed up in Christian love.* And,

1. *We may argue this from what reason teaches of the nature of love.* And if we duly consider its nature, two things will appear.

First, That love will *dispose to all proper acts of respect to both God and man.* This is evident because a true respect to either God or man *consists* in love. If a man sincerely loves God, it will dispose him to render all proper respect to him; and men need no other incitement to show each other all the respect that is due, than love. Love to God will dispose a man to honor him, to worship and adore him, and heartily to acknowledge his greatness, and glory, and dominion. And so it will dispose to all acts of obedience to God; for the servant that loves his master, and the subject that loves his sovereign, will be disposed to proper subjection and obedience. Love will dispose the Christian to behave toward God, as a child to a father; amid difficulties to resort to him for help, and put all his trust in him; just as it is natural for us, in case of need or affliction, to go to one that we love for pity and help. It will lead us, too, to give credit to his word, and to put confidence in him; for we are not apt to suspect the veracity of those we have entire friendship for. It will dispose us to praise God for the mercies we receive from him, just as we are disposed to gratitude for any kindness we receive from our fellow-men that we love. Love, again, will dispose our hearts to submission to the will of God, for we are more willing that the will of those we love should be done, than of others. We naturally desire that those we love should be suited, and that we should be agreeable to them·

and true affection and love to God will dispose the heart to acknowledge God's right to govern, and that he is worthy to do it, and so will dispose to submission. Love to God will dispose us to walk humbly with him, for he that loves God will be disposed to acknowledge the vast distance between God and himself. It will be agreeable to such an one, to exalt God, and set him on high above all, and to lie low before him. A true Christian delights to have God exalted on his own abasement, because he loves him. He is willing to own that God is worthy of this, and it is with delight that he casts himself in the dust before the Most High, from his sincere love to him.

And so a due consideration of the nature of love will show that it disposes men to all duties toward their neighbors. If men have a sincere love to their neighbors, it will dispose them to all acts of justice toward those neighbors—for real love and friendship always dispose us to give those we love their due, and never to wrong them. Rom. xiii. 10. "Love worketh no ill to his neighbor." And the same love will dispose to truth toward neighbors, and will tend to prevent all lying, and fraud, and deceit. Men are not disposed to exercise fraud and treachery toward those they love; for thus to treat men is to treat them like enemies, but love destroys enmity. Thus the apostle, makes use of the oneness that there ought to be among Christians, as an argument to induce them to truth between man and man. Ephesians iv. 25. Love will dispose to walk humbly amongst men, for a real and true love will incline us to high thoughts of others, and to think them better than ourselves. It will dispose men to honor one another, for all are naturally inclined to think highly of those they love, and to give them honor; so that by love are fulfilled those precepts, 1 Peter xi. 17, "Honor all men," and Phil. ii. 3, "Let nothing be done through strife or vain glory, but in lowliness of mind, let each esteem other better than themselves." Love will dispose to contentment in the sphere in which God hath placed us, without coveting any things that our neighbor possesses, or envying him on account of any good thing that he has. It will dispose men to meekness and gentleness in their carriage toward their neighbors, and not to treat them with passion, or violence, or heat of spirit, but with moderation, and calmness, and kindness. It will check and restrain everything like a bitter spirit; for love has no bitterness in it, but is a gentle and sweet disposition and affection of the soul. It will prevent broils and quarrels, and will dispose men to peaceableness, and to forgive injurious treatment received from others; as it is said in Proverbs x. 12, "Hatred stirreth up strifes, but love covereth all sins."

Love will dispose men to all acts of mercy toward their neighbors when they are under any affliction or calamity, for we are naturally disposed to pity those that we love when they are afflicted. It will dispose men to give to the poor, to bear one another's burdens, and to weep with those that weep, as well as to rejoice with those that do rejoice. It will dispose men to the duties they owe to one another in their several places and relations. It will dispose a people to all the duties they owe to their rulers, and to give them all that honor and subjection which are their due. And it will dispose rulers to rule the people over whom they are set, justly, seriously and faithfully, seeking their good, and not any by-ends of their own. It will dispose a people to all proper duty to their ministers, to hearken to their counsels and instructions, and to submit to them in the house of God, and to support and sympathize with and pray for them as those that watch for their souls; and it will dispose ministers faithfully and ceaselessly to seek the good of the souls of their people, watching for them as those that must give account. Love will dispose to suitable carriage between superiors and inferiors: it will dispose children to honor their parents, and servants to be obedient to their masters, not with eye service, but in singleness of heart; and it will dispose masters to exercise gentleness and goodness toward their servants.

Thus love would dispose to all duties both toward God, and toward man. And if it will thus dispose to all duties, then it follows, that it is the root, and spring, and, as it were, a comprehension of all virtues. It is a principle, which if it be implanted in the heart, is alone sufficient to produce all good practice; and every right disposition toward God and man is summed up in it, and comes from it, as the fruit from the tree, or the stream from the fountain.

Second, Reason teaches that *whatever performances or seeming virtues there are without love, are unsound and hypocritical.* If there be no love in what men do, then there is no true respect to God or men in their conduct; and if so, then certainly there is no sincerity. Religion is nothing without proper respect to God. The very notion of religion among mankind, is, that it is the creature's exercise and expression of such respect toward the creator. But if there be no true respect or love, then all that is called religion is but a seeming show, and there is no real religion in it, but it is unreal and vain. Thus if a man's faith be of such a sort that there is no true respect to God in it, reason teaches that it must be in vain; for if there be no love to God in it, there can be no true respect to him. From this it appears that love is al ways contained in a true and living faith, and that it is its true and proper life and soul, without which, faith is as dead as the body is without its soul; and that it is that which especially distinguishes a living faith from every other: but of this more particularly hereafter. Without love to God, again, there can be no true honor to him. A man is never hearty in the honor he seems to render to another whom he does not love; so that all the seeming honor or worship that is ever paid without love, is but hypocritical. And so reason teaches that there is no sincerity in the obedience that is performed without love, for if there be no love, nothing that is done can be spontaneous and free, but all must be forced. So without love, there can be no hearty submission to the will of God, and there can be no real and cordial trust and confidence in him. He that does not love God will not trust him: he never will, with true acquiescence of soul, cast himself into the hands of God, or into the arms of his mercy.

And so whatever good carriage there may be in men toward their neighbors, yet reason teaches that it is all unacceptable and in vain if at the same time there be no real respect in the heart toward those neighbors; if the outward conduct is not prompted by inward love. And from these two things taken together, viz., that love is of such a nature that it will produce all virtues, and dispose to all duties to God and men, and that without it there can be no sincere virtue, and no duty at all properly performed, the truth of the doctrine follows, that all true and distinguishing Christian virtue and grace may be summed up in love. In the

2. *The Scriptures teach us that love is the sum of all that is contained in the law of God, and of all the duties required in his word.* This the Scriptures teach of the law in general, and of each table of the law in particular.

First, The Scriptures teach this *of the law and word of God in general.* By the law, in the Scriptures, is sometimes meant the whole of the written word of God, as in John x. 34. " Is it not written in your law, I said ye are gods?" And sometimes by the law is meant the five books of Moses, as in Acts xxiv. 14, where it is named with the distinction of the "law" and the "prophets." And sometimes by the law, is meant the ten commandments, as containing the sum of all the duty of mankind, and all that is required as of universal and perpetual obligation. But whether we take the law as signifying only the ten commandments, or as including the whole written word of God, the Scriptures teach us that the sum of all that is required in it is love. Thus when by the law is meant the ten commandments, it is said in Romans xiii. 8, "He that loveth another hath fulfilled the law;" and therefore several of the commandments are rehearsed, and it is added, in the tenth verse, that "love" (which leads us to obey them all,) "is the fulfilling of the law." Now unless love was the sum of what the law requires, the law could not be wholly fulfilled in love; for a law is fulfilled only by obedience to the sum or whole of what it contains and enjoins. So the same apostle again declares, 1. Timothy, i. 5, "Now the end of the commandment is charity out of a pure heart, and of a good conscience, and of faith unfeigned, &c." Or if we take the law in a yet more extensive sense, as the whole written word of God, the Scriptures still teach us, that love is the sum of all that is required in it. In Matthew xxii. 40, Christ teaches, that on the two precepts of loving God with all the heart, and our neighbor as ourselves, hang all the law and the prophets; i. e. all the written word of God; for what was then called the law and the prophets, was the whole written word of God that was then extant. And,

Second, The Scriptures teach the same thing *of each table of the law in particular.* The command " Thou shalt love the Lord thy God with all thy heart," is declared by Christ, Matthew xxii. 38, to be the sum of the first table of the law, or the first great commandment; and in the next verse, to love our neighbor as ourself, is declared to be the sum of the second table ; as it is, also, in Romans xiii. 9, where the precepts of the second table of the law are particularly specified : and it is then added, " And if there be any other commandment, it is briefly comprehended in this saying, namely, Thou shalt love thy neighbor as thyself." And so in Galatians v. 14, " For all the law is fulfilled in one word, even in this, Thou shalt love thy neighbor as thyself." And the same seems to be stated in James ii. 8, "If ye fulfil the royal law, according to the Scripture, Thou shalt love thy neighbor as thyself, ye do well." Hence love appears to be the sum of all the virtue and duty that God requires of us, and therefore must undoubtedly be the most essential thing—the sum of all the virtue that is essential and distinguishing in real Christianity. That which is the sum of all duty, must be the sum of all real virtue.

3. *The truth of the doctrine as shown by the Scriptures, appears from this, that the apostle teaches us*, Galatians v. 6, *that "faith works by love."* A truly Christian faith is that which produces good works; but all the good works which it produces, are by love. By this, two things are evident to the present purpose.

First, That true love *is an ingredient in true and living faith, and is what is most essential and distinguishing in it.* Love is no ingredient in a merely speculative faith, but it is the life and soul of a practical faith. A truly practical or saving faith, is light and heat together, or rather light and love, while that which is only a speculative faith, is only light without heat; and in that it wants spiritual heat or divine love, is in vain and good for nothing. A speculative faith consists only in the assent of the understanding; but in a saving faith there is also the consent of the heart; and that faith which is only of the former kind, is no better than the faith of devils, for they have faith so far as it can exist without love, believing while they tremble. Now the true spiritual consent of the heart, cannot be distinguished from the love of the heart. He whose heart consents to Christ as a Saviour, has true love to him as such. For the heart sincerely to consent to the way of salvation by Christ, cannot be distinguished from loving that way of salvation, and resting in it. There is an act of choice or election in true saving faith, whereby the soul chooses Christ for its Saviour and portion, and accepts of and embraces him as such; but, as was observed before, an election or choice whereby it so chooses God and Christ, is an act of love—the love of a soul embracing him as its dearest friend and portion. Faith is a duty that God requires of every one. We are commanded to believe, and unbelief is a sin forbidden by God. Faith is a duty required in the first table of the law, and in the first command of that table; and therefore it will follow, that it is comprehended in the great commandment, "Thou shalt love the Lord thy God with all thy heart, &c.,"—and so it will follow that love is the most essential thing in a true faith. That love is the very life and spirit of a true faith, is especially evident from a comparison of this declaration of the apostle, that "faith works by love," and the last verse of the second chapter of the epistle of James, which declares, that "as the body without the spirit is dead, so faith without works is dead also." The working, active and acting nature of anything, is the life of it; and that which makes us call a thing alive, is, that we observe an active nature in it. This active, working nature in man, is the spirit which he has within him. And as his body without this spirit is dead, so faith without works is dead also. And if we would know what the working active thing in true faith is, the apostle tells us in Galatians v. 6, "Faith works by love." So that it is love which is the active working spirit in all true faith. This is its very soul, without which it is dead, as, in another form, he tells in the text, saying that faith without charity or love, is nothing, though it be to such a degree that it can remove mountains. And when he says, in the seventh verse of the context, that charity "believeth all things and hopeth all things," he probably refers to the great virtues of believing and hoping in the truth and grace of God, to which he compares charity in other parts of the chapter, and particularly in the last verse, "Now abideth faith, hope, charity, &c." For in the seventh verse he gives the preference to charity or love before the other virtues of faith and hope, because it includes them; for he says, "charity believeth all things and hopeth all things;" so that this seems to be his meaning, and not merely as it is vulgarly understood, that charity believeth and hopeth the best with regard to our neighbors. That a justifying faith, as a most distinguishing mark of Christianity, is comprehended in the great command of loving God, appears also, very plainly, from what Christ says to the Jews, John v. 40–43, &c.

Second, It is further manifest from this declaration of the apostle "that faith works by love," *that all Christian exercises of the heart, and works of the life are from love;* for we are abundantly taught in the New Testament, that all Christian holiness begins with faith in Jesus Christ. All christian obedience is in the Scriptures called the obedience of faith; as in Romans xvi. 26, the gospel is said to be "made known to all nations for the obedience of faith." The obedience here spoken of, is doubtless the same with that spoken of in the eighteenth verse of the preceding chapter, where Paul speaks of making "the Gentiles obedient by word and deed." And in Galatians ii. 20 he tells us, "The life which I now live in the flesh, I live by the faith of the Son of God," &c.; and we are often told that Christians, so far as they are Christians, "live by faith;" which is equivalent to saying that all gracious and holy exercises and virtues of the spiritual life are by faith. But how does faith work these things? Why, in this place in Galatians, it is expressly said, that it works whatsoever it does work *by love*. From which the truth of the doctrine follows, viz.: that all that is saving and distinguishing in Christianity does radically consist, and is summarily comprehended in love.

In the application of this subject, we may use it in the way of self-examination, instruction, and exhortation. And

1. *In view of it let us examine ourselves, and see if we have the spirit which it enjoins.* From love to God, springs love to man, as says the apostle, 1 John v. 1, "Whosoever believeth that Jesus is the Christ, is born of God: and every one that loveth him that be-

gat, loveth him also that is begotten of him." Have we this love to all who are the children of God? This love, also, leads those who possess it, to rejoice in God, and to worship and magnify him. Heaven is made up of such. Revelations xv. 2, 3, 4, "And I saw as it were a sea of glass mingled with fire; and them that had gotten the victory over the beast, and over his image, and over his mark, and over the number of his name, stand on the sea of glass, having the harps of God. And they sing the song of Moses the servant of God, and the song of the Lamb, saying, Great and marvellous are thy works, Lord God Almighty; just and true are thy ways, thou King of saints. Who shall not fear thee, O Lord, and glorify thy name? for thou only art holy: for all nations shall come and worship before thee; for thy judgments are made manifest." Do we thus delight in God, and rejoice in his worship, and in magnifying his holy name? This love, also, leads those who possess it, sincerely to desire, and earnestly to endeavor to do good to their fellow-men. 1 John iii. 16-19, "Hereby perceive we the love of God, because he laid down his life for us: and we ought to lay down our lives for the brethren. But whoso hath this world's good, and seeth his brother have need, and shutteth up his bowels of compassion from him, how dwelleth the love of God in him? My little children, let us not love in word, neither in tongue; but in deed and in truth. And hereby we know that we are of the truth, and shall assure our hearts before him." Is this spirit, which dwelt in Jesus Christ, the spirit that reigns in our hearts, and is seen in our daily life? The subject may, also, be of use,

2. *In the way of instruction.* And

First. This doctrine shows us *what is the right Christian spirit.* When the disciples, on their way to Jerusalem, desired Christ to call down fire from heaven to consume the Samaritans who would not receive him, he told them, Luke ix. 55, by way of rebuke, "Ye know not what manner of spirit ye are of;" by which we are to understand, not that they did not know their own hearts, but that they did not know and truly feel what kind of spirit was proper and becoming to their character and spirit as his professed disciples, and becoming that evangelical dispensation that he had come to establish, and under which they were now living. It might indeed be, and doubtless was true, that in many respects they did not know their own hearts. But what Christ here referred to was, not the want of self-knowledge in general, but the particular spirit they had manifested in desiring him to call down fire &c., a desire which showed not so much that they did not know what their own hearts or dispositions were, as that they did not seem to know what kind of spirit and temper was proper to the Christian dispensation that was henceforth to be established, and to the Christian character of which they were to be examples. They showed their ignorance of the true nature of Christ's kingdom; that it was to be a kingdom of love and peace; and that they did not know but that a revengeful spirit was a proper spirit for them as his disciples: and for this it is that he rebukes them.

And doubtless there are many, now-a-days, greatly to be rebuked for this, that though they have been so long in the school of Christ, and under the teachings of the gospel, yet they still remain under a great misapprehension as to what kind of a spirit a truly Christian spirit is, and what spirit is proper for the followers of Christ and the dispensation under which they live. But if we attend to the text and its doctrine, they will teach us what this spirit is, viz.: that in its very essence and savor it is the spirit of divine and Christian love. This may, by way of eminence, be called *the* Christian spirit; for it is much more insisted on in the New Testament, than anything that concerns either our duty or our moral state. The words of Christ whereby he taught men their duty, and gave his counsels and commands to his disciples and others, were spent very much on the precepts of love; and as the words that proceeded out of his mouth were so full of this sweet divine virtue, he thus most manifestly commends it to us. And after his ascension, the apostles were full of the same spirit, in their epistles abundantly recommending love, peace, gentleness, goodness, bowels of compassion and kindness, directing us by such things to express our love to God and to Christ, as well as to our fellow-men, and especially to all that are his followers. This spirit, even a spirit of love, is the spirit that God holds forth greater motives in the gospel to induce us to, than to any other thing whatever. The work of redemption which the gospel makes known, above all things affords motives to love; for that work was the most glorious and wonderful exhibition of love that ever was seen or heard of. Love is the principal thing that the gospel dwells on when speaking of God, and of Christ. It brings to light the love eternally existing between the Father and the Son, and declares how that same love has been manifested in many things; how that Christ is God's well-beloved Son, in whom he is ever well pleased; how he so loved him, that he has raised him to the throne of the mediatorial kingdom, and appointed him to be the judge of the world, and ordained that all mankind should stand before him in judgment. In the gospel, too, is revealed the love that Christ has to the Father, and the wonderful fruits of that love, particularly in his doing such great things, and suffering such great things in obedience to the Father's will, and for the honor of his justice, and law, and authority, as the great moral governor. There it is revealed how the Father and Son are one in love, that we might be induced, in the like spirit, to be one with them, and with one another, agreeably to Christ's prayer in John

xvii. 21-23, "That they all may be one; as thou, Father, art in me, and I in thee, that they also may be one in us: that the world may believe that thou hast sent me. And the glory which thou gavest me I have given them; that they may be one, even as we are one: I in them, and thou in me, that they may be made perfect in one; and that the world may know that thou hast sent me, and hast loved them, as thou hast loved me." The gospel also declares to us that the love of God was from everlasting, and reminds us that he loved those that are redeemed by Christ, before the foundation of the world; and that he gave them to the Son; and that the Son loved them as his own. It reveals, too, the wonderful love of both the Father and the Son to the saints now in glory—that Christ not only loved them while in the world, but that he loved them to the end. And all this love is spoken of as bestowed on us while we were wanderers, outcasts, worthless, guilty, and even enemies. This is love, such as was never elsewhere known, or conceived. John xv. 13, "Greater love hath no man than this, that a man lay down his life for his friends." Romans v. 7-10, "Scarcely for a righteous man will one die * * *. But God commendeth his love towards us, in that while we were yet sinners, Christ died for us; * * * when we were enemies."

God and Christ appear in the gospel revelation, as being clothed with love; as sitting as it were on a throne of mercy and grace, a seat of love, encompassed about with the sweet beams of love. Love is the light and glory that is round about the throne on which God is seated. This seems to be intended in the vision the apostle John, that loving and loved disciple, had of God in the isle of Patmos. Rev. iv. 3, "And there was a rainbow round about the throne, in sight like unto an emerald;" that is, round about the throne on which God was sitting. So that God appeared to him, as he sat on his throne, as encompassed with a circle of exceeding sweet and pleasant light, like the beautiful colors of the rainbow, and like an emerald, which is a precious stone of exceeding pleasant and beautiful color—thus representing that the light and glory with which God appears surrounded in the gospel, is especially the glory of his love and covenant grace, for the rainbow was given to Noah as a token of both these.

Therefore it is plain, that this spirit, even a spirit of love, is the spirit that the gospel revelation does especially hold forth motives and inducements to; and this is especially and eminently the Christian spirit—the right spirit of the gospel.

Second. If it is indeed so that all that is saving and distinguishing in a true Christian, is summarily comprehended in love, *then professors of Christianity may in this be taught as to their experiences, whether they are real Christian experiences or not.* If they are so, then love is the sum and substance of them. If persons have the true light of heaven let into their souls, it is not a light without heat. Divine knowledge and Divine love, go together. A spiritual view of divine things, always excites love in the soul, and draws forth the heart in love to every proper object. True discoveries of the divine character, dispose us to love God as the supreme good; they unite the heart in love to Christ; they incline the soul to flow out in love to God's people, and to all mankind. When persons have a true discovery of the excellency and sufficiency of Christ, this is the effect. When they experience a right belief of the truth of the gospel, such a belief is accompanied by love. They love him whom they believe to be the Christ, the Son of the living God. When the truth of the glorious doctrines and promises of the gospel is seen, these doctrines and promises are like so many cords which take hold of the heart, and draw it out in love to God and Christ. When persons experience a true trust and reliance on Christ, they rely on him with love, and so do it with delight and sweet acquiescence of soul. The spouse sat under Christ's shadow with great delight, and rested sweetly under his protection because she loved him, Cant. ii. 2. When persons experience true comfort and spiritual joy, their joy is the joy of faith and love. They do not rejoice in themselves, but it is God who is their exceeding joy.

Third. This doctrine shows *the amiableness of a Christian spirit.* A spirit of love is an amiable spirit. It is the spirit of Jesus Christ; it is the spirit of heaven.

Fourth. This doctrine shows *the pleasantness of a Christian life.* A life of love, is a pleasant life. Reason and the Scriptures alike teach us, that "Happy is the man that findeth wisdom," and that "Her ways are ways of pleasantness, and all her paths are peace.—Prov. iii. 13 and 17.

Fifth. Hence we may learn the reason *why contention tends so much to the ruin of religion.* The Scriptures tell us that it has this tendency: "where envying and strife is, there is confusion and every evil work."— James iii. 16. And so we find it by experience. When contention comes into a place, it seems to prevent all good. And if religion has been flourishing before, it presently seems to chill and deaden it; and everything that is bad begins to flourish. And in the light of our doctrine, we may plainly see the reason of all this. For contention is directly against that which is the very sum of all that is essential and distinguishing in true Christianity, even a spirit of love and peace. No wonder, therefore, that Christianity cannot flourish in a time of strife and contention among its professors. No wonder that religion and contention cannot live together.

Sixth. Hence, then, *what a watch and guard should Christians keep against envy, and malice, and every kind of bitterness of spirit towards their neighbors.* For these things are the very reverse of the real essence of Christianity. And it behooves Christians, as they would not, by their practice, directly contradict their profession, to take heed to themselves in this matter. They should suppress the first beginnings of ill-will, and bitterness, and envy; watch strictly against all occasions of such a spirit; strive and fight to the utmost against such a temper as tends that way; and avoid, as much as possible, all temptations that may lead to it. A Christian should at all times keep a strong guard against everything that tends to overthrow, or corrupt, or undermine a spirit of love. That which hinders love to men, will hinder the exercise of love to God; for, as was observed before, the principle of a truly Christian love, is one. If love is the sum of Christianity, surely those things which overthrow love, are exceedingly unbecoming Christians. An envious Christian, a malicious Christian, a cold and hard-hearted Christian, is the greatest absurdity and contradiction. It is as if one should speak of dark brightness, or a false truth!

Seventh. Hence it is *no wonder that Christianity so strongly requires us to love our enemies, even the worst of enemies* (as in Matthew v 44); for love is the very temper and spirit of a Christian: it is the sum of Christianity. And if we consider what incitements thus to love our enemies we have set before us in what the Gospel reveals of the love of God and Christ to their enemies, we cannot wonder that we are required to love our enemies, and to bless them, and do good to them, and pray for them, "that we may be the children of our Father which is in heaven, who maketh his sun to rise on the evil and the good, and sendeth rain on the just and on the unjust." In the

3. *Our subject exhorts us to seek a spirit of love; to grow in it more and more; and very much to abound in the works of love.* If love is so great a thing in Christianity, so essential and distinguishing, yea the very sum of all Christian virtue, then surely those that profess themselves Christians should live in love, and abound in the works of love, for no works are so becoming as those of love. If you call yourself a Christian, where are your works of love? Have you abounded, and do you abound in them? If this divine and holy principle is in you, and reigns in you, will it not appear in your life, in works of love?

Consider what deeds of love have you done? Do you love God? What have you done for him, for his glory, for the advancement of his kingdom in the world? And how much have you denied yourself to promote the Redeemer's interest among men? Do you love your fellow-men? What have you done for them? Consider your former defects in these respects, and how becoming it is in you as a Christian, hereafter to abound more in deeds of love. Do not make excuse that you have not opportunities to do anything for the glory of God, for the interest of the Redeemer's kingdom, and for the spiritual benefit of your neighbors. If your heart is full of love, it will find vent; you will find or make ways enough to express your love in deeds. When a fountain abounds in water, it will send forth streams. Consider that as a principle of love is the main principle in the heart of a real Christian, so the labor of love, is the main business of the Christian life. Let every Christian consider these things; and may the Lord give you understanding in all things, and make you sensible what spirit it becomes you to be of, and dispose you to such an excellent, amiable, and benevolent life, as is answerable to such a spirit, that you may not love only "in word and tongue, but in deed and in truth."

LECTURE II.

CHARITY MORE EXCELLENT THAN THE EXTRAORDINARY GIFTS OF THE SPIRIT.

"Though I speak with the tongues of men and of angels, and have not charity, I am become as sounding brass, or a tinkling cymbal. And though I have the gift of prophecy, and understand all mysteries, and all knowledge; and though I have all faith, so that I could remove mountains, and have not charity, I am nothing."—1 Cor. xiii. 1, 2.

Having in the last lecture shown, that all the virtue in the saints which is distinguishing and saving, may be summed up in Christian love, I would now consider what things are compared with it in the text, and to which of the two the preference is given.

The things compared together, in the text, are of two kinds: on the one hand, the extraordinary and miraculous gifts of the Spirit, such as the gift of tongues, the gift of prophecy, &c., which were frequent in that age, and particularly in the church at Corinth, and on the other hand, the effect of the ordinary influences of the same Spirit, in true Christians, viz. charity, or divine love.

That was an age of miracles. It was not then, as it had been of old among the Jews, when two or three, or at most a very few in the whole nation had the gift of prophecy: it rather seemed as if Moses' wish, recorded in Num. xi. 29, had become in a great measure fulfilled: "Would God that all the Lord's people were prophets." Not only some certain persons of great eminence were endowed with such gifts, but they were common to all sorts, old and young, men and women; according to the prophecy of the prophet Joel, who, speaking of those days, foretold beforehand that great event: "And it shall come to pass in the last days (saith God), I will pour out of my Spirit upon all flesh: and your sons and your daughters shall prophesy, and your young men shall see visions, and your old men shall dream dreams: and on my servants, and on my handmaidens I will pour out, in those days, of my Spirit, and they shall prophesy." Especially the church of Corinth was very eminent for such gifts. All sorts of miraculous gifts were, as is apparent from this Epistle, bestowed on that church, and the number who enjoyed these gifts was not small. "To one," says the Apostle, "is given by the Spirit, the word of wisdom: to another the word of knowledge by the same Spirit: to another faith by the same Spirit: to another the gifts of healing by the same Spirit: to another the working of miracles: to another prophecy, &c." "But all these worketh that one, and the self-same Spirit, dividing to every man severally as he will." And so some had one gift, and some another. "But," says the Apostle, "covet earnestly the best gifts; and yet show I unto you a more excellent way," *i. e.*, something more excellent than all these gifts put together, yea, something of so great importance, that all these gifts without it are nothing. For "though I speak with the tongues of men," as they did on the day of Pentecost, yea, "and of angels" too, "and have not charity, I am become" an empty worthless thing, "as sounding brass, or a tinkling cymbal. And though I have" not only one, but all the extraordinary gifts of the Spirit; and can not only speak with tongues, but "have the gift of all prophecy, and understand all mysteries, and all knowledge," to see 'nto all the deep things of God by immediate inspiration; "and though I have all faith," to work all sorts of miracles, yea, even "so that I could remove mountains, and have not charity, I am nothing." Charity, then, which is the fruit of the ordinary sanctifying influence of the Holy Spirit, is preferred, as being more excellent than any, yea, than all the extraordinary gifts of the Spirit, even Christian love, which, as has been shown, is the sum of all saving grace. Yea, so very much is it preferred, that all the extraordinary gifts of the Spirit, without it, are nothing, and can profit nothing. The doctrine taught, then, is: THAT THE ORDINARY INFLUENCE OF THE SPIRIT OF GOD, WORKING THE GRACE OF CHARITY IN THE HEART, IS A MORE EXCELLENT BLESSING THAN ANY OF THE EXTRAORDINARY GIFTS OF THE SPIRIT. Here I would endeavor to show, first, what is meant by the ordinary and extraordinary gifts of the Spirit; secondly, that the extraordinary gifts of the Spirit are indeed great privileges; and yet, thirdly, that the ordinary influence of the Spirit working the grace of charity or love in the heart is a more excellent blessing.

I. *I would briefly explain what is meant by the ordinary and extraordinary gifts of the Spirit;* for the gifts and operations of the

Spirit of God are by divines distinguished into *common* and *saving*, and into *ordinary* and *extraordinary*.

1. The gifts and operations of the Spirit of God are distinguished into those that are *common*, and those that are *saving*. By common gifts of the Spirit are meant, such as are common both to the godly and to the ungodly. There are certain ways in which the Spirit of God influences the minds of natural men, as well as the minds of the godly. Thus there are common convictions of sin, *i. e.*, such convictions as ungodly men may have as well as godly. So there are common illuminations, or enlightenings, *i. e.*, such as are common to both godly and ungodly. So there are common religious affections,—common gratitude, —common sorrow, and the like. But there are other gifts of the Spirit, which are peculiar to the godly, such as saving faith and love, and all the other saving graces of the Spirit.

2. *Ordinary and extraordinary.*—The extraordinary gifts of the Spirit, such as the gift of tongues, of miracles, of prophecy, &c., are called extraordinary, because they are such as are not given in the ordinary course of

God's providence. They are not bestowed in the way of God's ordinary providential dealing with his children, but only on extraordinary occasions, as they were bestowed on the Prophets and Apostles to enable them to reveal the mind and will of God before the canon of Scripture was complete, and so on the primitive church, in order to the founding and establishing of it in the world. But since the canon of Scripture has been completed, and the Christian church fully founded and established, these extraordinary gifts have ceased. But the ordinary gifts of the Spirit, are such as are continued to the church of God throughout all ages; such gifts as are granted in conviction and conversion, and such as appertain to the building up of the saints in holiness and comfort.

It may be observed then that the distinction of the gifts of the Spirit into ordinary and extraordinary, is very different from the other distinction into common and special; for some of the ordinary gifts, such as faith, hope, charity, are not common gifts. They are such gifts as God ordinarily bestows on his church in all ages, but they are not common to the godly and the ungodly; they are peculiar to the godly. And the extraordinary gifts of the Spirit are common gifts. The gifts of tongues, of miracles, of prophecy, &c., although they are not ordinarily bestowed on the Christian church, but only on extraordinary occasions, yet are not peculiar to the godly, for many ungodly men have had these gifts, Matt. vii. 22, 23: "Many will say to me in that day, Lord, Lord, have we not prophesied in thy name? and in thy name have cast out devils? and in thy name done many wonderful works? and then will I profess unto them, I never knew you: depart from me, ye that work iniquity." Having explained these terms, I proceed to show,

II. *That the extraordinary gifts of the Spirit of God are indeed great privileges.*—When God endows any one with a spirit of prophecy, favors him with immediate inspiration, or gives him power to work miracles, to heal the sick, to cast out devils, and the like, the privilege is great, yea, this is one of the highest kind of privileges that God ever bestows on men, next to saving grace. It is a great privilege to live in the enjoyment of the outward means of grace, and to belong to the visible church; but to be a prophet and a worker of miracles in the church, is a much greater privilege still. It is a great privilege to hear the word, which has been spoken by prophets and inspired persons; but a much greater to be a prophet, to preach the word, to be inspired by God to make known his mind and will to others. It was a great privilege that God bestowed on Moses, when he called him to be a prophet, and improved him as an instrument to reveal the law to the children of Israel, and to deliver to the church so great a part of the written word of God, even the first written revelation that ever was delivered to it; and when he used him as an instrument of working so many wonders in Egypt, at the Red Sea, and in the wilderness. Great was the privilege that God bestowed on David, in inspiring him, and making him the penman of so great and excellent a part of his word, for the use of the church in all ages. Great was the privilege that God bestowed on those two prophets, Elijah and Elisha, in enabling them to perform such miraculous and wonderful works. And the privilege was very great, that God bestowed on the prophet Daniel, in giving him so much of the extraordinary gifts of the Spirit, particularly such understanding in the visions of God. This procured him great honor among the heathen, and even in the court of the King of Babylon. Nebuchadnezzar, that great and mighty and haughty monarch, so admired Daniel for it, that he was once about to worship him as a god. He fell upon his face before him, and commanded that an oblation and sweet odors should be offered unto him, Dan. ii. 46. And Daniel was advanced to greater honor than all the wise men, the magicians, astrologers, and soothsayers of Babylon, in consequence of these extraordinary gifts which God bestowed upon him. Hear how the Queen speaks of him to Belshazzar, Dan. v. 11, 12: "There is a man in thy kingdom, in whom is the spirit of the holy gods: and in the days of thy father, light and understanding and wisdom, like the wisdom of the Gods, was found in him; whom the King Nebuchadnezzar thy father, the king, I say, thy father, made master of the magicians, astrologers, Chaldeans, and soothsayers; for as much as an excellent spirit, and knowledge, and understanding, interpreting dreams, and showing of hard sentences, and dissolving of doubts, were found in the same Daniel." This privilege was also the thing which gave Daniel honor in the Persian court. (Dan. vi. 1, 2, 3.) "It pleased Darius to set over the kingdom an hundred and twenty princes, which should be over the whole kingdom, and over these, three presidents, of whom Daniel was first, that the princes might give accounts unto them, and the king should have no damage. Then this Daniel was preferred above the presidents and princes, because an excellent spirit was in him; and the king thought to set him over the whole realm." By this excellent spirit was doubtless among other things meant the spirit of prophecy and divine inspiration, for which he had been so honored by the princes of Babylon.

It was a great privilege that Christ bestowed on the Apostles, in so filling them with the extraordinary gifts of the Holy Spirit, inspiring them to teach all nations, and making them as it were next to himself, and to be the twelve precious stones, that are considered as the twelve foundations of the church. Rev. xxi. 14: "And the wall of the city had twelve foundations, and in them the names of the twelve Apostles of the Lamb." Eph. ii. 20: "Built upon the foundation of the Apostles and Prophets, Jesus Christ himself being the chief corner-stone." And how highly was the Apostle John favored, when he was "in the Spirit on the Lord's day," and had such extraordinary visions, representing the great events of God's providence towards the church in all ages of it to the end of the world.

Such extraordinary gifts of the Spirit are spoken of in Scriptures as very great privileges. So was the privilege that God bestowed on Moses in speaking to him by way of extraordinary miraculous revelation, as it were, "face to face." And that outpouring of the Spirit in his extraordinary gifts which on the day of Pentecost was foretold and spoken of by the prophet Joel, as a very great privilege, in those forecited words in Joel ii. 28, 29. And Christ speaks of the gifts of miracles, and of tongues, as great privileges that he would bestow on them that should believe in him: Matt. xvi. 17, 18.

Such extraordinary gifts of the Spirit have been looked upon as a great honor. Moses and Aaron were envied in the camp because of the peculiar honor that God put upon them,

Psal. cvi. 16. And so Joshua was ready to envy Eldad and Medad because they prophesied in the camp: Num. xi. 27. And when the angels themselves have been sent to do the work of the prophets, to reveal things to come, it has set them in a very honorable point of light. Even the Apostle John himself, in his great surprise, was once and again ready to fall down and worship the angel, that was sent by Christ to reveal to him the future events of the church; but the angel forbids him, acknowledging that the privilege of the spirit of prophecy which he had, was not of himself, but that he had received it of Jesus Christ: Rev. xix. 10, and xxii. 8, 9. The heathen of the city of Lystra were so astonished at the power the Apostles Barnabas and Paul had to work miracles, that they were about to offer sacrifices to them as gods: Acts xiv. 11, 12, 13. And Simon the sorcerer had a great hankering after that gift that the Apostles had of conferring the Holy Ghost, by laying on their hands, and offered them money for it.

These extraordinary gifts are a great privilege, in that there is in them a conformity to Christ in his prophetical office. And the greatness of the privilege appears also in this, that though sometimes they have been bestowed on natural men, yet it has been very rarely; and commonly such as have had them bestowed on them have been saints, yea, and the most eminent saints. Thus it was on the day of Pentecost; and thus it was in more early ages. II. Pet. i. 21: "Holy men of God spake as they were moved by the Holy Ghost." These gifts have commonly been bestowed as tokens of God's extraordinary favor and love, as it was with Daniel. He was a man *greatly beloved*, and therefore he was admitted to such a great privilege, as that of having these revelations made to him: Dan. ix. 23, and x. 11, 19. And the Apostle John, as he was the disciple whom Jesus loved, so he was selected above all the other Apostles, to be the man to whom those great events were revealed that we have an account of in the book of the Revelation. I come now,

III. *To show, that though these are great privileges, yet that the ordinary influence of the Spirit of God, working the grace of charity in the heart, is a far more excellent privilege than any of them:* a greater blessing than the spirit of prophecy, or the gift of tongues, or of miracles, even to the removing of mountains; a greater blessing than all those miraculous gifts that Moses, and Elijah, and David, and the twelve Apostles were endowed with. This will appear, if we consider,

1. *This blessing of the saving grace of God is a quality inherent in the nature of him that is the subject of it.*—This gift of the Spirit of God, working a truly Christian temper in the soul, and exciting gracious exercises there, confers a blessing that has its seat in the heart, a blessing that makes a man's heart or nature excellent; yea, the very excellency of the nature does consist in it. Now it is not so with respect to these extraordinary gifts of the Spirit. They are excellent things, but not properly the excellency of a man's nature, for they are not things that are inherent in the nature. For instance, if a man is endowed with a gift of working miracles, this power is not anything inherent in his nature. It is not properly any quality of the heart and nature of the man, as true grace and holiness are; and though most commonly, those that have these extraordinary gifts of prophecy, speaking with tongues and working miracles, have been holy persons, yet their holiness did not

consist in their having these gifts. These extraordinary gifts are nothing properly inherent in the man. They are something adventitious. They are excellent things, but not excellences in the nature of the subject. They are like a beautiful garment, which does not alter the nature of the man that wears it. They are like precious jewels, with which the body may be adorned; but true grace is that whereby the very soul itself becomes as it were a precious jewel.

2. *The Spirit of God communicates himself much more in bestowing saving grace than in bestowing these extraordinary gifts.*—In the extraordinary gifts of the Spirit, the Holy Ghost does indeed produce effects, in men, or by men; but not so as properly to communicate himself, in his own proper nature, to men. A man may have an extraordinary impulse in his mind by the Spirit of God, whereby some future thing may be revealed to him; or he may have an extraordinary vision given him representing some future event; and yet the Spirit may not at all impart himself, in his holy nature, by that. The Spirit of God may produce effects in things in which he does not communicate himself to us. Thus the Spirit

of God moved on the face of the waters, but not so as to impart himself to the water. But when the Spirit, by his ordinary influences, bestows saving grace, he therein imparts himself to the soul in his own holy nature,—that nature of his, on the account of which, he is so often called in Scripture, the Holy Ghost, or the Holy Spirit. By his producing this effect, the Spirit becomes an indwelling vital principle in the soul, and the subject becomes spiritual, being denominated so from the Spirit of God that dwells in him, and whose nature he is partaker of. Yea, grace is, as it were, the holy nature of the Spirit imparted to the soul. But the extraordinary gifts of the Spirit, such as knowing things to come, or having power to work miracles, do not imply this holy nature. Not but that God, when he gives the extraordinary gifts of the Spirit, is commonly wont to give the sanctifying influences of the Spirit with them; but one does not imply the other. And if God gives only extraordinary gifts, such as the gift of prophecy, of miracles, &c., these alone will never make their receiver a partaker of the Spirit, so as to become spiritual in himself, *i. e.*, in his own nature.

3. *That grace or holiness, which is the effect of the ordinary influence of the Spirit of God in the hearts of the saints, is that wherein the spiritual image of God consists; and not in these extraordinary gifts of the Spirit.*—The spiritual image of God does not consist in having a power to work miracles, and foretell future events, but it consists in being holy as God is holy: in having a holy and divine principle in the heart, influencing us to holy and heavenly lives. Indeed, there is a kind of assimilation to Christ in having a power to work miracles, for Christ had such a power, and wrought a multitude of miracles, John xiv. 12: "The works that I do, shall he do also." But the moral image and likeness of Christ does much more consist in having *the same mind in us which was in Christ;* in being of the same Spirit that he was of; in being meek and lowly of heart; in having a spirit of Christian love, and walking as Christ walked. This makes a man more like Christ than if he could work ever so many miracles.

4. *That grace which is the effect of the ordinary influences of the Spirit of God, is a privilege which God bestows only on his own favorites and children, but the extraordinary*

gifts of the Spirit are not so.—It has been observed before, that though God most commonly has chosen saints and eminent saints to bestow extraordinary gifts of the Spirit upon, yet he has not always done so; but these gifts are sometimes bestowed on others. They have been common to both the godly and the ungodly. Balaam is stigmatized in Scripture as a wicked man, 2 Pet. ii. 15; Jude 11; Rev. ii. 14; and yet he had the extraordinary gifts of the Spirit of God for awhile. Saul was a wicked man, but we read, once and again, of his being *among the prophets.* Judas was one of those whom Christ sent forth to preach and work miracles : he was one of those twelve disciples, of whom it is said in Matt. x. 1 : " And when he had called unto him his twelve disciples, he gave them power against unclean spirits to cast them out, and to heal all manner of sickness, and all manner of disease." And in the next verses we are told who they were, their names are all rehearsed over, and " Judas Iscariot, who also betrayed him," among the rest. And in verse 8, Christ says to them, " Heal the sick, cleanse the lepers, raise the dead, cast out devils." The grace of God in the heart, is a gift of the Holy Ghost peculiar to the saints. It is a blessing that God reserves only for those who are the objects of his special and peculiar love. But the extraordinary gifts of the Spirit are what God sometimes bestows on those whom he does not love, but hates; which is a sure sign that the one is infinitely more precious and excellent than the other. That is the most precious gift, which is most of an evidence of God's love. But the extraordinary gifts of the Spirit were, in the days of inspiration and miracles, no sure sign of the love of God. The prophets were not wont to build their persuasion of the favor and love of God on their being prophets, and having revelations; but on their being sincere saints. Thus, it was with David. See Psal. xv. 1–5, and xvii. 1–3, and cxix. throughout: and indeed, the whole Book of Psalms bears witness to this. So the Apostle Paul, though he was so greatly privileged with the extraordinary gifts of the Spirit, was yet so far from making these the evidences of his good estate, that he expressly declares, that without charity they are all nothing. And hence we may argue,

5. *From the fruit and consequence of these two different things, that the one is infinitely*

more excellent than the other.—Eternal life is, by the promises of the gospel, constantly connected with the one, and never with the other. Salvation is promised to those who have the graces of the Spirit, but not to those who have merely the extraordinary gifts Many may have these last, and yet go to hell. Judas Iscariot had them, and is gone to hell. And Christ tells us, that many who have had them, will, at the last day, be bid to depart, as workers of iniquity, Matt. vii. 22, 23. And therefore when he promised his disciples these extraordinary gifts, he bade them rejoice, not because the devils were subject to them, but because their names were written in heaven, intimating that the one might be, and yet not the other, Luke x. 17, &c. And this shows that the one is an infinitely greater blessing than the other, as it carries eternal life in it. For eternal life is a thing of infinite worth and value, and that must be an excellent blessing indeed that has this infallibly connected with it, and of infinitely more worth than any privilege whatsoever, which a man may possess, and yet after all go to hell.

6. *Happiness itself does much more immediately and essentially consist in Christian*

grace, wrought by the ordinary influences of the Spirit, than in these extraordinary gifts. Man's highest happiness consists in holiness, for it is by this that the reasonable creature is united to God, the fountain of all good. Happiness doth so essentially consist in knowing, loving, and serving God, and having the holy and divine temper of soul, and the lively exercises of it, that these things will make a man happy without anything else; but no other enjoyments or privileges whatsoever will make a man happy without this.

7. *This divine temper of soul, which is the fruit of the ordinary sanctifying influences of the Spirit, is the end of all the extraordinary gifts of the Holy Ghost.*—The gift of prophecy, of miracles, of tongues, &c., God gave for this very end, to promote the propagation and establishment of the gospel in the world. And the end of the gospel is, to turn men from darkness to light, and from the power of sin and Satan to serve the living God, *i.e.*, to make men holy. The end of all the extraordinary gifts of the Spirit, is the conversion of sinners, and the building up of saints in that holiness which is the fruit of the ordinary influences of the Holy Ghost. For this, the Holy Spirit

was poured out on the Apostles after Christ's ascension; and they were enabled to speak with tongues, work miracles, &c.; and for this, very many others, in that age, were endued with the extraordinary gifts of the Holy Ghost, Eph. iv. 11: "And he gave some, Apostles: and some, Prophets: and some, Evangelists." Here the extraordinary gifts of the Spirit are referred to; and the end of all is expressed in the next words, viz.: "For the perfecting of the saints, for the work of the ministry, for the edifying of the body of Christ." And what sort of *edifying* of the body of Christ this is, we learn from verse 16: "Maketh increase of the body, unto the edifying of itself in love." In *love*, that is, in *charity*, the same that is spoken of in our text, for the word in the original is the same, and the same thing is meant. And so it is the same as in 1 Cor. viii. 1: *charity edifieth*.

But the end is always more excellent than the means: this is a maxim universally allowed; for means have no goodness in them any otherwise than as they are subordinate to the end. The end therefore must be considered as superior in excellency to the means.

8. *The extraordinary gifts of the Spirit*

will be so far from profiting without that grace which is the fruit of the ordinary influences of the Spirit, that they will but aggravate the condemnation of those that have them. Doubtless Judas' condemnation was exceedingly aggravated by his having been one that had had such privileges. And some, that have had such extraordinary gifts, have committed the sin against the Holy Ghost, and their privileges were a main thing that rendered their sin, the unpardonable sin; as appears from Heb. vi. 4, 5, 6: "For it is impossible for those who were once enlightened, and have tasted of the heavenly gift, and were made partakers of the Holy Ghost, and have tasted the good word of God, and the powers of the world to come, if they shall fall away, to renew them again unto repentance: seeing they crucify to themselves the Son of God afresh, and put him to an open shame." Those who *fell away*, were such as apostatized from Christianity after having made a public profession of it, and received the extraordinary gifts of the Holy Ghost, as most Christians did in those days. They were instructed in Christianity, and through the common influences of the Spirit they received the word with joy, like those in Matt. xiii. 20; and with a. received the extraordinary gifts of the Spirit: "were made partakers of the Holy Ghost, tasted of the heavenly gift, and the powers of the world to come;" spake with tongues; prophesied in Christ's name; and in his name cast out devils; and yet after all, openly renounced Christianity; joined to call Christ an impostor, as his murderers did; and so "crucified to themselves the Son of God afresh, and put him to an open shame." Of these it is that the Apostle says: "It is impossible to renew them again unto repentance." Such apostates, in their renouncing Christianity, must ascribe the miraculous powers which themselves had possessed to the devil. So their case became hopeless; and their condemnation must be exceedingly aggravated. And from this it appears that saving grace is of infinitely more worth and excellence, than the extraordinary gifts of the Spirit. And, lastly,

9. *Another thing that shows the preferableness of that saving grace, which is the fruit of the ordinary influences of the Holy Spirit, to the extraordinary gifts, is, that one will fail, and the other will not.*—This argument the Apostle makes use of, in the context, to

show that divine love is preferable to the extraordinary gifts of the Spirit, verse 8: "Charity never faileth: but whether there be prophecies, they shall fail; whether there be tongues, they shall cease; whether there be knowledge, it shall vanish away." Divine love will remain throughout all eternity, but the extraordinary gifts of the Spirit will fail in time. They are only of the nature of means, and when the end is obtained they shall cease; but divine love will remain forever. In the improvement of this subject, I remark:

1. *If saving grace is a greater blessing than the extraordinary gifts of the Spirit, we may doubtless hence argue, that it is the greatest privilege and blessing that ever God bestows on any person in this world.*—For these extraordinary gifts of the Holy Ghost, such as the gift of tongues, of miracles, of prophecy, &c., are the highest kind of privileges that God ever bestows on natural men, and privileges which have been very rarely bestowed on such, in any age of the world, the apostolic age excepted.

If what has been said be well considered, it will appear evident beyond all doubt, that the saving grace of God in the heart, working a holy and divine temper in the soul, is the greatest blessing that ever men receive in this world: greater than any natural gifts, greater than the greatest natural abilities, greater than any acquired endowments of mind, greater than the most universal learning, greater than any outward wealth and honor, greater than to be a king or an emperor, greater than to be taken from the sheepcote, as David was, and made king over all Israel; and all the riches and honor and magnificence of Solomon in all his glory, are not to be compared with it.

Great was the privilege that God bestowed on the blessed Virgin Mary, in granting that of her should be born the Son of God. That a person, who was infinitely more honorable than the angels, yea, who was the Creator and King of heaven and earth, the great sovereign of the world, that such an one should be conceived in her womb, born of her, and nursed at her breasts, was a greater privilege than for her to be the mother of the child of the greatest earthly prince that ever lived, yet even that was not so great a privilege, as to have the grace of God in the heart; to have Christ, as it were, born in the soul, as he himself doth expressly teach us, in Luke xi. 27, 28: "And it came to pass, as he spake these things, a certain woman of the company lifted up her voice, and said unto him, Blessed is the womb that bare thee, and the paps which thou hast sucked." But he said, "Yea, rather blessed are they that hear the word of God and keep it." And once when some told him, that his mother and his brethren stood without, desiring to speak with him, he thence took occasion to let them know, that there was a more blessed way of being related to him than that which consisted in being his mother and brethren according to the flesh, Matt. xii, 46, 47, 48, 49, 50: "Who is my mother?" said he, "and who are my brethren? and he stretched forth his hand toward his disciples, and said, Behold my mother and my brethren, For whosoever shall do the will of my Father which is in heaven, the same is my brother, and sister, and mother."

2. *Hence these two kinds of privileges are not to be confounded, by taking things that have some appearance of an extraordinary miraculous gift of the Spirit, for sure signs of grace.*—If persons at any time have some extraordinary impression made upon their

minds, which they think is from God, revealing something to them that shall come to pass hereafter, this, if it were real, would argue an extraordinary gift of the Holy Ghost, viz. the gift of prophecy; but, from what has been said, it is evident, that it would be no certain sign of grace, or of anything saving: even if it were real, I say, for indeed we have no reason to look on such things when pretended to, in these days, as any other than delusion. And the fact that such impressions are made by texts of Scripture coming suddenly to the mind, alters not the case; for a text of Scripture coming to the mind, proves no more to be true, than the reading of it proves. If reading any text of Scripture, at any time, and at all times, as it lies in the Bible, does not prove such a thing, then its coming suddenly to the mind does not prove it; for the Scripture speaks just the same thing at one time, as it does at another. The words have the same meaning when they are read along in course, as they have when they are suddenly brought to the mind. And if any man therefore argues anything further from them, he proceeds without warrant. For their coming suddenly to the mind does not give them a new meaning, which they had not before. So if a man thinks that he is in a good estate, because such a text of Scripture comes suddenly to his mind, if the text does not prove it, as it lies in the Bible, and if it would not have proved it, had he only read it, as he was reading along in course, then by such a text coming to his mind, he has no evidence that he is in a good estate. So if anything appears to persons, as though they had a vision of some visible form, and heard some voice, such things are not to be taken as signs of grace, for if they are real and from God, they are not grace, for the extraordinary influence of the Spirit, producing visions and dreams, such as the prophets of old had, are no sure signs of grace. All the fruits of the Spirit, which we are to lay weight upon as evidential of grace, are summed up in charity, or Christian love; because this is the sum of all grace. And the only way, therefore, in which any can know their good estate, is by discerning the exercises of this divine charity in their hearts, for without charity, let men have what gifts you please, they are nothing.

3. *If saving grace is more excellent than the extraordinary gifts of the Spirit, then we*

cannot conclude from what the Scripture says of the glory of the latter times of the church, that the extraordinary gifts of the Spirit will be granted to men in those times.—Many have been ready to think that, in those glorious times of the church, which shall be after the calling of the Jews, and the destruction of Antichrist, there will be many persons that will be inspired, and endued with a power of working miracles. But what the Scripture says concerning the glory of those times does not prove any such thing, or make it probable. For it has been shown, that the pouring out of the Spirit of God, in his ordinary and saving operations, to fill men's hearts with a Christian and holy temper, and lead them to the exercises of the divine life, is the most glorious way of pouring out the Spirit, that can be; more glorious, far more glorious, than a pouring out of the miraculous gifts of the Spirit. And therefore the glory of those times of the church does not require any such thing as those extraordinary gifts. Those times may be far the most glorious times of the church, that ever have been, without them. Their not having the gift of prophecy, of tongues, of healing, &c., as they had in the

Apostolic age, will not hinder there being far more glorious times than there were then, if the Spirit be poured out in greater measure in his sanctifying influences; for this, as the Apostle expressly asserts, is a more excellent way, 1 Cor. xii. 31. This glory is the greatest glory of the church of Christ; and the greatest glory which Christ's church will ever enjoy in any period. This is what will make the church more like the church in heaven, where charity or love hath a more perfect reign, than any number or degree of the extraordinary gifts of the Spirit could do. So that we have no reason on this account, and perhaps not on any other, to expect that the extraordinary gifts of the Spirit will be poured out in those glorious times which are yet to come. For in those times, there is no new dispensation to be introduced, and no new Bible to be given. Nor have we any reason to expect our present Scriptures are to be added to and enlarged; but rather in the end of the sacred writings which we now have, it seems to be intimated, that no addition is to be made till Christ comes. See Rev. xxii. 18–21.

4. *What cause have they to bless God, and*

to live to his glory, who have received such a privilege, as is implied in the influence of the Holy Spirit, working saving grace in the heart. If we do but seriously consider the state of the godly, of those who have been the subjects of this inexpressible blessing, we cannot but be astonished at the wonderful grace bestowed upon them. And the more we consider it, the more wonderful and inexpressible it will appear. When we read in the Scriptures of the great privileges conferred on the Virgin Mary, and on the Apostle Paul, when he was caught up into the third heaven, we are ready to admire such privileges as very great. But after all, they are as nothing compared with the privilege of being like Christ, and having his love in the heart. Let those, then, that hope they have this last blessing, consider more than they ever yet have done, how great a favor God has bestowed upon them, and how great their obligations to glorify him for the work he hath wrought in them, and to glorify Christ who hath purchased this blessing for them with his own blood, and to glorify the Holy Spirit who hath sealed it to their souls. What manner of persons ought such to be in all holy conversation and godliness! Consider, you that hope in God's mercy, how highly he hath advanced and exalted you; and will you not be diligent to live for him? Will you dishonor Christ so as to regard him but little, not giving him your whole heart, but going after the world, neglecting him, and his service, and his glory? Will you not be watchful against yourselves, against a corrupt, worldly, proud disposition, that might lead you away from God who has been so kind to you, and from the Saviour who has purchased such blessings for you, at the cost of his own agonies and death? Will you not every day make this your earnest inquiry, "What shall I render unto the Lord for all his benefits towards me?" What could God have done more for you than he has done? What privilege could he have bestowed, better in itself, or more worthy to engage your heart in thankfulness? And consider how you are living—how little you have done for him—how much you do for self—how little this divine love hath wrought in your heart to incline you to live for God and Christ, and for the extension of his kingdom? O! how should such as you, show your sense of your high privileges, by the exercises of love; love that is manifest toward God in obedience, submission, reverence, cheerfulness, joy and hope, and toward your neighbor, in meekness, sympathy, humility, charitableness, and doing good to all as you have opportunity. Finally,

5. *The subject exhorts all unrenewed persons, those who are strangers to this grace, to seek this most excellent blessing for themselves.* Consider how miserable you now are while wholly destitute of this love, far from righteousness, in love with the vanities of the world, and full of enmity against God. How will you endure when he shall deal with you according to what you are, coming forth in anger as your enemy, and executing his fierce wrath against you. Consider, too, that you are capable of this love; and Christ is able and willing to bestow it; and multitudes have obtained it, and been blessed in it. God is seeking your love, and you are under unspeakable obligation to render it. The Spirit of God has been poured out wonderfully here. Multitudes have been converted. Scarcely a family has been passed by. In almost every household some have been made nobles, kings, and priests unto God, sons and daughters of

the Lord Almighty! What manner of persons, then, ought all of us to be, how holy, serious, just, humble, charitable, devoted in God's service, and faithful to our fellow-men. As individuals and as a people, God has most richly blessed us, and as both individuals and a people, it becomes us to be a royal priesthood, an holy nation, a peculiar people, showing forth the praises of him that hath called us all out of darkness into his marvellous light. "Now consider this, ye that forget God, lest I tear you in pieces and there be none to deliver. Whoso offereth praise glorifieth me, and to him that ordereth his conversation aright, will I show the salvation of God!"

LECTURE III.

THE GREATEST PERFORMANCES OR SUFFERINGS IN VAIN WITHOUT CHARITY.

"And though I bestow all my goods to feed the poor, and though I give my body to be burned, and have not charity, it profiteth me nothing."—1 Cor. xiii. 3.

In the previous verses of this chapter, the necessity and excellence of charity are set forth, as we have seen, by its preference to the greatest privileges, and the utter vanity and insignificance of these privileges without it. The privileges particularly mentioned are those that consist in the extraordinary gifts of the Spirit of God. In this verse, things of another kind are mentioned, viz. those that are of a *moral* nature; and it is declared that none of these avail anything without charity. And, particularly,

First. That our *performances* are in vain without it. Here is one of the highest kinds of external performances mentioned, viz. giving all our goods to feed the poor. Giving to the poor, is a duty very much insisted on in the word of God, and particularly under the Christian dispensation. And in the primitive times of Christianity, the circumstances of the church were such, that persons were sometimes called to part with all they had, and give it away to others. This was partly because of the extreme necessities of those who were persecuted and in distress, and partly because the difficulties that attended being a follower of Christ and doing the work of the gospel were such, as to call for the disciples disentangling themselves from the care and burden of their worldly possessions, and going forth, as it were, without gold, or silver, or scrip, or their purses, or even two coats apiece. The Apostle Paul tells us, that he had suffered the loss of all things for Christ; and the primitive Christians, in the church at Jerusalem, sold all that they had, and gave it into a common fund, and " none said that aught that he had was his own, Acts iv. 32. The duty of giving to the poor, was a duty that the Christian Corinthians at this time had particular occasion to consider, not only because of the many troubles of the times, but by reason, also, of a great dearth or famine that sorely distressed the brethren in Judea; in view of which, the Apostle had already urged it on the Corinthians, as their duty, to send relief to them, speaking of it particularly in this Epistle, in the sixteenth chapter, and also in his second Epistle to the same church, in the eighth and ninth chapters. And yet, though he says so much in both these Epistles, to stir them up to the duty of giving to the poor, still he is very careful to inform them, that though they should go ever so far in it, yea, though they should bestow all their goods to feed the poor, and have not charity, it would profit them nothing.

Secondly. The Apostle teaches, that not only our performances, but also our *sufferings* are of no avail without charity. Men are ready to make much of what they *do*, but more of what they *suffer*. They are ready to think it a great thing when they put themselves out of their way, or are at great expense or suffering for their religion. The Apostle here mentions a suffering of the most extreme kind, suffering even to death, and that one of the most terrible forms of death, and says that even this is nothing without charity. When a man has given away all his goods, he has nothing else remaining that he can give, but himself. And the Apostle teaches, that when a man has given all his possessions, if he then goes on to give his own body, and that to be utterly consumed in the flames, it will avail nothing if it is not done from sincere love in the heart. The time when the Apostle wrote to the Corinthians, was a time when Christians were often called not only to give their goods, but their bodies, also, for Christ's sake; for the church then was generally under persecution, and multitudes were then or soon after put to very cruel deaths for the gospel's sake. But though they suffered in life, or endured the most agonizing death, it would be in vain without charity. What is meant by this charity, has already been explained in the former lectures on these verses, in which it has been shown that charity is the sum of all that is distinguishing in the religion of the heart. And therefore the doctrine that I would derive from these words is this,

THAT ALL THAT MEN CAN DO, AND ALL THAT THEY CAN SUFFER, CAN NEVER MAKE UP FOR

THE WANT OF SINCERE CHRISTIAN LOVE IN THE HEART.

I. *There may be great performances, and so there may be great sufferings without sincere Christian love in the heart.* And,

1. There may be great *performances* without it. The Apostle Paul, in the third chapter of the Epistle to the Philippians, tells us what things he did before his conversion, and while he remained a Pharisee. In the fourth verse, he says, "If any other man thinketh that he hath whereof he might trust in the flesh, I more." Many of the Pharisees did great things, and abounded in religious performances. The Pharisee mentioned in Luke xviii. 11, 12, boasted of the great things he had done, both towards God and men, and thanked God, that he so exceeded other men in his doings. And many of the heathen have been eminent for their great performances; some for their integrity, or for their justice, and others for their great deeds done for the public good. Many men without any sincerity of love in their hearts, have been exceeding magnificent in their gifts for pious and charitable uses, and have thus gotten to themselves great fame, and had their names

handed down in history to posterity with great glory. Many have done great things from fear of hell, hoping thereby to appease the Deity and make atonement for their sins, and many have done great things from pride, and from a desire for reputation and honor among men. And though these motives are not wont to influence men to a constant and universal observance of God's commands, and to go on with a course of Christian performances, and with the practice of all duties towards God and man through life, yet it is hard to say how far such natural principles may carry men in particular duties and performances. And so,

2. There may be great *sufferings* for religion, and yet no sincerity of love in the heart. Persons may undergo great sufferings in life, just as some of the Pharisees used themselves to great severities, and to penances and voluntary inflictions. Many have undertaken wearisome pilgrimages, and have shut themselves out from the benefits and pleasures of the society of mankind, or have spent their lives in deserts and solitudes, and some have suffered death, of whom we have no reason to think that they had any sincere love to

God in their hearts. Multitudes among the Papists, have voluntarily gone and ventured their lives in bloody wars, in hopes of meriting heaven by it. In the wars carried on with the Turks and Saracens, called the Holy Wars, or Crusades, thousands went voluntarily to all the dangers of the conflict, in the hope of thus securing the pardon of their sins, and the rewards of glory hereafter; and many thousands, yea, some millions, in this way lost their lives, even to the depopulation, in a considerable measure, of many parts of Europe. And the Turks were many of them enraged by this exceedingly, so as to venture their lives, and rush, as it were, upon the very points of the swords of their enemies, because Mahomet has promised that all that die in war, in defence of the Mahometan faith, shall go at once to Paradise. And history tells us of some, that have yielded themselves to voluntary death, out of mere obstinacy and sturdiness of spirit, rather than yield to the demand of others, when they might, without dishonor, have saved their lives. Many among the heathen have died for their country; and many, as martyrs for a false faith, though not in any wise in such numbers, nor in such a manner, as those that have died as martyrs for the true religion. And in all these cases, many doubtless have endured their sufferings, or met death, without having any sincere divine love in their hearts. But,

II. *Whatever men may do or suffer, they cannot by all their performances and sufferings, make up for the want of sincere love in the heart.*—If they lay themselves out ever so much in the things of religion, and are ever so much engaged in acts of justice and kindness and devotion; and if their prayers and fastings are ever so much multiplied; or if they should spend their time ever so much in the forms of religious worship, giving days and nights to it, and denying sleep to their eyes and slumber to their eyelids, that they might be the more laborious in religious exercises; and if the things that they should do in religion were such as to get them a name throughout the world, and make them famous to all future generations, it would all be in vain without sincere love to God in the heart. And so if a man should give most bounteously to religious or charitable uses; and if possessing the riches of a kingdom he should give it all, and from the splendor of an earthly prince should reduce himself to the level of beggars; and if he should not stop there, but when he has done all this, should yield himself to undergo the fiercest sufferings, giving up not only all his possessions, but also giving his body to be clothed in rags, or to be mangled and burned and tormented as much as the wit of man could conceive, all, even all this, would not make up for the want of sincere love to God in the heart. And it is plain that it would not for the following reasons:—

1. *It is not the external work done, or the suffering endured, that is, in itself, worth anything in the sight of God.*—The motions and exercise of the body, or anything that may be done by it, if considered separately from the heart—the inward part of the man, is of no more consequence or worth in the sight of God, than the motions of anything without life. If anything be offered or given, though it be silver, or gold, or the cattle on a thousand hills, though it be a thousand rams, or ten thousands of rivers of oil, there is nothing of value in it, as an external thing, in God's sight. If God were in need of these things, they might be of value to him in themselves considered, independently of the motives of

the heart that led to their being offered. We often stand in need of external good things, and therefore such things offered or given to us, may and do have a value to us, in themselves considered. But God stands in need of nothing. He is all-sufficient in himself. He is not fed by the sacrifices of beasts, nor enriched by the gift of silver, or gold, or pearls, "Every beast of the forest is mine, and the cattle upon a thousand hills. If I were hungry, I would not tell thee, for the world is mine, and the fulness thereof," Psalm l. 10, 12. "All things come of thee, and of thine own, have we given thee. O, Lord, our God, all this store that we have prepared to build thee an house for thine holy name, cometh of thine hand, and is all thine own," 1 Chronicles xxix. 14, 16. And as there is nothing profitable to God in any of our services or performances, so there can be nothing acceptable in his sight in a mere external action without sincere love in the heart, " for the Lord seeth not as men seeth ; for man looketh on the outward appearance, but God looketh on the heart." The heart is just as naked and open to him as the external actions. And therefore he sees our actions, and all our conduct, not merely as the external motions of a machine, but as the actions of rational, intelligent creatures, and voluntary free agents, and therefore there can be, in his estimation, no excellence or amiableness in anything we can do, if the heart be not right with him.

And so God takes no pleasure in any sufferings that we may endure, in themselves considered. He is not profited by the torments men may undergo, nor does he delight to see them putting themselves to suffering, unless it be from some good motive, or to some good purpose and end. We sometimes may need that our fellow-men, our friends and neighbors should suffer for us, and should help us bear our burdens, and put themselves to inconvenience for our sake. But God stands in no such need of us, and therefore our sufferings are not acceptable to him, considered merely as sufferings endured by us; and are of no account apart from the motive that leads us to endure them. No matter what may be done or suffered, neither doings nor sufferings will make up for the want of love to God in the soul. They are not profitable to God, or lovely for their own sake in his sight; nor can they ever make up for the absence of that love to God and love to men, which is the sum of all that God requires of his moral creatures.

2. *Whatever is done or suffered, yet if the heart is withheld from God, there is nothing really given to him.*—The act of the individual, in what he does or suffers, is in every case, looked upon not as the act of a lifeless engine or machine, but as the act of an intelligent, voluntary, moral being. For surely a machine is not properly capable of giving anything: and if any such machine, that is without life, being moved by springs, or weights, places anything before us, it cannot properly be said to give it to us. Harps, and cymbals, and other instruments of music, were of old made use of in praising God in the temple and elsewhere. But these lifeless instruments could not be said to give praise to God, because they had no thought, nor understanding, or will, or heart, to give value to their pleasant sounds. And so though a man has a heart, and an understanding, and a will, yet if when he gives anything to God, he gives it without his heart, there is no more truly given to God, than is given by the instrument of music.

He that has no sincerity in his heart, has

no real respect to God in what he seems to give, or in all his performances or sufferings; and therefore God is not his great end in what he does or gives. What is given, is given to that which the individual makes his great end in giving. If his end be only himself, then it is given only to himself, and not to God;—and if his aim be his own honor or ease, or worldly profit, then the gift is but an offering to these things. The gift is an offering to him to whom the giver's heart devotes, and for whom he designs it. It is the aim of the heart that makes the reality of the gift; and if the sincere aim of the heart be not to God, then there is in reality nothing given to him, no matter what is performed or suffered. So that it would be a great absurdity to suppose, that anything that can be offered or given to God, can make up for the absence of love in the heart to him; for without this, nothing is truly given, and the seeming gift is but mockery of the Most High. This further appears,

3. *From the fact, that this love or charity is the sum of all that God requires of us.*—And it is absurd to suppose that anything can make up for the want of that which is the sum of *all* that God requires. Charity or love is some-

thing that has its seat in the heart, and in which, as we have seen, consists all that is saving and distinguishing in Christian character. This love it is, of which our Saviour speaks as the sum of all required in the two tables of the law; and which the Apostle declares is the fulfilling of the law; and how can we make up for the defect, when by withholding it, we do, in effect, withhold the sum total of all that God requires of us. It would be absurd to suppose that we can make up for one thing that is required, by offering another that is required—that we can make up for one debt by paying another. But it is still more absurd to suppose, that we can make up for the whole debt without paying anything, but by continuing still to withhold all that is required. As to external things without the heart, God speaks of them as not being the things that he has required (Isaiah i. 12), and demands that the heart be given to him, if we would have the external offering accepted.

4. *If we make a great show of respect and love to God, in the outward actions, while there is no sincerity in the heart, it is but hypocrisy and practical lying unto the Holy One.*—To pretend to such respect and love, when it is

not felt in the heart, is to act as if we thought we could deceive God. It is to do as Israel did in the desert, after they had been delivered from Egypt, when they are said to have "flattered God with their mouth, and to have lied unto him with their tongues," Ps. lxxviii. 36. But surely it is as absurd to suppose that we can make up for the want of sincere respect by flattery and guile, as to suppose we can make up for the want of truth by falsehood and lying.

5. *Whatever may be done or suffered, if there be no sincerity in the heart, it is all but an offering to some idol.*—As observed before, there is nothing, in the case supposed, really offered to God, and therefore it will follow, that it is offered to some other being or object or end; and whatever that may be, it is what the Scriptures call an idol. In all such offerings, something is virtually worshipped, and whatever it is, be it self, or our fellow-men, or the world, *that* is allowed to usurp the place that should be given to God, and to receive the offerings that should be made to him. And how absurd to suppose we can make up for withholding from God that which is his due, by offering something to our idol. It is

as absurd as it is to suppose that the wife can make up for want of love to her husband, by giving that affection which is due to him, to another man who is a stranger; or that she can make up for her want of faithfulness to him, by the guilt of adultery.

In the application of this subject, it becomes us to use it,

1. *In the way of self-examination.*—If it be indeed so, that all that we can do or suffer is in vain, if we have not sincere love to God in the heart, then it should put us upon searching ourselves whether or no we have this love in sincerity in our hearts. There are many that make a profession and show of religion, and some that do many of the outward things which it requires; and possibly they may think that they have done and suffered much for God and his service. But the great inquiry is, has the heart been sincere in it all, and has all been suffered or done from a regard to the divine glory. Doubtless if we examine ourselves we may see much of hypocrisy. But is there any sincerity? God abominates the greatest things without sincerity, but he accepts of and delights in little things when they spring from sincere love to himself. A

cup of cold water given to a disciple in sincere love, is worth more in God's sight, than all one's goods given to feed the poor, yea, than the wealth of a kingdom given away, or a body offered up in the flames without love. And God accepts of even a little sincere love. Though there be a great deal of imperfection, yet if there be any true sincerity in our love, that little shall not be rejected because there is some hypocrisy with it. And here it may be profitable to observe, that there are these four things that belong to the nature of sincerity, viz, truth, freedom, integrity and purity. And,

First, *truth*.—That is, that there be that truly in the heart, of which there is the appearance and show in the outward action. Where there is, indeed, true respect to God, the love that honors him will be felt in the heart, just as extensively as there is a show made of it in the words and actions. In this sense it is said in the fifty-first psalm, "Behold thou desirest truth in the inward parts." And in this view, it is, that sincerity is spoken of in the Scriptures as the opposite of hypocrisy, and that a sincere Christian is said to be one that is such indeed as he appears to be—one "without guile," John i. 47. Examine yourself, therefore, with respect to this matter. If in your outward actions, there is an appearance or show of respect to God, inquire if it be only external, or if it be sincerely felt in your heart; for without real love or charity you are nothing. The

Second thing, in the nature of sincerity, is *freedom.* On this account, especially, the obedience of Christians is called filial, or the obedience of children, because it is an ingenuous, free obedience, and not legal, slavish, and forced, but that which is performed from love and with delight. God is chosen for his own sake; and holiness for its sake, and for God's sake. Christ is chosen and followed because he is loved, and religion because it is loved, and the soul rejoices in it, finding in its duties its highest happiness and delight. Examine yourself faithfully on this point, whether or no this spirit is yours. The

Third thing, belonging to the nature of this sincerity, is *integrity.* The word signifies *wholeness,* intimating that where this sincerity exists, God is sought, and religion is chosen and embraced with the whole heart, and adhered to with the whole soul. Holiness is chosen with the whole heart. The whole of duty is embraced, and entered upon most cordially, whether it have respect to God or to man, whether it be easy or difficult, whether it have reference to little things or great. There is a proportion and fulness in the character. The whole man is renewed. The whole body, and soul, and spirit are sanctified. Every member is yielded to the obedience of Christ. All the parts of the new creature are brought into subjection to his will. The seeds of all holy dispositions are implanted in the soul, and they will more and more bear fruit in the performance of duty and for the glory of God. The

Fourth thing, that belongs to the nature of sincerity, is *purity*. The word sincere often signifies pure. So in 1 Peter ii. 2, " As newborn babes, desire the sincere milk of the word, that ye may grow thereby ;" *i. e.* pure, unmixed, unadulterated. This appears in the opposition of virtue to sin. The one is spoken of as defilement, and impurity, and uncleanness: the other, as that which is free from these things. The apostle compares sin to a body of death, or a dead body, which of all things is most polluting and defiling, while holiness is spoken of as purity, and holy pleasures as pure pleasures, and the saints in heaven as without spot before the throne of God. Inquire then, whether this purity is yours, and whether in its possession you find the evidence that you sincerely love God. This subject may, also,

2. *Convince those who are still in an unregenerate state, of their lost condition.*—If it be indeed so, that by all you can either do or suffer, you cannot make up for the want of a holy, sincere principle of love in your heart, then it will follow that you are in an undone condition till you have obtained God's regenerating grace to renew a right spirit within you; and that do what you will, or undergo and suffer what you will, you cannot be delivered from your wickedness without the converting grace of God. If you make ever so many prayers, that will not make your case less miserable, unless God, by his mighty power, is pleased to give you a new heart. If you take ever so much pains in religion, and cross and deny yourself, and do or suffer ever so much, all will not avail without this. Therefore whatever you have done, though you can look back upon a great many prayers

offered, and much time spent in reading and meditation, you have no reason to think that these things have made any atonement for your sins, or rendered your case any the less deplorable, or left you any other than a wretched, lost, miserable, guilty and ruined creature.

Natural, unrenewed men, would be glad to have something to make up for the want of sincere love and real grace in their hearts; and many do great things to make up for the want of it, while others are willing to suffer great things. But alas! how little does it all signify! No matter what they may do or suffer, it does not change their character; and if they build their hopes upon it, they do but delude themselves, and feed upon the East wind. If such be your case, consider how miserable you will be while you live without hope in the only true source of hope, and how miserable when you come to die, when the sight of the king of terrors will show the nothingness and vanity of all your doings! How miserable when you see Christ coming to judgment in the clouds of heaven! Then you will be willing to do and suffer anything, that you may be accepted by him. But doings or sufferings will not avail. They will not atone for your sins, or give you God's favor, or save you from the overwhelming storms of his wrath. Rest, then, on nothing that you have done or suffered, or that you can do or suffer; but rest on Christ. Let your heart be filled with sincere love to him; and then, at the last great day, he will own you as his follower and as his friend. The subject,

3. *Exhorts all, earnestly to cherish sincere Christian love in their hearts.*—If it be so, that this is of such great and absolute necessity, then let it be the one great thing that you seek. Seek it with diligence and prayer; and seek it of God, and not of yourself. He only can bestow it. It is something far above the unassisted power of nature; for though there may be great performances, and great sufferings, too, yet without sincere love they are all in vain. Such doings and sufferings may, indeed, be required of us, as the followers of Christ, and in the way of duty; but we are not to rest in them, or feel that they have any merit or worthiness in themselves. At best they are but the outward evidence and the outflowing of a right spirit in the heart. Be exhorted, then, as the great thing, to cherish

sincere love, or Christian charity in the heart. It is that which you must have; and there is nothing that will help your case without it. Without it, all will, in some respects, but tend to deepen your condemnation, and to sink you to but lower depths in the world of despair!

LECTURE IV.

CHARITY DISPOSES US MEEKLY TO BEAR THE INJURIES RECEIVED FROM OTHERS.

"Charity suffereth long and is kind."—1 CORINTHIANS xiii. 4.

THE Apostle, in the previous verses, as we have seen, sets forth how great and essential a thing charity, or a spirit of Christian love, is, in Christianity: that it is far more necessary and excellent than any of the extraordinary gifts of the Spirit; that it far exceeds all external performances and sufferings; and, in short, that it is the sum of all that is distinguishing and saving in Christianity—the very life and soul of all religion, without which, though we give all our goods to feed the poor, and our bodies to be burned, we are nothing. And now he proceeds, as his subject naturally leads him, to show the excellent nature of charity, by describing its several amiable and excellent fruits. In the text two of these fruits are mentioned : *suffering long*, which has respect to the evil or injury received from others ; and *being kind*, which has respect to the good to be done to others. Dwelling, for the present, on the first of these points, I would endeavor to show,

THAT CHARITY, OR A TRULY CHRISTIAN SPIRIT, WILL DISPOSE US MEEKLY TO BEAR THE EVIL THAT IS RECEIVED FROM OTHERS, OR THE INJURIES THAT OTHERS MAY DO TO US.

Meekness is a great part of the Christian spirit. Christ, in that earnest and touching call and invitation of his that we have in the eleventh chapter of Matthew, in which he invites all that labor and are heavy-laden to come to himself for rest, particularly mentions, that he would have them come, to *learn* of him ; for he adds, "I am meek and lowly of heart." And meekness, as it respects injuries received from men, is called *long-suffering* in the Scriptures, and is often mentioned as an exercise, or fruit of the Christian spirit (Galatians, v. 22) : "But the fruit of the Spirit is love, joy, peace, long-suffering ;" and (Ephesians iv. 1, 2) : "I, therefore, the prisoner of the Lord, beseech you that ye walk worthy of the vocation wherewith ye are called, with all lowliness, and meekness, with long-suffering, &c.;" and Colosians iii. 12, 13 : "Put on therefore, as the elect of God, holy and beloved, bowels of mercies, kindness, humbleness of mind, meekness, long-suffering; forbearing one another, and forgiving one another, if any man have a quarrel against any; even as Christ forgave you, so also do ye."

In dwelling more fully on this point, I would, 1. Take notice of some of the various kinds of injuries that we may receive from others; 2. Show what is meant by meekly bearing such injuries; and, 3. How that love which is the sum of the Christian spirit, will dispose us to do this. And,

I. *I would briefly notice some of the various kinds of injuries that we may or do receive from others.*—Some injure others in their estates, by unfairness and dishonesty in their dealings, by being fraudulent and deceitful with them, or at least by leading them to act in the dark, and taking advantage of their ignorance; or by oppressing them, taking advantage of their necessities; or by unfaithfulness towards them, not fulfilling their promises and engagements, and being slack and slighting in any business they are employed in by their neighbors, aiming at nothing but just to meet the letter of their engagements, and not being careful to improve their time to the utmost in accomplishing that which they are engaged to do; or by asking unreasonable prices for what they do; or by withholding what is due, from their neighbors, unjustly, neglecting to pay their debts, or unnecessarily putting their neighbors to trouble and difficulty to get what is due from them. And besides these, there are many other methods in which men injure one another in their dealings, by an abundance of crooked and perverse ways in which they are far from doing to others as they would have them do to themselves, and by which they provoke, and irritate, and injure one another.

Some injure others in their good name, by reproaching or speaking evil of them behind their backs. No injury is more common, and no iniquity more frequent or base than this. Other ways of injury are abundant; but the amount of injury by evil-speaking of this kind, is beyond account. Some injure others by making or spreading false reports about them, and so cruelly slandering them. Others, without saying that which is directly false, greatly misrepresent things, picturing out everything respecting their neighbors in the worst colors, exaggerating their faults, and setting them forth as far greater than they really are, always speaking of them in an unfair and unjust manner. A great deal of injury is done among neighbors by thus uncharitably judging one another, and putting injurious and evil constructions on one another's words and actions.

Persons may greatly injure others in their thoughts, by unjustly entertaining mean thoughts, or a low esteem of them. Some are deeply and continually injurious to others, by the contempt they habitually have of them in their hearts, and by their willingness to think the worst about them. And, as the outflowing of the thoughts, a great deal is done to the injury of others by the words;—for the tongue is but too ready to be the wicked instrument of expressing the evil thoughts and feelings of the soul, and hence in the Scriptures (Job v. 21), it is called a scourge, and is compared (Ps. cxl. 3) to the fangs of some very poisonous kinds of serpents, whose bite is supposed to cause death.

Sometimes men injure others in their treatment and actions towards them, and in the injurious deeds they do them. If clothed with authority, they sometimes carry themselves very injuriously toward those over whom their authority extends, by behaving very assumingly, and magisterially, and tyrannically toward them; and sometimes those who are under authority, carry themselves very injuriously toward those who are over them, by denying them that respect and honor which are due to their places, and thus to themselves while they occupy them. Some carry themselves very injuriously toward others by the exercise of a very selfish spirit, seeming to be all for themselves, and apparently having no regard to the good or benefit of their neighbor, but all their contrivance is only to better their own interests. Some carry themselves injuriously in the manifestation of a very haughty and proud spirit, as though they thought they were more excellent than all others, and that nobody was at all to be regarded except themselves alone; and this appears in their air, and talk, and actions, and their greatly assuming behavior in general, all of which are such, that those about them feel and justly feel, that they are injured by them. Some carry themselves very injuriously by the exercise of a very wilful spirit, being so desperately set on having their own way, that they will, if possible, bend everything to their own will, and never will alter their career, or yield to the wishes of others: they shut their eyes against the light or motives others may offer, and have no regard to any one's inclination but their own, being always perverse and wilful in having their own way. Some carry themselves injuriously in the course they take in public affairs, acting not so much from a regard for the public good, as from the spirit of opposition to some party, or to some particular person; so that the party or person opposed is injured, and oftentimes is greatly provoked and exasperated. Some injure others by the malicious and wicked spirit they cherish against them, whether with or without cause. It is not an uncommon thing for neighbors to dislike and even hate one another; not cherishing anything like love to each other in their hearts, but whether they acknowledge it or not, in reality hating one another, having no delight in each other's honor and prosperity, but, on the contrary, being pleased when they are cast down and in adversity, foolishly and wickedly thinking, perhaps, that another's fall is their own elevation, which it never is. Some injure others by the spirit of envy they show toward them, cherishing ill-will toward them for no other reason than for the honor and prosperity they enjoy. Many injure others from a spirit of revenge, deliberately returning evil for evil, for real or imaginary injuries received from them; and some, as long as they live, will keep up a grudge in their hearts against their neighbor, and whenever an opportunity offers, will act it out in injury to him in the spirit of malice. And in innumerable other particular ways which might be mentioned, do men injure one another; though these may suffice for our present purpose. But,

II. *I would go on to show what is meant by meekly bearing such injuries, or how they ought meekly to be borne.*—And here I would show, first, the nature of the duty enjoined; and then why it is called long-suffering, or suffering long. And,

1. *I would show the nature of the duty of meekly bearing the injuries we suffer from others.* And,

First, It implies that injuries offered *should be borne without doing anything to revenge them*.—There are many ways in which men do that which is revengeful; not merely by actually bringing some immediate suffering on the one that may have injured them, but by anything either in speech or behavior, which shows a bitterness of spirit against him for what he has done. Thus, if after we are offended or injured, we speak reproachfully to our neighbor, or of him to others, with a design to lower or injure him, and that we may gratify the bitter spirit we feel in our hearts for the injury that neighbor has done us, this is revenge. He, therefore, that exercises a Christian long-suffering toward his neighbor, will bear the injuries received from him without revenging or retaliating, either by injurious deeds or bitter words. He will bear it without doing anything against his neighbor that shall manifest the spirit of resentment, without speaking to him, or of him, with revengeful words, and without allowing a revengeful spirit in his heart, or manifesting it in his behavior. He will receive all with a calm, undisturbed countenance, and with a soul full of meekness, quietness and goodness;

and this he will manifest in all his behavior to the one that has injured him, whether to his face or behind his back. Hence, it is, that this virtue is recommended in the Scriptures under the names of gentleness, or as always connected with it, as may be seen in James iii. 17, and Galatians v. 22. In him that exercises the Christian spirit as he ought, there will not be a passionate, rash, or hasty expression, or a bitter, exasperated countenance, or an air of violence in the talk or behavior; but, on the contrary, the countenance and words and demeanor, will all manifest the savor of peaceableness and calmness and gentleness. He may perhaps reprove his neighbor. This may clearly be his duty. But if he does, it will be without impoliteness, and without that severity that can tend only to exasperate; and though it may be with strength of reason and argument, and with plain and decided expostulation, it will still be without angry reflections, or contemptuous language. He may show a disapprobation of what has been done; but it will be not with an appearance of high resentment, but as reproving the offender for a sin against God, rather than as for the offence against himself; as lamenting his calamity, more than resenting his injury; as seeking his good, not his hurt; and as one that more desires to deliver the offender out of the error into which he has fallen, than to be even with him for the injury done to himself. The duty enjoined also implies,

Secondly, That injuries be borne *with the continuance of love in the heart, and without those inward emotions and passions that tend to interrupt and destroy it.*—Injuries should be borne, where we are called to suffer them, not only without manifesting an evil and revengeful spirit in our words and actions, but also without such a spirit in the heart. We should not only control our passions when we are injured, and refrain from giving vent to outward revenge, but the injury should be borne without the spirit of revenge in the heart. Not only a smooth external behavior should be continued, but also a sincere love with it. We should not cease to love our neighbor because he has injured us. We may pity, but not hate him for it. The duty enjoined also implies,

Thirdly, That injuries be borne *without our losing the quietness and repose of our own*

minds and hearts.—They should not only be borne without a rough behavior, but with a continuance of inward calmness and repose of spirit. When the injuries we suffer are allowed to disturb our calmness of mind, and put us into an excitement and tumult, then we cease to bear them in the true spirit of long-suffering. If the injury is permitted to discompose and disquiet us, and to break up our inward rest, we cannot enjoy ourselves, and are not in a state to engage properly in our various duties; and especially we are not in a state for religious duties—for prayer and meditation. And such a state of mind is the contrary of the spirit of long-suffering and meekly bearing of injuries that is spoken of in the text. Christians ought still to keep the calmness and serenity of their minds undisturbed, whatever injuries they may suffer. Their souls should be serene, and not like the unstable surface of the water, disturbed by every wind that blows. No matter what evils they may suffer, or what injuries may be inflicted on them, they should still act on the principle of the words of the Saviour to his disciples (Luke xxi. 19): "In your patience, possess ye your souls." The duty we are speaking of, also implies, once more,

Fourthly, That in many cases when we are injured, *we should be willing to suffer much in our interests and feelings for the sake of peace, rather than do what we have opportunity, and perhaps the right to do in defending ourselves.*—When we suffer injuries from others, the case is often such that a Christian spirit, if we did but exercise it as we ought, would dispose us to forbear taking the advantage we may have to vindicate and right ourselves. For by doing otherwise, we may be the means of bringing very great calamity on him that has injured us; and tenderness toward him may and ought to dispose us to a great deal of forbearance, and to suffer somewhat ourselves, rather than bring so much suffering on him. And besides, such a course would probably lead to a violation of peace, and to an established hostility, whereas in this way, there may be hope of gaining our neighbor, and from an enemy making him a friend. These things are manifest from what the apostle says to the Corinthians concerning going to law one with another. "Now, therefore, there is utterly a fault among you, because ye go to law one with another. Why do ye not rather take wrong? Why do ye not rather suffer yourselves to be defrauded?" 1 Corinthians vi. 7. Not that all endeavors in men to defend and right themselves, when they are injured by others, are censurable, or that they should suffer all the injuries that their enemies please to bring upon them, rather than improve an opportunity they have to defend and vindicate themselves, even though it be to the damage of him that injures them. But in many and probably in most cases, men ought to suffer long first, in the spirit of the long-suffering charity of the text. And the case may often be such, that they may be called to suffer considerably, as charity and prudence shall direct, for the sake of peace, and from a sincere Christian love to the one that injures them, rather than deliver themselves in the way they may have opportunity for. Having thus shown what is implied in this virtue, I would now show, briefly,

2. *Why it is called long-suffering, or suffering long.*—And it seems to be so called, especially on two accounts:—

First, Because we ought meekly to bear not only a small injury, but also a good deal *of injurious treatment from others.* We should persevere, and continue in a quiet frame, without ceasing still to love our neighbor, not only when he injures us a little, but when he injures us much, and the injuries he does us are great. And we should not only thus bear a few injuries, but a great many, and though our neighbor continues his injurious treatment to us for a long time. When it is said that charity suffers long, we cannot infer from this, that we are to bear injuries meekly for a season, and that after that season we may cease thus to bear them. The meaning is not that we must, indeed, bear injuries for a long time, but may cease to bear them at last. But it is that we should meekly continue to bear them, though they are long continued, even to the end. The spirit of long-suffering should never cease. And it is called long-suffering,

Secondly, Because in some cases we should be willing to *suffer a great while in our interests, before we improve opportunities of righting ourselves.* Though we may defend ourselves at last, when we are driven, as it were, by necessity to it, yet we are not to do it out of revenge, or to injure him that has injured us, but only for needful self-defence; and even this, in many cases, is to be given up for peace, and out of a Christian spirit toward him that has injured us, and lest we should do injury to him. Having thus shown in what ways we are often injured by others, and what is implied in meekly bearing the injuries thus inflicted, I come now to show,

III. *How that love or charity which is the sum of the Christian spirit, will dispose us meekly to bear such injuries.*—And this may be shown both in reference to love to God, and love to our neighbors. And,

1. *Love to God and the Lord Jesus Christ, has a tendency to dispose us to this.* For,

First, Love to God disposes us to *imitate* him, and therefore disposes us to such long-suffering as he manifests. Long-suffering is often spoken of as one of the attributes of God. In Exodus xxxiv. 6, it is said, "And the Lord passed by before him, and proclaimed, the Lord, the Lord God, merciful and gracious, long-suffering, &c." And in Romans ii. 4, the apostle asks, " Despisest thou the riches of his goodness, and forbearance, and long-suffering?" The long-suffering of God is very wonderfully manifest in his bearing innumerable injuries from men, and injuries that are very great, and long continued. If we consider the wickedness that there is in the world, and then consider how God continues the world in existence, and does not destroy it, but showers upon it innumerable mercies, the bounties of his daily providence and grace, causing his sun to rise on the evil and on the good, and sending rain alike upon the just and the unjust, and offering his spiritual blessings ceaselessly and to all, we shall perceive how abundant is his long-suffering toward us. And if we consider his long-suffering to some of the great and populous cities of the world, and think how constantly the gifts of his goodness are bestowed on and consumed by them, and then consider how great the wickedness of these very cities, it will show us how amazingly great is his long-suffering. And the same long-suffering has been manifest to very many particular persons, in all ages of the world. He is long-suffering to the sinners that he spares, and to whom he offers his mercy, even while they are rebelling against him. And he is long-suffering toward his own elect people, many of whom long lived in sin, and despised alike his goodness and his wrath: and yet he bore long with them, even to the end, till they were brought to repentance, and made, through his grace, vessels of mercy and glory. And this mercy he showed to them even while they were enemies and rebels, as the apostle tells us was the case with himself. "And I thank Christ Jesus our Lord, who hath enabled me, for that he counted me faithful, putting me into the ministry; who was before a blasphemer, and a persecutor, and injurious; but I obtained mercy, because I did it ignorantly in unbelief. And the grace of our Lord was exceeding abundant with faith and love which is in Christ Jesus. This is a faithful saying, and worthy of all acceptation, that Christ Jesus came into the world to save sinners; of whom I am chief. Howbeit for this cause I obtained mercy, that in me first Jesus Christ might show forth all long-suffering, for a pattern to them which should hereafter believe on him to life everlasting" 1 Timothy i. 12-16. Now it is the nature of love, at least in reference to a superior, that it always inclines and disposes to imitation of him. A child's love to his father disposes him to imitate his father, and especially does the love of God's children dispose them to imitate their heavenly Father And as he is long-suffering, so they should be. And,

Secondly, Love to God will dispose us thus *to express our gratitude* for his long-suffering, exercised toward us. Love not only disposes to imitate, but it works by gratitude. And they that love God, will be thankful to him for the abundant long-suffering that he has exercised toward them in particular. They that love God as they ought, will have such a sense of his wonderful long-suffering toward them under the many injuries they have offered to him, that it will seem to them but a small thing to bear with the injuries that have been offered to them by their fellow-men. All the injuries they have ever received from others, in comparison with those they have offered to God, will appear less than a few pence in comparison with ten thousand talents. And as they thankfully accept of and admire God's long-suffering toward themselves, so they cannot but testify their approbation of it, and their gratitude for it, by manifesting, so far as they are able, the same long-suffering to others. For if they should refuse to exercise long-suffering toward those that have injured them, they would practically disapprove of God's long-suffering toward themselves; for what we truly approve of and delight in, we shall not practically reject. And then gratitude for God's long-suffering, will also dispose us to obedience to God in this particular, when he commands us to be long-suffering toward others. And so, again,

Thirdly, Love to God *tends to humility*, which is one main root of a meek and long-suffering spirit. Love to God, as it exalts him, tends to low thoughts and estimates of ourselves, and leads to a deep sense of our unworthiness and our desert of ill; because he that loves God is sensible of the hatefulness and vileness of sin committed against the being that he loves. And discerning an abundance of this in himself, he abhors himself in his own eyes, as unworthy of any good, and deserving of all evil. Humility is always found connected with long-suffering, as says the apostle, Ephesians iv. 2: "With all lowliness and meekness, with long-suffering, forbearing one another in love." An humble spirit disinclines us to indulge resentment of injuries; for he that is little and unworthy in his own eyes, will not think so much of an injury offered to him, as he that has high thoughts of himself, for it is deemed a greater and higher enormity to offend one that is great and high, than one that is mean and vile. It is pride or self-conceit, that is very much the foundation of a high and bitter resentment, and of an unforgiving and revengeful spirit. Again,

Fourthly, Love to God disposes men to have *regard to the hand of God in the injuries they suffer*, and not only to the hand of man, and meekly to submit to his will therein. Love to God disposes men to see his hand in everything; to own him as the governor of the world, and the director of providence; and to acknowledge his disposal in everything that takes place. And the fact that the hand of God is a great deal more concerned in all that happens to us than the treatment of men is, should lead us, in a great measure, not to think of things as from men, but to have respect to them chiefly as from God—as ordered by his love and wisdom, even when their immediate source may be the malice or heedlessness of a fellow-man. And if we indeed consider and feel that they are from the hand of God, then we shall be disposed meekly to receive and quietly to submit to them, and to own that the greatest injuries received from men are justly and even kindly ordered of God, and so be far from any ruffle or tumult of mind on account of them. It was with this view, that David so meekly and quietly bore the curses of Shimei, when he came forth and cursed and cast stones at him, 2 Samuel xvi. 5, 10; saying that the Lord had bid him do it, and therefore forbidding his followers to avenge it. And once more,

Fifthly, Love to God disposes us meekly to bear injuries from others, because it *sets us very much above the injuries of men*. And it does so in two respects. In the first place it sets us above the reach of injuries from others, because nothing can ever really hurt those that are the true friends of God. Their life is hid with Christ in God; and he as their protector and friend, will carry them on high as on the wings of eagles; and all things shall work together for their good; Romans viii. 28, and none shall be permitted really to harm them, while they are followers of that which is good, 1 Peter iii. 13. And then, in the next place, as love to God prevails, it tends to set persons above human injuries, in this sense, that the more they love God the more they will place all their happiness in him. They will look to God as their all, and seek their happiness and portion in his favor, and thus not in the allotments of his providence alone. The more they love God, the less they set their hearts on their worldly interests, which are all that their enemies can touch. Men can injure God's people only with respect to worldly good. But the more a man loves God, the less is his heart set on the things of the world, and the less he feels the injuries that his enemies may inflict, because they cannot reach beyond these things. And so it often is the case, that the friends of God hardly think the injuries they receive from men are worthy of the name of injuries; and the calm and quietness of their minds are scarcely disturbed by them. And as long as they have the favor and friendship of God, they are not much concerned about the evil work and injuries of men. Love to God and a sense of his favor, disposes them to say of the injuries of men, when they would take from them their worldly enjoyments, as Mephibosheth did of Ziba's taking the land (2 Samuel xix. 30): "Yea, let him take all, forasmuch as my lord the king is come again in peace unto his own house." And as love to God will, in these several respects, dispose us to long-suffering under injuries from others, so,

2. *Love to our neighbor will dispose us to the same.*—In this sense, charity suffers long,—long-suffering and forbearance are always the fruit of love. As the Apostle intimates (Ephesians iv. 1, 2), it is a part of our walking worthily of the Christian vocation, that we walk " with all lowliness and meekness, with long-suffering, forbearing one another in love." Love will bear with a multitude of faults and offences, and will incline us (Proverbs x. 12) to cover all sins. So we see by abundant observation and experience. Those that we have a great and strong affection for, we always bear a great deal more from, than from those that we dislike, or to whom we are indifferent. A parent will bear many things in his own child that he would greatly reprobate in the child of another, and a friend tolerates many things in the friend that he would not in a stranger. But there is no need to multiply words, or reasons, on this branch of the subject, for it is exceedingly plain to all

All know that love is of such a nature, that it is directly contrary both to resentment and revenge; for these imply ill-will, which is the very reverse of love, and cannot exist with it. Without dwelling, then, on this point, I pass, in conclusion, to make some brief improvement of the subject. And,

1. *It exhorts us all to the duty of meekly bearing the injuries that may be received from others.*—Let what has been said be improved by us to suppress all wrath, revenge, and bitterness of spirit, toward those that have injured, or that may at any time injure us: whether they injure us in our estates, or good names, or whether they abuse us with their tongues or with their hands, and whether those that injure us are our superiors, inferiors or equals. Let us not say in our heart, I will do to him, as he hath done to me. Let us not endeavor, as is sometimes said, "to be even with him," by some kind of retaliation, or so much as suffer any hatred or bitterness or vindictiveness of spirit to rise in our hearts. Let us endeavor, under all injuries, to preserve the calmness and quiet of our spirits; and be ready rather to suffer considerably in our just rights, than to do anything that may

occasion our stirring up, and living in strife and contention. To this end I would offer for consideration the following motives.

First, Consider the *example that Christ has set us.* He was of a meek and quiet spirit, and of a most long-suffering behavior. In 2 Corinthians x. 1, we are told by the Apostle, of the meekness and gentleness of Christ. He meekly bore innumerable and very great injuries from men. He was very much the object of bitter contempt and reproach, and slighted and despised as of but little account. Though he was the Lord of glory, yet he was set at naught and rejected and disesteemed of men. He was the object of the spite, and malice, and bitter revilings of the very ones he came to save. He endured the contradiction of sinners against himself. He was called a glutton, and a drunkard; and though holy, harmless, undefiled, and separate from sinners, yet he was charged with being a friend of publicans and sinners. He was called a deceiver of the people, and oftentimes (as in John x. 20, and vii. 20) he was said to be mad, and possessed with the devil. Sometimes they reproached him (John viii. 48) with being a Samaritan and having a devil;

the former being esteemed by the Jews as the highest reproach, and the latter as implying the most diabolical wickedness. He was sometimes charged (John x. 33) with being a wicked blasphemer, and one that deserved death on that account. Sometimes they charged him with working miracles by the power and aid of Beelzebub the prince of devils, and even called him (Matthew x. 25) a devil himself. And such was their spite against him, that they had agreed (John ix. 22) to excommunicate or cast out of the synagogue any one that should say that he was the Christ. They hated him with a mortal hatred, and wished he was dead, and from time to time endeavored to murder him, yea, were almost always endeavoring to imbrue their hands in his blood. His very life was an annoyance to them, and they hated him so (Psalm xli. 5) that they could not bear that he should live. We very often read (as in John v. 16), of their seeking to kill him. And what pains did many of them take to watch him in his words, that they might have something of which to accuse him, and thus be able, with the show of reason, to put him to death. And many times they combined together to take his life in this manner. They often actually took up stones to stone him, and once led him to the brow of a hill that they might cast him down, and thus dash him to pieces. And yet Christ meekly bore all these injuries, without resentment or one word of reproach; and with a heavenly quietness of spirit passed through them all. And at last, when he was most ignominiously dealt with of all, when his professed friend betrayed, and his enemies seized him, and led him away to scourging and the death of the cross, he went as a lamb to the slaughter, opening not his mouth. Not one word of bitterness escaped him. There was no interruption of the calmness of his mind under his heavy distress and sufferings; nor was there the least desire for revenge. But on the contrary, he prayed for his murderers that they might be forgiven, even when they were about nailing him to the cross; and not only prayed for them, but pleaded in their behalf with his Father, that they knew not what they did. The sufferings of his life, and the agonies of his death, did not interrupt his long-suffering toward those that injured him.

Second, If we are not disposed meekly to bear injuries, *we are not fitted to live in the world*, for in it we must expect to meet with many injuries from men. We do not dwell in a world of purity and innocence and love, but in one that is fallen and corrupt, and miserable, and wicked, and that is very much under the reign and dominion of sin. The principle of divine love that was once in the heart of man, is extinguished, and now reigns in but few, and in them in a very imperfect degree. And those principles that tend to malice and injuriousness, are the principles that the generality of the world are under the power of. This world is a place, where the devil, who is called the god of this world, has influence and dominion, and where multitudes are possessed of his spirit. All men, as the Apostle says (2 Thessalonians iii. 2), have not faith; and indeed but few have that spirit of faith in the heart which leads to the life being governed by the rules of justice and kindness toward others. The aspect of the world is too much that of which our Saviour spoke, when in sending out his disciples, he said (Matthew x. 16): "Behold I send you forth as sheep in the midst of wolves." And therefore those that have not a spirit with meekness and calmness and long-suffering and composedness of soul to bear injuries in such a world, are miserable indeed, and are like to be wretched at every step of their way through life. If every injury we must meet, and every reproach and malicious and unjust deed is to put our minds and hearts into a ruffle and tumult, and disturb the calm and peace in which we may enjoy ourselves, then we can have no possession or enjoyment of spirit, but shall be kept in a perpetual turmoil and tumult, like the bark that is driven to and fro continually on the stormy ocean. Men that have their spirits heated and enraged, and rising in bitter resentment when they are injured, act as if they thought some strange thing had happened to them, whereas they are very foolish in so thinking; for it is no strange thing at all, but only what was to be expected in a world like this. They, therefore, do not act wisely that allow their spirits to be ruffled by the injuries they suffer; for a wise man doth but expect more or less injury in the world, and is prepared for it, and in meekness of spirit is prepared to endure it.

Third, In this way *we shall be most above injuries.* He that has established such a spirit and disposition of mind that the injuries received from others do not exasperate and provoke him, or disturb the calmness of his mind, lives, as it were, above injuries and out of their reach. He conquers them, and rides over and above them as in triumph, exalted above their power. He that has so much of the exercise of a Christian spirit, as to be able meekly to bear all injuries done him, dwells on high where no enemy can reach him. History tells us that when the Persians besieged Babylon, the walls of the city were so exceeding high, that the inhabitants used to stand on the top of them, and laugh at their enemies; and so one whose soul is fortified with a spirit of Christian meekness, and a disposition calmly to bear all injuries, may laugh at the enemy that would injure him. If any that have an ill spirit against us, and are therefore disposed to do us an injury by reproaching us or otherwise, see that by so doing they can disturb and vex us, they are gratified thereby; but if they see that by all they can do they cannot interrupt the calm of our minds, or break up our serenity of soul, then they are frustrated in their aim, and the shafts with which they would wound us, fall back without doing the execution they intended: while on the other hand, just in proportion as we allow our minds to be disturbed and embarrassed by the injuries offered by an adversary, just in the same proportion do we fall under his power.

Fourth, The spirit of Christian long-suffering and of meekness in bearing injuries, *is a mark of true greatness of soul.* It shows a true and noble nature, and real greatness of spirit, thus to maintain the calmness of the mind in the midst of injuries and evils. It is an evidence of excellence of temper, and of inward fortitude and strength. "He that is slow to anger," says Solomon (Proverbs xvi. 32), "is better than the mighty, and he that ruleth his spirit than he that taketh a city;" that is, he shows a more noble and excellent nature, and more true greatness of spirit, than the greatest conquerors of the earth. It is from littleness of mind that the soul is easily disturbed and put out of repose by the reproaches and ill-treatment of men; just as little streams of water are much disturbed by the small unevennesses and obstacles they meet with in their course, and make a great deal of noise as they pass over them, whereas great and mighty streams pass over the same obstacles calmly and quietly, without a ripple on the surface to show they are disturbed. He that possesses his soul after such a manner that when others harm and injure him, he can, notwithstanding, remain in calmness and hearty good-will toward them, pitying and forgiving them from the heart, manifests therein a godlike greatness of spirit. Such a meek and quiet and long-suffering spirit, shows a true greatness of soul, in that it shows great and true wisdom, as says the Apostle (James iii. 13): "Who is a wise man and endued with knowledge among you? Let him show, out of a good conversation, his works with meekness of wisdom." And the wise Solomon, who well knew what belonged to wisdom, often speaks of the wisdom of such a spirit: declaring (Proverbs xiii. 10) that "only by pride cometh contention; but with the well advised, is wisdom;" and again (xxix. 8), that "wise men turn away wrath;" and still again (xix. 11); that "the discretion of a man deferreth his anger." On the contrary, those that are apt highly to resent injuries, and to be greatly angered and vexed by them, are spoken of in the Scriptures as of a little and foolish spirit. "He that is slow to wrath," says Solomon (Proverbs xiv. 29), "is of great understanding; but he that is hasty of spirit, exalteth folly;" and again (Ecclesiastes vii. 8, 9), "The patient in spirit, is better than the proud in spirit. Be not hasty in thy spirit to be angry; for anger resteth in the bosom of fools;" and still again (Proverbs xiv. 16, 17, 18), "The fool rageth, and is confident. He that is soon angry, dealeth foolishly; and a man of wicked devices is hated. The simple inherit folly." And on the other hand, a meek spirit is expressly spoken of in the Scripture, as an honorable spirit; as in Proverbs xx. 3 : "It is an honor to a man to cease from strife."

Fifth, The spirit of Christian long-suffering and meekness *is commended to us by the example of the saints*. The example of Christ alone might be, and is sufficient; since it is the example of him who is our head and Lord and master, whose followers we profess to be, and whose example we believe to be perfect. And yet some may be ready to say with regard to the example of Christ, that he was sinless, and had no corruption in his heart, and that it cannot be expected of us that we should do in all things as he did. Now though this is no reasonable objection, yet the example of saints who were men of like passions with ourselves, is not without its special use, and may in some respects have a peculiar influence. Many of the saints have set bright examples of this long-suffering that has been recommended. With what meekness, for instance, did David bear the injurious treatment that he received from Saul, when he was hunted by him as a partridge on the mountains, and pursued with the most unreasonable envy and malice, and with murderous designs, though he had ever behaved himself dutifully toward him. And when he had the opportunity put into his hands of cutting him off, and at once delivering himself from his power, and others around him were ready to think it very lawful and commendable to do so, yet as Saul was the Lord's anointed, he chose rather to commit himself and all his interests to God, and venture his life in his hands, and suffer his enemy still to live. And when, after this, he saw that his forbearance and goodness did not overcome Saul, but that he still pursued him, and when again he had the opportunity of destroying him, he chose rather to go out as a wanderer and an outcast, than to injure the one that would have destroyed him.

Another instance is that of Stephen, of whom we are told (Acts vii. 59, 60) that when his persecutors were venting their rage upon him by stoning him to death, "he kneeled down, and cried with a loud voice, Lord, lay not this sin to their charge." This prayer is mentioned as that which he made with his expiring breath, and as the last words that he uttered after praying the Lord Jesus to receive his spirit; and immediately after making this prayer for his persecutors, we are told that he fell asleep, thus forgiving them and commending them to God's blessing as the last act of his life on earth. Another example, is that of the Apostle Paul, who was the subject of numberless injuries from wicked and unreasonable men. Of these injuries and his manner of behavior under them, he gives us some account in 1 Corinthians iv. 11, 12, 13: "Even unto this present hour we both hunger, and thirst, and are naked, and are buffeted, and have no certain dwelling-place; and labor, working with our own hands. Being reviled, we bless; being persecuted, we suffer it; being defamed, we entreat; we are made as the filth of the world, and are the off-scouring of all things unto this day." Thus he manifested a meek and long-suffering spirit, under all the injuries that were heaped upon him. And not only do we have these records respecting inspired men; but we have accounts in uninspired and mere human histories, of the remarkable heroism and long-suffering of martyrs and other Christians, under the most unreasonable and wicked treatment and injuries received from men: all of which should lead us to the same meek and long-suffering spirit.

Sixth, This is the way *to be rewarded with the exercise of the divine long-suffering toward us.* We are often informed in the Scriptures, that men are to be dealt with by God hereafter according to their way of dealing with others. Thus we are told (Psalm xviii. 25, 26) "that with the merciful God will show himself merciful, and with an upright man, upright; that with the pure, he will show himself pure, and with the froward, he will show himself froward." And again (Matthew vii. 2), "with what judgment ye judge, ye shall be judged: and with what measure ye mete, it shall be measured to you again;" and still again

(vi. 14, 15), "that if we forgive men their trespasses, our heavenly Father will also forgive us, but if we forgive not men their trespasses, neither will our Father forgive our trespasses." By trespasses, here, is meant the same as injuries done to us; so that if we do not bear with men's injuries against us, neither will our heavenly Father bear with our injuries against him; and if we do not exercise long-suffering toward men, we cannot expect that God will exercise long-suffering toward us. But let us consider how greatly we stand in need of God's long-suffering with regard to our injuries toward him. How often and how greatly are we injuriously behaving ourselves toward God, and how ill is our treatment of him every day! And if God did not bear with us, and exercise wonderful long-suffering toward us, how miserable should we be, and what would become of us! Let this consideration, therefore, influence all of us to seek such an excellent spirit as that which has been spoken of, and to disallow and suppress anything of the contrary spirit or practice. It would have a most happy influence on us as individuals, and on our families, and so on all our public associations and affairs, if such a spirit as this prevailed. It would prevent contention and strife, and diffuse gentleness and kindness, and harmony and love. It would do away with bitterness and confusion, and every evil work. Our affairs would all be carried on, both in public and private, without fierceness, or edge, or bitterness of spirit; without harsh and opprobrious expressions to others; and without any of the malignant backbiting and contemptuous speech, that so often are heard among men, and which at the same time do great injury in society, and are making fearful work for the judgment.

But some, in their hearts, may be ready to object against such a meek and quiet bearing of injuries as has been spoken of; and some of these objections it may be profitable briefly to mention and answer:—

Objection 1. Some may be ready to say, *that the injuries they receive from men are intolerable;* that the one who has injured them has been so unreasonable in what he has said or done, and it is so unjust and injurious and unjustifiable, and the like, that it is more than flesh and blood can bear; that they are treated with so much injustice that it is enough to pro voke a stone : or that they are treated with such contempt, that they are actually trampled on, and they cannot but resent it. But in answer to this objection, I would ask a few questions. And,

First, Do you think the injuries you have received from your fellow-man, are more than you have offered to God? Has your enemy been more base, more unreasonable, more ungrateful, than you have to the High and Holy One? Have his offences been more heinous or aggravated, or more in number, than yours have been against your creator, benefactor, and redeemer? Have they been more provoking, and exasperating, than your sinful conduct has been to Him who is the author of all our mercies, and to whom you are under the highest obligations?

Second, Do you not hope that as God hitherto has, so he will still bear with you in all this, and that notwithstanding all, he will exercise toward you his infinite love and favor? Do you not hope that God will have mercy upon you, and that Christ will embrace you in his dying love; though you have been such an injurious enemy; and that through his grace, he will blot out your transgressions and all your offences against him, and make you eternally his child, and an heir of his kingdom?

Third, When you think of such long-suffering on God's part, do you not approve of it, and think well of it, and that it is not only worthy and excellent, but exceeding glorious? And do you not approve of it, that Christ should have died for you, and that God, through him, should offer you pardon and salvation? Or do you disapprove of this? And would you have liked God better, if he had not borne with you, but had long since cut you off in his wrath?

Fourth, If such a course be excellent and worthy to be approved of in God, why is it not in yourself? Why should you not imitate it? Is God too kind in forgiving injuries? Is it less heinous to offend the Lord of heaven and earth, than for a man to offend you? Is it well for you to be forgiven, and that you should pray to God for pardon, and yet that you should not extend it to your fellow-men that have injured you?

Fifth, Would you be willing, for all the future, that God should no longer bear with the injuries you may offer him, and the offences you commit against him? Are you willing to go, and ask God to deal with yourself for the future, as in holding this objection, you think of dealing with your fellow-men?

Sixth, Did Christ turn again upon those who injured, and insulted, and trod on him, when he was here below; and was he not injured far more grievously than ever you have been? And have not you more truly trodden under foot the Son of God, than you were ever trodden on by others? And is it a more provoking thing for men to tread on and injure you, than for you to tread on and injure Christ? These questions may sufficiently answer your objection.

Objection 2. But you may still further say, that *those who have injured you, persist in it, and do not at all repent, but go on doing it still.* But what opportunity could there be for long-suffering, if injury were not persisted in long? If injuries are continued, it may be for the very purpose, in providence, of trying whether you will exercise long-suffering and meekness, and that forbearance that has been spoken of. And did not God bear with you, when you persisted in offending him? When you have been obstinate, and self-wil'ed, and persevering in your injuries against him, has he ceased to exercise his long-suffering toward you?

Objection 3. *But you may object, again, that your enemies will be encouraged to go on with their injuries;* excusing yourself by saying, that if you bear injury, you will only be injured the more. But you do not know this, for you have not an insight into the future, or into the hearts of men. And, beside, God will undertake for you, if you obey his commands; and he is more able to put a stop to the wrath of man than you are. He hath said (Romans xii. 19), "Vengeance is mine, I will repay, saith the Lord." He interposed wonderfully for David, as he has for very many of his saints; and if you do but obey him, he will take part with you against all that rise up against you. And in the observation and experience of men, it is generally found, that a meek and long-suffering spirit puts an end to injuries, while a revengeful spirit does but provoke them. Cherish, then, the spirit of long-suffering meekness, and forbearance, and you shall possess your soul in patience and happiness, and none shall be permitted to harm you more than God in wisdom and kindness may permit.

LECTURE V.

CHARITY DISPOSES US TO DO GOOD.

" Charity suffereth long and is kind."—1 CORINTHIANS xiii. 4.

In the last lecture from these words, it was shown, that charity or Christian love is long-suffering, or that it disposes us meekly to bear the injuries received from others. And now it is proposed to show that it is kind, or in other words,

THAT CHARITY, OR A TRULY CHRISTIAN SPIRIT, WILL DISPOSE US FREELY TO DO GOOD TO OTHERS.

In dwelling on this point, I would, 1, briefly open the nature of the duty of doing good to others, and 2, show that a Christian spirit will dispose us to it.

I. *I would briefly open the nature of the duty of doing good to others.*—And here, three things are to be considered, viz.: the *act*, doing good; the *objects*, or those to whom we should do good; and the *manner* in which it should be done, freely. And,

1. *The act which is the matter of the duty, which is, doing good to others.*—There are many ways in which persons may do good to others, and in which they are obliged so to do, as they have opportunity. And,

First, Persons may do good *to the souls of others,* which is the most excellent way of doing good. Men may be, and oftentimes are the instruments of spiritual and eternal good to others; and wherein any are so, they are the instruments of greater good to them than if they had given them the riches of the universe. And we may do good to the souls of others, by taking pains to instruct the ignorant, and to lead them to the knowledge of the great things of religion; and by counselling and warning others, and stirring them up to their duty, and to a seasonable and thorough care for their soul's welfare; and so again, by Christian reproof of those that may be out of the way of duty; and by setting them good examples, which is a thing the most needful of all, and commonly the most effectual of all for the promotion of the good of their souls. Such an example must accompany the other means of doing good to the souls of men, such as instructing, counselling, warning and reproving, and is needful to give force to such means, and to make them take effect; and it is more likely to render them effectual, than anything else whatsoever; and without it, they will be likely to be in vain.

Men may do good to the souls of vicious persons, by being the means of reclaiming them from their vicious courses; or to the souls of neglecters of the sanctuary, by persuading them to go to the house of God; or to the souls of secure and careless sinners, by putting them in mind of their misery and danger; and so may be the instruments of awakening them, and the means of their conversion, and of bringing them home to Christ. Thus they may be of the number of those, of whom we read (Daniel xii. 3), "that turn many to righteousness," and who "shall shine as stars forever and ever." Saints, too, may be the instruments of comforting and establishing one another, and of strengthening one another in faith and obedience; of quickening, and animating, and edifying one another; of raising one another out of dull and dead frames, and helping one another out of temptations, and onward in the divine life; of directing one another in doubtful and difficult cases; of encouraging one another under darkness or in trial; and generally, of promoting each other's spiritual joy and strength, and thus being mutually fellow-helpers on their way to glory.

Second, Persons may do good to others *in outward things, and for this world*. They may help others in their external difficulties and calamities; for there are innumerable kinds of temporal calamities to which mankind are liable, and in which they stand much in need of the help of their neighbors and friends. Many are hungry, or thirsty, or strangers, or naked, or sick, or in prison (Matthew xxv. 35, 36), or in suffering of some other kind; and to all such we may minister. We may do good to others, by furthering their outward estate or substance; or in aiding their good name, and thus promoting their esteem and acceptance among men; or by anything that may truly add to their comfort and happiness in the world, whether it be in the kind word, or the considerate and benevolent deed. And by endeavoring thus to do good to them externally, we are under the greater advantage to do good to their souls; for when our instructions, counsels, warnings, and good examples are accompanied with such outward kindness, the latter tends to open the way for the better effect of the former, and to give them their full force, and to lead such persons to appreciate our efforts when we seek their spiritual good. And we may thus contribute to the good of others, in three ways: by *giving to them*, of those things that they need and we possess; by *doing for them*, and taking pains to help them and promote their welfare; and by *suffering for them*, and aiding them to bear their burdens, and doing all in our power to make those burdens light. In each of these ways, Christianity requires us to do good to others. It requires us to *give* to others, Luke vi. 38, "Give and it shall be given unto you." It requires us to *do* for others, and to labor for them, 1 Thess. ii. 9: "For ye remember, brethren, our labor and travail; for laboring night and day, because we would not be chargeable unto any of you, we preached unto you the gospel of God;" and Hebrews vi. 10: "For God is not unrighteous to forget your work and labor of love, &c." And it requires us, if need be, to *suffer* for others, Galatians vi. 2 : "Bear ye one another's burdens, and so fulfil the law of Christ;" and 1 John iii. 16: "Hereby perceive we the love of God, because he laid down his life for us; and we ought to lay down our lives for the brethren." So that in all these ways the Scriptures require us to do good to all. I pass, then, to speak,

2. *Of the objects of this act, or of those to whom we should do good.* These are often spoken of in the Scriptures, by the expression, "our neighbor;" for the duty before us, is implied in the command, that we love our neighbor as ourselves. But here, perhaps, we may be ready with the young lawyer that came to Christ (Luke x. 29, &c.), to ask, "who is our neighbor?"—And as Christ's answer taught him that the Samaritan was neighbor to the Jew, though the Samaritans and Jews were each esteemed by the other vile, and accursed, and as bitter enemies, so we may be taught who those are to whom we are to do good, in three respects :—

First, We are to do good both to the *good* and to the *bad.* This we are to do, as we would imitate our heavenly Father, for "he

(Matthew v. 45) maketh his sun to rise on the evil and the good, and sendeth rain on the just and on the unjust." The world is full of various kind of persons; some good, and some evil; and we should do good to all. We should, indeed, especially, "do good to them that are of the household of faith," or that we have reason, in the exercise of charity, to regard as saints. But though we should most abound in beneficence to them, yet our doing good should not be confined to them, but we should do good to all men as we have opportunity. While we live in the world, we must expect to meet with some men of very evil properties, and hateful dispositions and practices. Some are proud, some immoral, some covetous, some profane, some unjust or severe, and some despisers of God. But any or all these bad qualities should not hinder our beneficence, or prevent our doing them good as we have opportunity. On this very account we should the rather be diligent to benefit them, that we may win them to Christ; and especially should we be diligent to benefit them in spiritual things.

Second, We should do good both to *friends* and *enemies*. We are obliged to do good to our friends, not only from the obligation we are under to do good to them as our fellow-creatures, and those that are made in the image of God, but from the obligations of friendship, and gratitude, and the affection we bear them. And we are also obliged to do good to our enemies; for our Saviour says (Matthew v. 44): "But I say unto you, love your enemies; bless them that curse you; do good to them that hate you; and pray for them that despitefully use you, and persecute you." To do good to those that do ill to us, is the only retaliation that becomes us as Christians; for we are taught (Romans xii. 17, 21) to "recompense to no man evil for evil," but on the contrary to "overcome evil with good;" and again it is written (1 Thessalonians v. 15): "See that none render evil for evil unto any man, but ever follow that which is good, both among yourselves and to all men;" and still again (1 Peter iii. 9): "Not rendering evil for evil, or railing for railing, but contrariwise, blessing; knowing that ye are thereunto called, that ye should inherit a blessing." And,

Third, We should do good both to the *thankful* and the *unthankful*. This we are obliged to do by the example of our heavenly Father, for he (Luke vi. 35) "is kind unto the unthankful and to the evil;" and the command is, that we "be merciful as he also is merciful." Many make an objection against doing good to others, saying, "If I do, they will never thank me for it; and for my kindness, they will return abuse and injury:" and thus they are ready to excuse themselves from the exercise of kindness, especially to those who may have shown themselves ungrateful. But such persons do not sufficiently look at Christ; and they either show their want of acquaintance with the rules of Christianity, or their unwillingness to cherish its spirit. Having thus spoken of the duty of doing good, and the persons to whom we are to do it, I pass, as proposed, to speak,

3. *Of the manner in which we should do good to others.*—This is expressed in the single word "*freely.*" This seems implied in the words of the text; for to be kind, is to have a disposition freely to do good. Whatever good is done, there is no proper kindness in the doer of it, unless it be done freely. And this doing good freely, implies three things:—

First, That our doing good *be not in a mer*-

cenary spirit. We are not to do it for the sake of any reward received or expected from the one to whom we do the good. The command is (Luke vi. 35): "Do good, and lend, hoping for nothing again." Oftentimes men will do good to others, expecting to receive as much again; but we should do good to the poor and needy from whom we can expect nothing in return. The command of Christ, is (Luke xiv. 12, 13, 14.): "When thou makest a dinner or a supper, call not thy friends, nor thy brethren, neither thy kinsmen, nor thy rich neighbors; lest they also bid thee again; and a recompense be made thee. But when thou makest a feast, call the poor, the maimed, the lame, the blind; and thou shalt be blessed; for they cannot recompense thee: for thou shalt be recompensed at the resurrection of the just." That our doing good be free, and not mercenary, it is necessary that what we do, be done, not for the sake of any temporal good, or to promote our temporal interest, or honor, or profit, but from the spirit of love.

Second, That our doing good be free, it is requisite that we do it *cheerfully or heartily*, and with real good will to the one we would benefit. What is done heartily, is done from love; and what is done from love, is done with delight, and not grudgingly or with backwardness and reluctance of spirit. "Use hospitality," says the Apostle (1 Peter iv. 9): "one to another, without grudging;" and says Paul (2 Corinthians ix. 7): "Every man, according as he purposeth in his heart, so let him give; not grudgingly, or of necessity: for God loveth a cheerful giver." This requisite or qualification for our doing good, is much insisted on in the Scriptures. "He that giveth," says the Apostle (Romans xii. 8) "let him do it with simplicity; he that ruleth, with diligence; he that showeth mercy, with cheerfulness." And God gives a strict charge (Deuteronomy xv. 10): that we shall not be grieved in our heart when we give to our neighbor. And in a word, the very idea of giving acceptably, is presented throughout the Bible, as implying that we give with a cordial and cheerful spirit. Doing good freely also implies,

Third, That we do it *liberally and bountifully*. We are not to be scant and sparing in our gifts or efforts, but to be open-hearted and open-handed. We are to "abound every good work" (2 Corinthians ix. 8, 11), "being enriched in everything, to all bountifulness." Thus God requires that when we give to the poor, we should "open our hand wide unto him" (Deuteronomy xv. 8); and we are told (Proverbs xi. 25), that "the liberal soul shall be made fat;" and the Apostle would have the Corinthians be bountiful in their contributions for the poor saints in Judea, assuring them (2 Corinthians ix. 6) that "he that soweth sparingly, shall reap also sparingly, and he that soweth bountifully, shall reap also bountifully." Having thus explained the nature of this duty of freely doing good to others, I now proceed, to show,

II. *That a Christian spirit will dispose us thus to do good to others.*—And this appears from two considerations:—

1. *The main thing in that love which is the sum of the Christian spirit, is benevolence or good-will to others.*—We have already seen what Christian love is, and how it is variously denominated according to its various objects and exercises; and particularly how as it respects the good enjoyed, or to be enjoyed *by* the beloved object, it is called the love of *benevolence,* and as it respects the good to be enjoyed

in the beloved object, it is called the love of *complacence.* Love of benevolence is that disposition which leads us to have a desire for, or delight in the good of another; and that is the main thing in Christian love, yea the most essential thing in it, and that whereby our love is most of an imitation of the eternal love and grace of God, and of the dying love of Christ which consists in benevolence or goodwill to men, as was sung by the angels at his birth, Luke ii. 14. So that the main thing in Christian love, is good-will, or a spirit to delight in, and seek the good of those who are the objects of that love.

2. *The most proper and conclusive evidence that such a principle is real and sincere, is, its being effectual.*—The proper and conclusive evidence of our wishing or willing to do good to another, is, to do it. In every case, nothing can be plainer, than that the proper and conclusive evidence of the will, is the act; and the act always follows the will, where there is power to act. The proper and conclusive evidence of a man's sincerely desiring the good of another, is his seeking it in his practice:— for whatever we truly desire, we do thus seek. The Scriptures, therefore, speak of doing good,

as the proper and full evidence of love; and they often speak of loving in the deed or practice, as being the same thing as loving in truth and reality:—1 John iii. 18, 19: "My little children, let us not love in word, neither in tongue, but in deed and in truth:" "hereby we know that we are of the truth;" *i. e.* know that we are sincere. And again (James ii. 15, 16): "If a brother or sister be naked, and destitute of daily food, and one of you say unto them, Depart in peace, be ye warmed and filled, notwithstanding ye give them not those things which are needful to the body, what doth it profit?" There is no profit to them; and so there is no evidence of sincerity on your part, and that you really desire that they should be clothed and fed. Sincerity of desire would lead not merely to *words*, but to the *deeds* of benevolence. In the application of this subject, in conclusion, we may use it,

1. *In the way of reproof.*—If a truly Christian spirit disposes persons freely to do good to others, then all those that are of a contrary spirit and practice, may by it be reproved. A malignant and malicious spirit is the very contrary of the former, for it disposes men to

do evil to others, and not good; and so, also, is a close and selfish spirit, whereby men are wholly bent on their own interests, and unwilling in anything to forego their own ends for the sake of others. And they, also, are of a spirit and practice the very opposite of a spirit of love, who show an exorbitantly grasping and avaricious spirit, and who take every opportunity to get all they possibly can from their neighbors in their dealings with them; asking them more for what they do for, or sell to them, than it is truly worth, and extorting to the utmost from them by unreasonable demands; having no regard to value of the thing to their neighbor, but, as it were, forcing out of him all they can get for it. And they who do these things, are generally very selfish, also, in buying from their neighbors, grinding and pinching them down to the lowest prices, and being very backward to give what the thing purchased is really worth. Such a spirit and practice, are the very opposite of a Christian spirit, and are severely reproved by the great law of love, viz.: that we do to others, as we would have them do to us. The subject we have been considering, also,

2. *Exhorts all to the duty of freely doing*

good to others.—Seeing that this is a Christian duty, and a virtue becoming the gospel, and to which, a Christian spirit, if we possess it, will dispose us, let us seek, as we have opportunity, to do good to the souls and bodies of others, endeavoring to be a blessing to them for time and eternity. Let us, to this end, be willing to do, or give, or suffer, that we may do good alike to friends and enemies, to the evil and the good, to the thankful and the unthankful. Let our benevolence and beneficence be universal, constant, free, habitual, and according to our opportunities and ability; for this is essential to true piety, and required by the commands of God! And here several things are to be considered:—

First, What a *great honor* it is, to be made an instrument of good in the world. When we fill up our lives with doing good, God puts the high honor upon us, of making us a blessing to the world; an honor like that which he put upon Abraham, when he said (Genesis xii. 2), "I will bless thee, and make thy name great, and thou shalt be a blessing." The very light of nature teaches, that this is a great honor; and therefore the Eastern kings and governors used to assume to themselves the title of benefactors, that is "doers of good," as the most honorable they could think of (Luke xxii. 25); and it was a common thing in heathen lands, when those that had done a great deal of good in their life-time were dead, for the people, among whom they dwelt, to reckon them as gods, and build temples to their honor and for their worship. So far as God makes men the instruments of doing good to others, he makes them like the heavenly bodies, the sun and moon and stars, that bless the world by shedding down their light: he makes them like the angels, who are ministering spirits to others for their good: yea, he makes them like himself, the great fountain of all good, who is forever pouring down his blessings on mankind.

Second, Thus freely to do good to others, is but *to do to them as we would have them do to us.* If others have a hearty good-will to us, and show us a great deal of kindness, and are ready to help us when we stand in need, and for that end are free to do, or give, or suffer for us, and to bear our burdens, and feel for us in our calamities, and are warm-hearted and liberal in all this, we most highly approve of their spirit and conduct. And we not only approve, but we highly commend, and perhaps make occasions to speak well of such persons; never thinking, however, that they exceed their duty, but that they act as it becomes them to do. Let us, then, remember, that if this is so noble and so much to be commended in others when we are its objects, then we ought to do the same to them, and to all about us. What we thus approve, we should exemplify in our own conduct.

Third, Let us consider *how kind God and Christ have been to us*, and how much good we have received from them. Their kindness in things pertaining to this world has been very great. The divine mercies are new to us every morning, and fresh every evening: they are as ceaseless as our being. And still greater good things has God bestowed for our spiritual and eternal good. He has given us what is of more value than all the kingdoms of the earth. He has given his only-begotten and well-beloved son, the greatest gift he could bestow. And Christ has not only done, but he has suffered great things, and given himself to die for us; and all freely, and without grudging, or hope of reward. "Though he was rich," with all the riches of the universe, "yet for our sakes he became poor, that we through his poverty might be rich" (2 Corinthians viii. 9). And what great things hath God done for those of us who are converted, and have been brought home to Christ; delivering us from sin, justifying and sanctifying us, making us kings and priests unto God, and giving us a title "to an inheritance that is incorruptible, and undefiled, and that fadeth not away" (1 Peter i. 4). And all this, when we were not good, but evil, and unthankful, and in ourselves deserving only of wrath. And,

Fourth, Let us consider what *great rewards are promised to those that freely do good to others.* God hath promised that to "the merciful he will show himself merciful" (Psalm xviii. 25); and there is scarcely any duty spoken of throughout the Bible, that has so many promises of reward as this, whether for this world, or the world to come. For this world, as our Saviour declares (Acts xx. 35), "It is more blessed to give than to receive." He that gives bountifully, is more blessed in the bountiful gifts that he parts with, than he that receives the bounty. What is bestowed in doing good to others, is not lost, as if it were thrown into the ocean. It is rather, as Solomon tells us (Ecclesiastes xi. 1), like the seed which the Orientals plant by scattering it on the waters when the floods are up, and which sinking to the bottom, there takes root, and springing up, is found again in the abundant harvest after many days. What is so given, is loaned to the Lord (Proverbs xix. 17); and what we have thus lent him, he will pay us again. And he will not only repay it, but will greatly increase its amount; for if we give, it is declared (Luke vi. 38), that it shall be "given to us again, good measure, pressed down, shaken together, and running over." Indeed this is the very way to increase; for it is said (Proverbs xi. 24), "There is that scattereth, and yet increaseth, and there is that withholdeth more than is meet, and it tendeth to poverty;" and again (Isaiah xxxii. 8), "The liberal deviseth liberal things, and by liberal things shall he stand." What even unregenerate men do give in this way, God often seems to reward with great temporal blessings. His own declaration is (Proverbs xxviii. 27) that "he that giveth to the poor shall not lack," and the promise is not restricted to the saints: and our observation of providence shows, that men's gifts to the poor are almost as surely prospered of God to themselves, as the seed which they sow in the field. It is easy for God to make up, and more than make up to us all that we thus give for the good of others. It is of this very kind of giving, that the Apostle tells the Corinthians (2 Corinthians ix. 6–8) that "he that soweth bountifully shall reap also bountifully;" adding that "God loveth the cheerful giver," and that he "is able to make all grace abound toward them;" that is, to make all their gifts abound to themselves. Many persons do but little consider how much their prosperity depends on Providence. And yet, even for this world, "it is the blessing of God that that maketh rich" (Proverbs x. 22); and of him that considereth the poor, it is written (Psalm xli. 1) that "the Lord will deliver him in time of trouble." And if we give in the way and with the spirit of Christian charity, we shall thus lay up treasure in heaven, and receive at last the rewards of eternity. This is that laying up of treasures that fail not, of which Christ speaks (Luke xii. 33), and as to which he declares (Luke xiv. 13, 14, 15), that though the poor whom we benefit cannot recompense us, "we shall be recompensed at the resurrection of the just." This, then, is the best way of laying up for time or for eternity. It is the best way of laying up for ourselves, and the best way of laying up for our posterity; for of the good man, who showeth favor and lendeth, it is written (Psalm cxii.) that "his horn shall be exalted with honor," and that "his seed shall be mighty upon earth, and wealth and riches shall be in his house, and his righteousness endureth forever." And when Christ shall come to judgment, and all people shall be gathered before him, then to those who were kind and benevolent, in the true spirit of Christian love, to the suffering and the poor, he shall say (Matthew xxv. 34, 35, 36, 40), " Come ye blessed of my father, inherit the kingdom prepared for you from the foundation of the world: for I was an hungered, and ye gave me meat; I was thirsty, and ye gave me drink; I was a stranger, and ye took me in; naked, and ye clothed me; I was sick, and ye visited me; I was in prison, and ye came unto me." "Verily, I say unto you, inasmuch as ye have done it unto one of the least of these, my brethren, *ye have done it unto me!*"

LECTURE VI.

CHARITY INCONSISTENT WITH AN ENVIOUS SPIRIT.

"Charity envieth not."—1 Cor. xiii. 4.

Having already seen the nature and tendency of Christian charity, or divine love, with respect to the evil received from others, that it "*suffers long*," and also with respect to doing good to others, that it "*is kind*," we now come to the feelings and conduct to which the same charity will lead us in respect to the good possessed by others, and that possessed by ourselves. And in reference to the good possessed by others, the Apostle declares it to be the nature and tendency of charity, or true Christian love, not to envy them the possession of any good whatever which is theirs. "*Charity envieth not.*" The teaching of these words plainly is,

That charity or a truly Christian spirit, is the very opposite of an envious spirit

In dwelling on this thought, I would show, 1, What is the nature of an envious spirit; 2, Wherein a Christian spirit is the opposite of such a spirit; 3, The reason and evidence of the doctrine. And,

I. *The nature of envy.*—Envy may be defined to be a spirit of dissatisfaction with and opposition to the prosperity and happiness of others as compared with our own. The thing that the envious person is opposed to and dislikes, is, the comparative superiority of the state of honor, or prosperity or happiness, that another may enjoy, over that which he possesses. And this spirit is especially called envy, when we dislike and are opposed to another's honor or prosperity, because, in general, it is greater than our own, or because, in particular, they have some honor or enjoyment that we have not. It is a disposition natural in men, that they love to be uppermost; and this disposition is directly crossed, when they see others above them. And it is from this spirit, that men dislike and are opposed to the prosperity of others, because they think it makes those who possess it, superior, in some respect, to themselves. And from this same disposition, a person may dislike another's being equal to himself in honor or happiness, or in having the same sources of enjoyments that he has; for as men very commonly are, they cannot bear a rival, much, if any better than a superior, for they love to be singular and alone in their eminence and advancement. Such a spirit is called envy in the Scriptures. Thus Moses speaks of Joshua's envying for his sake, when Eldad and Medad were admitted to the same privilege with himself in having the spirit of prophecy given them, saying (Numbers xi. 29), "Enviest thou for my sake? Would God that all the Lord's people were prophets, and that the Lord would put his spirit upon them." And Joseph's brethren, we are told (Genesis xxvii. 11), envied him when they had heard his dream, which implied that his parents and brethren were yet to bow down before him, and that he was to have power over them. From such a spirit, persons are not only unwilling that others should be above them or equal to them, but that they should be near them; for the desire to be distinguished in prosperity and honor, is the more gratified just in proportion as they are elevated and others are below them, so that their comparative eminence may be marked and visible to all. And this disposition may be exercised, either in reference to the prosperity that others may obtain and of which they are capable, or in reference to that which they actually have obtained. In the latter form, which is the most common, the feeling of envy will be manifest in two respects, first, in respect to their prosperity, and next in respect to themselves. And,

1. It will be manifest in an *uneasiness and dissatisfaction with the prosperity* of others. Instead of rejoicing in the prosperity of others, the envious man will be troubled with it. It will be a grievance to his spirit to see them rise so high, and come to such honors and advancement. It is no comfortable feeling to him to hear of their having obtained such and such advantages and honors and preferments, but on the contrary very uncomfortable. He is very much of the spirit of Haman, who in view of all "the glory of his riches, and the multitude of his children, and all the things wherein the king had promoted him," still could say (Esther v. 13), "yet all this availeth me nothing, so long as I see Mordecai the Jew sitting in the king's gate." From such a spirit, the envious person stands

ready to rejoice at anything that happens to diminish the honor and comfort of others. He is glad to see them brought down, and will even study how to lower their estate, as Haman did how to humble and bring down Mordecai. And often, like Haman, he will show his uneasiness, not only by planning and scheming, but by actual endeavors of one kind or another, to bring them down; and the very first opportunity of pulling them down that offers, he will gladly embrace. And it is from this disposition, that the sight, even, of others' prosperity, often sets the envious on talking against them and speaking evil of them, even when perhaps they do not know them. Envying them the prominence they have obtained, they hope, by speaking evil of them, in some measure to diminish their honors, and lower them in the esteem of men. This suggests, again,

2. That the opposition of the envious to the prosperity of others will be manifest *in a dislike of their persons for it*. Seeing how others prosper, and what honors they attain, the envious dislike, and even hate them, on account of their honor and prosperity. They entertain and cherish an evil spirit toward them,

for no other reason but that they are prospered. They are embittered against them in spirit, only because they are eminent in name or fortune. Thus Haman, it is said (Esther v. 9), "Was full of indignation against Mordecai," because he saw him "in the king's gate," and because "he stood not up, nor moved for him;" and Joseph's brethren (Genesis xxxvii. 4, 5) "hated him and could not speak peaceably unto him," because his father loved him; and when he had dreamed a dream implying their inferiority, "they hated him yet the more." And so the envious generally resent the prosperity of others and their coming to honor, as if in it they were guilty of some injury to themselves. Sometimes there is a settled hatred toward others upon this account, leading as in the case of Joseph's brethren (Genesis xxxvii. 19–28), to acts of the greatest cruelty and wickedness. But this may suffice for the nature of this envy; and I proceed to show,

II. *Wherein a Christian spirit is the opposite of such a spirit of envy.* And,

1. A Christian spirit *disallows of the exercise and expressions of such a spirit.* He that is influenced in the course of his life and ac-

tions by Christian principles, though he may have envy as well as other corrupt feelings in his heart, yet abhors its spirit as unbecoming in himself as a Christian, and contrary to the nature and will and spirit of God. He sees it to be a most odious and hateful spirit, and he sees its odiousness not only in others, but also and equally in himself. And therefore whenever he perceives its emotions rising within him on any occasion, or toward any person, so far as he is influenced by a Christian spirit he will be alarmed at it, and will fight against, and will not allow its exercise for a moment. He will not suffer it to break forth and show itself in words or actions; and he will be grieved at whatever he sees of its movements in his heart, and will crucify within him the hateful disposition, and do all in his power to go contrary to it in his outward actions.

2. A Christian spirit not only opposes the exercise and outward expressions of an envious spirit, *but it tends to mortify its principle and disposition in the heart.* So far as a Christian spirit prevails, it not only checks the outward actings of envy, but it tends to mortify and subdue the very principle itself

in the heart; so that just in proportion to the power of the former, the individual will cease to feel any inclination to be grieved at the prosperity of others, and still more will cease to dislike them, or entertain any ill-will toward them on account of it. A Christian spirit disposes us to feel contentment with our own condition, and with the state which God has given us among men, and to a quietness and satisfaction of spirit with regard to the allotments and distributions of stations and possessions which God in his wise and kind providence has made to ourselves and others. Whether our rank be as high as that of the angels, or as low as that of the beggar at the rich man's gate (Luke xvi. 20), we shall equally be satisfied with it as the post in which God hath placed us, and shall equally respect ourselves if we are endeavoring faithfully to serve him in it. Like the Apostle (Philippians iv. 11), we shall learn, if we do but have a Christian spirit, "in whatsoever state we are, therewith to be content." But,

3. A Christian spirit not only disallows the exercise and expression of envy, and tends to mortify its principle and disposition in the heart, but *it disposes us to rejoice in the pros*

perity of others. It disposes us to a cheerful and habitual compliance with that rule given by the Apostle (Romans xii. 10) that we "rejoice with them that do rejoice, and weep with them that weep;"—*i. e.* that we sympathize with their estate and condition, in the spirit we should feel if it were our own. Such a spirit of benevolence and good-will, will cast out the evil spirit of envy, and enable us to find happiness in seeing our neighbor prospered. I now proceed as proposed, to show,

III. *The reason and evidence of the doctrine stated; or to show that it is so, and why it is so, that a Christian spirit is thus the opposite of a spirit of envy.*—And this will appear if we consider three things: *first*, how much a spirit and practice contrary to an envious spirit, is insisted on in the precepts that Christ has given; *second*, how much the history and doctrines of the gospel hold forth to enforce these precepts; and, *third*, how much a spirit of Christian love will dispose us to yield to the authority of these precepts, and the influence of the motives enforcing them. And,

1. *A spirit and practice entirely contrary to an envious spirit, is much insisted on in the precepts of Christ.*—The New Testament is

full of precepts of good-will to others, and of precepts enjoining the principles of meekness, humility, and beneficence, all of which are opposed to a spirit of envy; and in addition to these, we have many particular warnings against envy itself. The Apostle exhorts (Romans xiii. 13) that we " walk honestly, as in the day, not in strife and *envying;*" and again (1 Corinthians iii. 3), he blames the Corinthians as being yet carnal, because there was *envying* among them; and still again (2 Corinthians xii. 20), he mentions his fears concerning them, lest he should find among them *envyings*, and that too coupled, as envyings too often are, with " wraths, strifes, backbitings, whisperings, swellings, tumults;" and again (Galatians v. 21), *envy* is ranked among the abominable works of the flesh, such as " murders, drunkenness, revellings, &c.;" and again (1 Timothy vi. 4), it is condemned as implying great wickedness; and again (Titus iii. 3), it is mentioned as one of the hateful sins that Christians had lived in before their conversion, but which they are now redeemed from, and therefore should confess and forsake. And in the same spirit, the Apostle James (iii. 14, 16), speaks of *envy* as exceed ing contrary to Christianity, and as connected with every evil work, being earthly, sensual, devilish; and he warns us against it (v. 9) saying, "Grudge not one against another, brethren, lest ye be condemned: behold the judge standeth before the door;" and to quote but one more instance, the Apostle Peter (1 Peter ii. 1 and 2) warns us against all *envies*, as connected with various other evils, and as preventing our growth in divine things. Thus we see that the New Testament is full of precepts which Christ has left us, which enjoin the very opposite of the spirit of envy. And these precepts,

2. *Are strongly enforced by the doctrines and history of the gospel.*—If we consider the Christian scheme of *doctrine*, we shall find that it tends strongly to enforce the precepts we have considered; for all of it, from beginning to end, strongly tends to the contrary of an envious spirit. In all its bearings and teachings, the Christian form of doctrine militates against a spirit of envy. The things it teaches as to God are exceeding contrary to it; for there we are told how far God was from begrudging us the most exceeding honor and blessedness, and how he has withheld

nothing as too much to be done for us, or as too great or good to be given us. He has not begrudged us his only-begotten and well-beloved son, who was dearer to him than everything beside; nor hath he begrudged us the highest honor and blessedness in and through him. The doctrines of the gospel also teach us, how far Christ was from begrudging us anything that he could do for, or give us. He did not begrudge us a life spent in labor and suffering, or his own precious blood which he shed for us on the cross; nor will he begrudge us a throne of glory with him in the heavens, where we shall live and reign with him for ever. The Christian scheme of doctrine teaches us how Christ came into the world to deliver us from the power of Satan's envy toward us; for the devil, with miserable baseness, envied mankind the happiness that they at first had, and could not bear to see them in their happy state in Eden, and therefore exerted himself to the utmost for their ruin, which he accomplished. And the gospel also teaches, how Christ came into the world to destroy the works of the devil, and deliver us from that misery into which his envy hath brought us, and to purify our natures from every trace of the same spirit, that we may be fitted for heaven.

And if in addition to the doctrine of the gospel, we consider its *history*, we shall find that it also tends greatly to enforce those precepts that forbid envy. And particularly is this true of the history of the life of Christ, and the example he has set us. How far was he from a spirit of envy! How contented in the low and afflictive circumstances in which he voluntarily placed himself for our sakes! And how far was he from envying those that were of worldly wealth and honor, or coveting their condition! He rather chose to continue in his own low estate; and when the multitude, filled with admiration of his teaching and his miracles, on one occasion stood ready to make him a king, he refused the high honor they intended to put upon him, and withdrew himself to be out of their way (John vi. 15), and went away into a mountain alone. And when John the Baptist was so greatly honored by the people as a distinguished prophet, and all Judea and Jerusalem went out to hear him and to be baptized of him. Christ envied him not, but himself went out to be baptized of him in Jordan, though he was John's lord and master; and John, as he himself testified, had need to be baptized of him. And so far was he from begrudging to his disciples any honors or privileges as too great for them, that he told and promised them (John xiv. 12), that after his death and ascension, they should do greater works than he had done while he remained with them. And, as we find in the Acts of the Apostles, all that he foretold, in a little while came true. And,

3. *The true spirit of Christian love will dispose us to yield to the authority of these precepts, and to the influence of the motives enforcing them.*—And the spirit of love will dispose us to this, directly, or by its immediate tendency; and indirectly, as it teaches and leads us to humility.

First, Christian love disposes us to hearken to the precepts that forbid envy, and to the gospel motives against it, *by its own immediate tendency.* The nature of charity or Christian love to men is directly contrary to envy; for love does not grudge, but rejoices at the good of those who are loved. And surely love to our neighbor does not dispose us to hate him for his prosperity, or be unhappy at his good. And love to God, also, has a direct tendency to influence us to obey his commands. The natural, genuine, uniform fruit of love to God, is, obedience; and therefore it will tend to obedience to those commands wherein he forbids envy, as much as others, yea, to them more especially, because love delights to obey no commands so much as those that require love. And so love to God will dispose us to follow his example, in that he has not begrudged us our manifold blessings, but has rejoiced in our enjoyment; and it will dispose us to imitate the example of Christ in not begrudging his life for our sakes, and to imitate the example he set us in the whole course of his life on earth. And,

Second, A spirit of Christian love disposes to the same, also, indirectly, *by inclining us to humility*. It is pride that is the great root and source of envy. It is because of the pride of men's hearts, that they have such a burning desire to be distinguished, and to be superior to all others in honor and prosperity, and which makes them so uneasy and dissatisfied in seeing others above them. But a spirit of love tends to mortify pride, and to work humility in the heart. Love to God tends to this, as it implies a sense of God's infinite excellence, and therefore tends to a sense of our comparative nothingness and unworthiness. And love to men tends to an humble behavior among men, as it disposes us to acknowledge the excellencies of others, and that the honors bestowed on them are their due, and to esteem them better than ourselves, and thus more deserving of distinction than we are. But I will not now dwell more particularly on this point, as in a future lecture I shall have occasion more fully to show how Christian love tends to humility. Passing then, in conclusion, to the application of the subject, I remark,

1. *It should lead us to examine ourselves, whether we are in any degree under the influence of an envious spirit.*—Let us examine ourselves as to time past and look over our past behavior among men. Many of us have long been members of human society, having lived by others, and having had to do with them in very many ways, and being connected with them on many occasions both in public and private affairs. And we have seen others in prosperity, and it may be prospering in their affairs more than ourselves.

They have had more of the world, and have been possessed of greater riches, and have lived in greater ease, and in much more honorable circumstances than we have enjoyed. And perhaps some that heretofore we used to look upon as our equals, or even as inferiors, we may have seen growing in wealth, or advancing in honor and prosperity while we have been left behind, until now they have reached a station far superior to our own. It may be that we have seen such changes, and been called to bear such trials through a great part of the course of our life; and certainly we have often seen others abounding in all that the world esteems of value, while we have been comparatively destitute of these things. And now let us inquire how these things have affected us, and how have our hearts stood, and what has been our behavior in these circumstances? Has there not been a great deal of uneasiness, dissatisfaction, and uncomfortable feeling, and of a desire to see those who were prosperous brought down? Have we not been glad to hear of anything to their disadvantage; and in the forebodings we have expressed about them, have we not in reality spoken out our wishes; and in word or deed, have we not been ready to do that which might in some respect lessen their prosperity or honor? Have we ever cherished a bitter or unkind spirit toward another because of his prosperity, or been ready on account of it to look upon him with an evil eye, or to oppose him in public affairs, or from an envious spirit to act with the party that might be against him? As we look back on the past, do we not see that in these and many other kindred things we have often exercised and allowed an envious spirit, and many times have not our hearts burned with it toward others?

And turning from the past to the present, what spirit do you now find as you search your heart? Do you carry any old grudge in your heart against this or that man that you see sitting with you from Sabbath to Sabbath in the house of God, and from time to time sitting with you at the Lord's table? Is not the prosperity of one and another, an eye-sore to you; and does it not make your life uncomfortable that they are higher than you; and would it not be truly a comfort to you to see them brought down, so that their losses and depression would be a source of inward joy and gladness to your heart? And does not this same spirit lead you often to think evil, or to speak with contempt, or unkindness, or severity of such to those about you? And let those who are above others in prosperity, inquire, whether they do not allow and exercise a spirit of opposition to the comparative happiness of those below them? Is there not a disposition in you to pride yourself on being above them, and a desire that they should not rise higher, lest they come to be equal or superior to you: and from this are you not willing to see them down, and even to help them down to the utmost, lest at some time they may get above you? And does not all this show, that you are very much under the influence of an envious spirit? But it may be that in all this you may justify yourself, not giving it the name of envy, but some other name, and having various excuses for your envious spirit by which you account yourself justified in its exercise. Some are ready to say of others that they are not worthy of the honor and prosperity they have; that they have not half the fitness or worthiness of the honor and advancement they have, that many of their neighbors have who are below them.

And where, I ask, is the man in the world who envies another for his honor or prosperity, but is ready to think or say, that that other is not worthy of his prosperity and honors? Did Joseph's brethren esteem him worthy of the peculiar love of his father? Did Haman think Mordecai worthy of the honor the king conferred on him? Or did the Jews think the Gentiles worthy of the privileges extended to them under the gospel, when they were so filled with envy on this account, as is related in the Acts of the Apostles, xiii. 45, and xvii. 5? It is generally the case, that when others are promoted to honor, or in any respect come to remarkable prosperity, some are always ready to improve the occasion to tell of their faults, and set forth their unworthiness, and rake up all possible evil about them. Whereas it is not so much that they have faults, for these would often be unnoticed if they were in obscurity, as it is that they are prospered, and those who talk about their faults are envious of their prosperity, and therefore speak against them. And I would desire such persons as think that they are to be justified in their opposition to others because they are not worthy of their prosperity, diligently to inquire which it is that pains and troubles them most, their neighbor's faults, or his prosperity. If it be their faults, then you would be grieved on account of them whether the persons were prospered or not; and if truly grieved with their faults, then you would be very slow to speak of them except to themselves, and then in the true spirit of Christian compassion and friendship. But you may say, they make a bad use of their prosperity and honor; that they are lifted up by it, and cannot bear, or do not know how to manage it; that they are insufferable, and scornful, and there is no doing anything with them in their prosperity; and it is best they should be brought down; that this will tend to humble them, and that the best thing for their own good, is, to bring them down to the place where they belong, and which is fittest for them. But here let me urge you strictly to inquire whether you do in truth lament the injury their prosperity does them, and whether you mourn it for their sakes, and because you love them? Do your lamentations spring from pity, or from envy? If you dislike their prosperity because it is not best for them, but does them hurt, then you will grieve for their calamity, and not at their prosperity. You will sincerely love them; and out of this love, will be heartily sorry for their calamity, and feel a true compassion of heart for them that the disadvantages of their prosperous state are so much greater than its advantages. But is this in truth your real feeling? Do not deceive yourself. Is it their calamity that you are grieved at, or is it merely that they are prospered? Is it that you are grieved for them, that their prosperity injures them, or for yourself, that their prosperity is not yours? And here also let every one inquire, whether they do not sometimes envy others for their spiritual prosperity? You remember what was the spirit of Cain toward Abel, of the seed of the serpent toward the seed of the woman, of Ishmael toward Isaac, of the Jews toward Christ, of the elder brother toward the prodigal. Beware that you cherish not their spirit; but rather rejoice in the good estate of others, as much as if it were your own.

2. *The subject also exhorts us to disallow and put away everything approaching to an envious spirit.*—So contrary is the spirit of envy to a Christian spirit, so evil in itself, and so injurious to others, that it should be disal-

lowed and put away by all, and especially by those who profess to be Christians. Great numbers cherish the hope that this is their character, and that they have been endued with a new spirit, even the spirit of Christ. Let it then be evident to all that such is your spirit by the exercise of that charity that envieth not. In the language of the Apostle (James iii. 13, 14, 15, 16), "Who is a wise man, and endued with knowledge among you? Let him show, out of a good conversation, his works with meekness of wisdom. But if ye have bitter *envying* and strife in your hearts, glory not, and lie not against the truth. This wisdom descendeth not from above, but is earthly, sensual, devilish; for where envying and strife is, there is confusion and every evil work." The spirit of envy is the very contrary of the spirit of heaven, where all rejoice in the happiness of others; and it is the very spirit of hell itself, which is a most hateful spirit, and one that feeds itself on the ruin of the prosperity and happiness of others, on which account some have compared envious persons to caterpillars, which delight most in devouring the most flourishing trees and plants. And as an envious disposition is most hateful in itself, so it is most uncomfortable and uneasy to its possessor. As it is the disposition of the devil, and partakes of his likeness, so it is the disposition of hell, and partakes of its misery. In the strong language of Solomon (Proverbs xiv. 30): "A sound heart is the life of the flesh, but envy the rottenness of the bones." It is like a powerful eating cancer, preying on the vitals, offensive and full of corruption. And it is the most foolish kind of self-injury; for the envious make themselves trouble most needlessly, being uncomfortable only because of others' prosperity, when that prosperity does not injure themselves, or diminish their enjoyments and blessings. But they are not willing to enjoy what they have, because others are enjoying also. Let, then, the consideration of the foolishness, the baseness, the infamy of so wicked a spirit, cause us to abhor it, and to shun its excuses, and earnestly to seek the spirit of Christian love, that excellent spirit of divine charity which will lead us always to rejoice in the welfare of others, and which will fill our own hearts with happiness. This love "is of God" (1 John iv. 7); and he that dwelleth in it, "dwelleth in God, and God in him." 1 John iv. 16.

LECTURE VII.

THE SPIRIT OF CHARITY IS AN HUMBLE SPIRIT.

"Charity vaunteth not itself; is not puffed up; doth not behave itself unseemly."—1 Corinthians xiii. 4, 5.

Having shown the nature and tendency of charity or Christian love, in respect to our receiving injury, and doing good to others, that it "*suffers long and is kind;*" and also with respect to the good possessed by others as compared with that possessed by ourselves, that charity "*envieth not;*" the Apostle now proceeds to show, that in reference to what we ourselves may be or have, charity *is not proud;* that "it vaunteth not itself, is not puffed up, doth not behave itself unseemly." As, on the one hand, it prevents us from envying others what they possess, so on the other, it keeps us from glorying in what we possess ourselves. Paul had just declared that charity was contrary to a spirit of envy, and now he declares that it is equally contrary to that spirit which specially provokes men to envy others, and which they often make a pretence or apology for envying them, viz. : that they are puffed up with their honors and prosperity, and vaunt themselves on their possession of these things. When men have obtained prosperity or are advanced, and others observe that they are puffed up and vaunt themselves in it, this tends to provoke envy and make others uneasy at the sight of their prosperity. But if a man has prosperity or advancement and yet does not vaunt himself or behave in an unseemly manner on account of it, this tends to reconcile others to his high circumstances, and make them satisfied that he should enjoy his elevation. As already observed, when men envy another, they are prone to excuse and justify themselves in so doing, by the pretence that he does not make a good improvement of his prosperity, but is proud of it and puffed up on account of it. But the Apostle shows how Christian love, or charity, tends to make all behave suitably to their condition, whatever it may be ; if below others, not to envy them, and if above others, not to be proud or puffed up with the prosperity.

In the words of the text, we may observe, that a spirit of Christian love is spoken of as the opposite of *a proud behavior*, and that two degrees of such a behavior are mentioned. The higher degree is expressed by a man's "vaunting himself," that is, by his so carrying himself as to show plainly that he glories in what he has, or is; and the lower degree is expressed by his "behaving himself unseemly," that is, by his not conducting himself in a becoming and decent manner in the enjoyment of his prosperity, but so acting as to show that he thinks the mere fact of his being prosperous exalts him above others. And the spirit of charity or love is spoken of as opposed not only to a proud behavior, but to a *proud spirit*, or pride in the heart, for charity "is not puffed up." The doctrine we are taught, then, in these words, is this:—

THAT THE SPIRIT OF CHARITY, OR CHRISTIAN LOVE, IS AN HUMBLE SPIRIT.—In speaking to this doctrine, I would show, 1, What humility is; and 2, How a Christian spirit, or the spirit of charity, is an humble spirit. And,

I. *I would show what humility is.*—Humility may be defined to be, a habit of mind and heart corresponding to our comparative unworthiness and vileness before God, or a sense of our own comparative meanness in his sight, with the disposition to a behavior answerable thereto. It consists partly in the understanding, or in the thought and knowledge we have of ourselves; partly in the will; partly in the sense or estimate we have of ourselves; and partly in the disposition we have to a behavior answerable to this sense or estimate. And the first thing in humility, is,

1. *A sense of our own comparative meanness.*—I say *comparative* meanness, because humility is a grace proper for beings that are glorious and excellent in very many respects. Thus the saints and angels in heaven excel in humility; and humility is proper and suitable in them, though they are pure, spotless, and glorious beings, perfect in holiness, and excelling in mind and strength. But though they are thus glorious, yet they have a comparative meanness before God, of which they are sensible; for he is said (Psalm cxiii. 6), "to humble himself to behold the things that are in heaven." So the man Christ Jesus, who is the most excellent and glorious of all crea-

tures, is yet meek and lowly of heart, and excels all other beings in humility. Humility is one of the excellences of Christ, because he is not only God but man, and as a man he was humble: for humility is not, and cannot be an attribute of the divine nature. God's nature is indeed infinitely opposite to pride, and yet humility cannot properly be predicated of him; for if it could, this would argue imperfection, which is impossible in God. God who is infinite in excellence and glory, and infinitely above all things, cannot have any comparative meanness, and of course cannot have any such comparative meanness to be sensible of, and therefore cannot be humble. But humility is an excellence proper to all created intelligent beings, for they are all infinitely little and mean before God, and most of them are in some way mean and low in comparison with some of their fellow-creatures. Humility implies a compliance with that rule of the Apostle (Romans xii. 3), that we think not of ourselves more highly than we ought to think, but that we think soberly, according as God hath dealt to every one of us the measure not only of faith, but of other things. And this humility, as a virtue in men, implies a sense of their own comparative meanness, both as compared with God, and as compared with their fellow-creatures. And,

First, Humility doth primarily and chiefly consist in *a sense of our meanness as compared with God*, or a sense of the infinite distance there is between God and ourselves. We are little, despicable creatures, even worms of the dust, and we should feel that we are as nothing and less than nothing in comparison with the majesty of heaven and earth. Such a sense of his nothingness Abraham expressed, when he said (Genesis xviii. 27), "Behold now, I have taken upon me to speak unto the Lord, which am but dust and ashes." There is no true humility without somewhat of this spirit; for however sensible we may be of our meanness as compared with some of our fellow-creatures, we are not truly humble, unless we have a sense of our nothingness as compared with God. Some have a low thought of themselves as compared with other men, from the meanness of their circumstances, or from a melancholy and despondent temperament which is natural to them, or from some other cause, while still they know nothing of the infinite distance there is between them and God; and though they may be ready to look upon themselves as humble-spirited, yet they have no true humility. That which above all other things it concerns us to know of ourselves, is, what we are in comparison with God, who is our creator, and the one in whom we live, and move, and have our being, and who is infinitely perfect in all things. And if we are ignorant of our meanness as compared with him, then the most essential thing, and that which is indispensable in true humility, is wanting. But where this is truly felt, there arises from it,

Secondly, A sense of our own meanness as compared with many of our fellow-creatures. For man is not only a mean creature in comparison with God, but he is very mean as compared with multitudes of creatures of a superior rank in the universe; and most men are mean in comparison with many of their fellow-men. And when a sense of this comparative meanness arises from a just sense of our meanness as God sees it, then it is of the nature of true humility. He that has a right sense and estimate of himself in comparison with God, will be likely to have his eyes open to see himself aright in all respects. Seeing truly how he stands with respect to the first and highest of all beings, will tend greatly to help him to a just apprehension of the place he stands in among creatures. And he that does not rightly know the first and greatest of beings, who is the fountain and source of all other beings, cannot truly know anything aright; but so far as he has come to a knowledge of the former, so far is he prepared for and led unto the knowledge of other things, and so of himself as related to others, and as standing among them.

All this would apply to men considered as unfallen beings, and would have been true of our race if our first parents had not fallen, and thus involved their posterity in sin. But humility in *fallen* men, implies a sense of a ten-fold meanness, both before God and men. Man's *natural* meanness consists in his being infinitely below God in natural perfection, and in God's being infinitely above him in greatness, power, wisdom, majesty, &c. And a truly humble man is sensible of the small extent of his own knowledge, and the great extent of his ignorance, and of the small extent of his understanding as compared with the understanding of God. He is sensible of his weakness; how little his strength is, and how little he is able to do. He is sensible of his natural distance from God; of his dependence on him; of the insufficiency of his own power and wisdom, and that it is by God's power that he is upheld and provided for, and that he needs God's wisdom to lead and guide him, and his might to enable him to do what he ought to do for him. He is sensible of his subjection to God, and that God's greatness does properly consist in his authority, whereby he is the sovereign Lord and king over all; and he is willing to be subject to that authority, as feeling that it becomes him to submit to the divine will, and yield in all things to God's authority. Man had this sort of comparative littleness before the fall. He was then infinitely little and mean in comparison with God; but his natural meanness is become much greater since the fall, for the moral ruin of his nature has greatly impaired his natural faculties, though it has not extinguished them.

The truly humble man, since the fall, is also sensible of his *moral* meanness and vileness. This consists in his sinfulness. His *natural* meanness, is his *littleness as a crea-*

ture; his *moral* meanness is his *vileness and filthiness as a sinner.* Unfallen man was infinitely distant from God in his natural qualities or attributes: fallen man is infinitely distant from him, also, as sinful and thus filthy. And a truly humble person is in some measure sensible of his comparative meanness in this respect, that he sees how exceedingly polluted he is before an infinitely holy God, in whose sight the heavens are not clean. He sees how pure God is, and how filthy and abominable he is before him. Such a sense of his comparative meanness Isaiah had, when he saw God's glory, and cried out (Isaiah vi. 5): "Woe is me! for I am undone; because I am a man of unclean lips, and I dwell in the midst of a people of unclean lips, for mine eyes have seen the king, the Lord of Hosts!" An humble sense of our meanness in this respect, implies self-abhorrence, such as led Job to exclaim (Job xlii. 5, 6): "I have heard of thee by the hearing of the ear; but now mine eye seeth thee. Wherefore I abhor myself, and repent in dust and ashes." It implies, also, such contrition and brokenness of heart, as David speaks of when he says (Psalm li. 17), "The sacrifices of God, are a broken spirit; a broken and a contrite heart, O God, thou wilt not despise;" and such, too, as Isaiah contemplated when he declared (Isaiah lvii. 15), "Thus saith the high and lofty One that inhabiteth eternity, whose name is Holy, I dwell in the high and holy place; with him, also, that is of a contrite and humble spirit, to revive the spirit of the humble, and to revive the heart of the contrite ones." And both the sense of our own littleness, and the sense of our moral vileness before God, are implied in that poverty of spirit, which the Saviour speaks of when he says (Matthew v. 3), "Blessed are the poor in spirit, for theirs is the kingdom of heaven."

And in order to this sense of our own meanness and unworthiness that is implied in humility, it is not only necessary that we should know God, and have a sense of his greatness, without which we cannot know ourselves, but we must have a right sense, also, of his excellence and loveliness. The devils and damned spirits see a great deal of God's greatness, of his wisdom, omnipotence, &c. God makes them sensible of it by what they see in his dealings, and feel in their own sufferings. However unwilling they are to know it, God makes them know how much he is above them now, and they shall know and feel it still more, at and after the judgment. But they have no humility, nor will they ever have, because though they see and feel God's greatness, yet they see and feel nothing of his loveliness. And without this there can be no true humility, for that cannot exist unless the creature feels his distance from God, not only with respect to his greatness, but also his loveliness. The angels and ransomed spirits in heaven see both these things; not only how much greater God is than they are, but how much more lovely he is also; so that though they have no absolute defilement and filthiness as fallen men have, yet as compared with God, it is said (Job xv. 15, and iv. 18), "The heavens are not clean in his sight," and "his angels he charged with folly." From such a sense of their comparative meanness, persons are made sensible how unworthy they are of God's mercy, or gracious notice. Such a sense Jacob expressed, when he said (Genesis xxxii. 10), "I am not worthy of the least of all the mercies, and of all the truth which thou hast showed unto thy servant;" and David, when he exclaimed (2 Samuel vii. 18),

"Who am I, O Lord God, and what is my house, that thou hast brought me hitherto?" And such a sense have all who are truly humble before God. But as humility consists in a sense of our comparative meanness, so it implies,

2. *A disposition to a corresponding behavior and conduct.*—Without this there is no true humility. If it could be so that our understanding could be enlightened to see our own meanness, and at the same time the will and disposition of the soul did not comply with, and conform to that which is answerable to our sense of it, but opposed it, then there would be no humility. As was just now said, the devils and damned spirits see much of their comparative littleness before God in some respects. They know that God is infinitely above them in power, and knowledge, and majesty. And yet not knowing and feeling his loveliness and excellence, their wills and dispositions by no means comply with, and conform to what is becoming their meanness; and so they have no humility, but are full of pride. Without pretending to mention everything in our behavior answerable to a proper sense of our meanness and vileness to

which humility would dispose us, for that would include the whole of our duty toward God and man, I would specify some things that are worthy of notice, both in reference to God, and in reference to man. And,

First, Some things *in our behavior toward God*, to which humility will dispose us. As the first of these, humility disposes a person *heartily and freely to acknowledge his meanness or littleness before God*. He sees how fit and suitable it is that he should do this; and he does it willingly, and even with delight. He freely confesses his own nothingness and vileness, and owns himself unworthy of any mercy, and deserving of all misery. It is the disposition of the humble soul, to lie low before God, and to humble himself in the dust in his presence. Humility, also, disposes one *to be distrustful of himself, and to depend only on God*. The proud man, that has a high opinion of his own wisdom, or strength, or righteousness, is self-confident. But the humble are not disposed to trust in themselves, but are diffident of their own sufficiency; and it is their disposition to rely on God, and with delight to cast themselves wholly on him as their refuge, and righteousness, and strength.

The humble man is further disposed *to renounce all the glory of the good he has or does, and to give it all to God.* If there be anything that is good in him, or any good done by him, it is not his disposition to glory or vaunt himself in it before God, but to ascribe all to God, and in the language of the Psalmist (Psalm cxv. 1) to say, "Not unto us, O Lord, not unto us, but unto thy name give glory, for thy mercy and for thy truth's sake." It is the disposition, again, of the humble person, *wholly to subject himself to God.* His heart is not opposed to a full and absolute subjection to the divine will, but inclined to it. He is disposed to be subject to the commands and laws of God, for he sees it to be right and best that he who is so infinitely inferior to God, should be thus subject; and that it is an honor that belongs to God, to reign over, and give laws to him. And he is equally disposed to be subject to the providence, and daily disposal of God, and to submit cheerfully to his will as manifested in what he orders for him; and though God orders affliction, and low and depressed circumstances as his lot in the world, he does not murmur, but feeling his meanness and unworthiness, he is sensible that afflictive and trying dispensations are what he deserves, and that his circumstances are better than he merits. And however dark the divine dealings, with the faith which we so often see manifested in those who are eminent in grace, he is ready to say with Job (Job xiii. 15), "Though he slay me, yet will I trust in him." And as humility implies a disposition to such a behavior toward God, so,

Secondly, It disposes to *a behavior toward men* answerable to our comparative meanness. And this I shall show by pointing out what kind of behavior humility tends to prevent. And it tends in the first place, to prevent *an aspiring and ambitious behavior amongst men*. The man that is under the influence of an humble spirit, is content with such a situation amongst men as God is pleased to allot to him, and is not greedy of honor, and does not affect to appear uppermost and exalted above his neighbors. He acts on the principle of that saying of the prophet (Jeremiah xlv. 5), "Seekest thou great things for thyself? Seek them not;" and also of that injunction of the Apostle (Romans xii. 16), "Mind not high things." Humility tends also *to prevent an ostentatious behavior.* If the truly humble man has any advantage or benefit of any kind, either temporal or spiritual, above his neighbors, he will not affect to make a show of it. If he has greater natural abilities than others, he will not be forward to parade and display them, or be careful that others shall know his superiority in this respect. If he has a remarkable spiritual experience, he will not be solicitous that men should know it for the sake of the honor he may obtain by it; nor does he affect to be esteemed of men as an eminent saint and a faithful servant of heaven; for it is a small thing with him what men may think of him. If he does anything well, or does his duty in any respect with difficulty and self-denial, he does not affect that men should take notice of it, nor is he careful lest they should not observe it. He is not of the behavior of the Pharisees, who, it is said (Matthew xxiii. 5), did "all their works to be seen of men;" but if he has done anything in sincerity, he is content that the great Being who sees in secret beholds and will approve it.

Humility tends, also, to prevent *an arrogant and assuming behavior.* He that is under the influence of an humble spirit, is not forward to take too much upon him; and when he is amongst others, he does not carry it toward them as if he expected and insisted that a great deal of regard should be shown to himself. His behavior does not carry with it the idea that he is the best amongst those about him, and that he is the one to whom the chief regard should be shown, and whose judgment is most to be sought and followed. He does not carry it as if he expected that everybody should bow and truckle to him, and give place to him as if no one was of as much consequence as himself. He does not put on assuming airs in his common conversation, nor in the management of his business, nor in the duties of religion. He is not forward to take upon himself that which does not belong to him, as though he had power where indeed he has not, as if the earth ought to be subject to his bidding, and must comply with his inclination and purposes. On the contrary, he gives all due deference to the judgment and inclinations of others, and his behavior carries with it the impression, that he sincerely receives and acts on that teaching of the Apostle (Philippians ii. 3), " Let nothing be done through strife, or vain glory, but in lowliness of mind, let each esteem other better than themselves." In talking of the things of religion, he has not the air, either in his speech or behavior, of one that esteems himself one of the best saints in the whole company, but he rather carries himself as if he thought, in the expression of the Apostle (Ephesians iii. 8), that he was " less than the least of all saints."

Humility tends, also, *to prevent a scornful behavior.* Treating others with scorn and contempt, is one of the worst and most offensive manifestations of pride toward them. But they that are under the influence of an humble spirit, are far from such a behavior. They do not despise, or look down on those that are below them, with a haughty supercilious air, as though they were scarce worthy to come nigh them, or to have any regard from them. They are sensible that there is no such vast difference between themselves and their fellow-men as warrants such a behavior. They are not found treating with scorn and contempt what others say, or speaking of what they do with ridicule and sneering reflections, or sitting and relating what others may have spoken or done, only to make sport of it. On the contrary, humility disposes a person to a condescending behavior to the meekest and lowest, and to treat inferiors with courtesy and affability, as being sensible of his own weakness and despicableness before God, and that it is God alone that makes him in any respect to differ from others, or gives him the advantage over them. The truly humble will (Romans xii. 16) always have the spirit to "condescend to men of low estate." Even if they are great men, and in places of public trust and honor, humility will dispose them to treat their inferiors in such a manner as has been spoken of, and not in a haughty and scornful manner, as vaunting themselves on their greatness.

Humility tends, also, *to prevent a wilful and stubborn behavior*. They that are under the influence of an humble spirit, will not set up their own will either in public or private affairs. They will not be stiff and inflexible, and insist that everything must go according to what they happen first to propose, and manifest a disposition by no means to be easy, but to make all the difficulty they can, and to make others uneasy as well as themselves, and to prevent anything being done with any quietness, if it be not according to their own mind and will. They are not as some that the Apostle Peter describes (2 Peter ii. 10), "presumptuous and self-willed," always bent on carrying their own points, and if this cannot be done, then bent on opposing and annoying others. On the contrary, humility disposes men to be of a yielding spirit to others, ready, for the sake of peace, and to gratify others, to comply in many things with their inclinations, and to yield to their judgments wherein they are not inconsistent with truth and holiness. A truly humble man, is inflexible in nothing but in the cause of his Lord and master, which is the cause of truth and virtue. In this he is inflexible because God and conscience require it; but in things of lesser moment, and which do not involve his principles as a follower of Christ, and in things that only concern his own private interests, he is apt to yield to others. And if he sees that others are stubborn and unreasonable in their wilfulness, he does not allow that to provoke him to be stubborn and wilful in his opposition to them; but he rather acts on the principles taught in such passages as Romans xii. 19; 1 Corinthians vi. 7; and

Matthew v. 40, 41 : "Dearly beloved, avenge not yourselves, but rather give place unto wrath ;" "Why do ye not rather take wrong? Why do ye not rather suffer yourselves to be defrauded?" "If any man will sue thee at the law, and take away thy coat, let him have thy cloak also ; and whosoever shall compel thee to go a mile, go with him twain."

Humility will further tend *to prevent a levelling behavior*. Some persons are always ready to level those above them down to themselves, while they are never willing to level those below them up to their own position. But he that is under the influence of humility will avoid both these extremes. On the one hand, he will be willing that all should rise just so far as their diligence and worth of character entitle them to ; and on the other hand, he will be willing that his superiors should be known and acknowledged in their place, and have rendered to them all the honors that are their due. He will not desire that all should stand upon the same level, for he knows it is best that there should be gradations in society ; that some should be above others, and should be honored and submitted to as such. And therefore he is willing to be content with this divine arrangement, and agreeably to it, to conform both his spirit and behavior to such precepts as the following: " Render therefore to all their dues; tribute, to whom tribute is due; custom, to whom custom; fear, to whom fear; honor, to whom honor" (Romans xiii. 7); " Put them in mind to be subject to principalities and powers, to obey magistrates, to be ready to every good work" (Titus iii. 1). Humility also tends, once more, *to prevent a self-justifying behavior.* He that is under the influence of an humble spirit, if he has fallen into a fault, as all are liable at some time to fall, or if in anything he has injured another, or dishonored the Christian name and character, will be willing to acknowledge his fault, and take the shame of it to himself. He will not be hard to be brought to a sense of his fault, nor to testify that sense by a suitable acknowledgment of his error. He will be inwardly humbled for it, and ready to show his humility in the manner which the Apostle points out, when he says (James v. 16), " Confess your faults one to another." It is pride that makes men so exceedingly backward to confess their fault when they have fallen into one, and that makes them think that to be their shame, which is in truth their highest honor. But humility in the behavior, makes men prompt to their duty in this respect, and if it prevails as it should, will lead them to do it with alacrity and even delight. And when any one shall give such a person a Christian admonition or reproof for any fault, humility will dispose him to take it kindly, and even thankfully. It is pride that makes men to be so uneasy when they are reproved by any of their neighbors, so that oftentimes they will not bear it, but become angry, and manifest great bitterness of spirit. Humility, on the contrary, will dispose them not only to tolerate such reproofs, but to esteem and prize them as marks of kindness and friendship. "Let the righteous smite me;" says the Psalmist (Psalm clxi. 5), "it shall be a kindness; and let him reprove me; it shall be an excellent oil which shall not break my head." Having thus shown what humility is in its nature, and to what it will lead us both in spirit and behavior, in respect both to God and to our fellow-men, I proceed, as proposed, to show,

II. *That the spirit of charity is an humble spirit.*—And this I would do in two particulars: first, by showing how the spirit of charity or divine love, implies and tends to humility, and then by showing how such exercises of this charity as the gospel tends to draw forth, do especially imply and tend to it. And,

1. *A spirit of charity or divine love implies and tends to humility.*

First, It *implies* humility. The spirit of charity or divine love, as has already been shown, is the sum of the Christian spirit, and of course implies humility in it, as an essential qualification. True divine love, is an humble love; and that love which is not humble, is not truly divine. And this appears plain from two considerations: because a sense of the loveliness of God is peculiarly that discovery of God that works humility, and because when God is truly loved, he is loved as an infinite superior. In the first place,

Because a sense of the loveliness of God, is peculiarly that discovery of God that works humility. A sense or discovery of God's greatness, without the sight of his loveliness, will not do it, but it is the discovery of his loveliness that effects it, and that makes the soul truly humble. All grace is wrought in the heart through the knowledge of God, or by the clear discovery of his perfections; and the knowledge of these perfections is the foundation of all grace. And it is the discovery or sense of God as lovely, and not only as lovely, but as infinitely above us in loveliness, that works humility in the heart. Merely having a sense of the fact that God is infinitely above us, and that there is an infinite distance between him and us in greatness, will not work humility. It will effect nothing toward making the heart humble, unless we are also sensible that there is an infinite distance between him and us in his loveliness. And this is evident from the work of the law on the heart of the sinner, and from the experience of devils and damned spirits. Under the work of the law on the heart, persons may have a sense of the awful greatness of God, and yet have no humility because they have no sense of his loveliness. All the work of the spirit, and of the law and gospel in the heart, is wrought by conviction; and there is a kind of conviction that natural men have as to God, that awakens them, and makes them feel their danger; and this is a conviction of the terrible greatness of God, revealing himself in the requirements and denunciations of his law. But this they may and often do have, and yet have no humility; and the reason is, that they have no sense of how much God is above them in loveliness. This is the only thing wanting; and without this, they will not be humble.

And the same is manifest from the experience of devils and damned spirits. They have a clear sense of God's being infinitely above them in greatness, but they have no humility, because they do not feel how much he is above them in loveliness. As was observed, God makes the devils and lost spirits know and feel that he is above them in greatness and power, and that they are as nothing in his hands; and yet they are proud, and have no humility. And at and after the day of judgment, they will see still more of his greatness. When Christ shall come in the clouds of heaven, surrounded by his angels, and with the glory of his Father, then shall the wicked, even the kings, and great rulers, and the rich captains, and the mighty men of the world, see that he is infinitely above them in greatness; and as they see his terrible majesty, they shall hide themselves from his face. And the devils, too, will see it, and will tremble at that time, a great deal more than they tremble now at the thoughts of it. And the devils and wicked men shall be made to know that he is the Lord. They shall know it with a witness. They shall know by what they see, and by what they feel when the sentence comes to be executed on them, that God is indeed above them, and they are as nothing before him, as is said by the prophet (Ezekiel vii. 27): "According to their deserts will I judge them, and they shall know that I am the Lord." But though they shall so clearly, and so terribly see that God is infinitely above them in greatness, yet they will have no humility. They will see themselves at an infinite distance from God, but their hearts will not comply with that distance and feel as is answerable to it. Because they will not see God's loveliness, they will not know their infinite distance from him in this respect, and therefore will not be led to humility. And this their experience shows, that it is a sense of the infinite distance of the creature from the Creator in loveliness, that causes true humility. This it is that causes humility in the angels in heaven, and in the saints on earth. And since it is a sense of God's loveliness that works humility, we may hence learn that divine love implies humility, for love is but the disposition of the heart toward God as lovely. If the knowledge of God as lovely, causes humility, then a respect to God as lovely, implies humility. And from this love to God, arises a Christian love to man; and therefore it follows, that both love to God, and love to man, the union of which is the very thing the Apostle calls charity, alike imply humility.

And it further appears that divine love implies humility, because when God is truly loved, he is loved as an infinite superior. True love to God, is not love to him as an equal; for every one that truly loves God, honors him as God, that is, as a being infinitely superior to all others in greatness and excellence. It is love to a being who is infinitely perfect in all his attributes, the supreme Lord, and absolute sovereign of the universe. But if we love God as infinitely superior to ourselves, then love is exercised in us as infinite inferiors, and therefore it is an humble love. In exercising it, we look upon ourselves as infinitely mean and low before God, and love proceeds from us as such. But to love God in this manner, is to love him in humility, and with an humble love. Thus divine love *implies* humility. But,

Secondly, It also *tends to* humility. Humility is not only a quality in divine love, but it is also an effect of it. Divine love does not only imply humility in its nature, but also tends to cherish and produce it, and to call forth its exercises as consequences and fruits of love. And humility is not only implied in, and is as it were a part of love, but it is a fruit and uniform production of love. And that, especially, in two ways. In the first place, love inclines the heart to *that spirit and behavior that are becoming the distance from the beloved*. It is enmity against God that makes men's hearts so opposed to love to him, and to such a behavior as carries in it a full and proper acknowledgment of the distance between themselves and him. Those that men have a great love to, they are willing to honor, and willing to acknowledge their superiority to themselves, and that they themselves are far below them; and they are willing to give them the honor of such an acknowledgment, especially if they are very much their superiors. The devils know their distance from God, but they are not reconciled to it; and the chief of devils affected to be equal with God, and even above him, because he had no love to him. And so in a measure it is with men, while they are without divine love. But when love enters the heart, then the inclination of the soul is to all that humble respect that becomes the distance between God and us. And so love to man, arising from love to God, disposes to a humble behavior toward them, inclining us to give them all the honor and respect that are their due. And so in the next place, love to God tends *to an abhorrence of sin against God*, and so to our being humbled before him for it. So much as anything is loved, so much will its contrary be hated. And therefore just in proportion as we love God, in the same proportion shall we have an abhorrence of sin against him. And having an abhorrence of sin against God, this will lead us to abhor ourselves for it, and so to humble ourselves for it before God. Having thus shown how divine love, which is the sum of the Christian temper, implies and tends to humility, I come now to show,

2. *How the gospel tends to draw forth such exercises of love as do especially imply and tend to it.*—A Christian spirit and a gospel spirit are the same. That is a Christian spirit, which the Christian revelation tends to lead to; but the Christian revelation is the same as the gospel. Now such a kind of exercises of love as the gospel tends to draw forth, do, in a special manner, tend to, and imply humility; and that on several accounts. And,

First, Because the gospel leads us *to love God as an infinitely condescending God.* The gospel above all things in the world, holds forth the exceeding condescension of God. No other manifestation that ever God made of himself, exhibits such wonderful condescension as the Christian revelation does. The gospel teaches how God, who humbles himself to behold things that are in heaven and earth, stooped so low as to take an infinitely gracious notice of poor vile worms of the dust, and to concern himself for their salvation, and so as to send his only-begotten Son to die for them, that they might be forgiven, and elevated, and honored, and brought into eternal fellowship with him, and to the perfect enjoyment of himself in heaven forever. So that the love the Christian revelation leads us to, is love to God as such a condescending God, and to such exercises of love as it becomes us to have toward a God of such infinite condescension; and such acts of love are, of necessity, humble acts of love, for there is no disposition in the creature, that is more adapted to condescension in the creator, than humility is. The condescension of God, is not properly humility, because, for the reasons already given, humility is a virtue only of those beings that have comparative meanness. And yet God, by his infinite condescension, shows his nature to be infinitely far from, and hostile to pride, and therefore his condescension is sometimes spoken of as humility; and humility on our part is the most proper conformity to God's condescension that there can be in a creature. His condescension tends to draws forth humility on our part.

Secondly, The gospel leads us *to love Christ as an humble person.* Christ is the God-man, including both the divine and the human nature; and so has not only condescension which is a divine perfection, but also humility which is a creature excellency. Now the gospel holds forth Christ to us as one that is **meek and lowly of heart**; as the most perfect and excellent instance of humility that ever existed; as one in whom the greatest performances and expressions of humility were manifest in his abasement of himself. Though he was "in the form of God," he "made himself of no reputation, and took upon him the form of a servant, and humbled himself, and became obedient unto death, even the death of the cross" (Philippians ii. 6, 7, 8). Now the gospel leads us to love Christ as such an humble person; and therefore to love him with such a love as is proper to be exercised toward such an one, is to exercise an humble love. And this is the more true, because the gospel leads us to love Christ not only as an humble person, but as an humble Saviour and Lord, and head. If our Lord and master is humble, and we love him as such, certainly it becomes us who are his disciples, and servants, to be so too; for surely it does not become the servant to be prouder, or less abased than his master. As Christ himself tells us (Matthew x. 24, 25), "The disciple is not above his master, nor the servant above his Lord. It is enough for the disciple that he be as his master, and the servant as his Lord." And again, he tells us (John xiii. 13-16), that his own example of humility was intended for our imitation; and still again declares to his disciples (Matthew xx. 25-28), "Ye know that the princes of the Gentiles exercise dominion over them, and they that are great, exercise authority upon them; but it shall not be so among you. But whosoever will be great among you, let him be your minister; and whosoever will be chief among you, let him be your servant: even as the Son of Man came not to be ministered unto, but to minister, and to give his life a ransom for many."

Thirdly, The gospel leads us *to love Christ as a crucified Saviour.* As our Saviour and Lord, he suffered the greatest ignominy, and was put to the most ignominious death, though he was the Lord of glory. This may well kindle the humility of his followers, and lead them to an humble love to him. For by God sending his Son into the world to suffer such an ignominious death, he did, as it were, pour contempt on all the earthly glory that men are wont to be proud of, in that he gave him, as the Saviour and head of all his elect people, to appear in circumstances so far from earthly glory, and in circumstances of the greatest earthly ignominy and shame. And Christ, by being willing thus to be abased, and thus to suffer, not only cast contempt on all worldly glory and greatness, but he showed his humility in the clearest manner. If we, then, consider ourselves as the followers of the meek, and lowly, and crucified Jesus, we shall walk humbly before God and man, all the days of our life on earth.

Fourthly, The gospel still further tends to lead us to humble exercises of love, because it leads us *to love Christ as one that was crucified for our sakes.* The mere fact that Christ was crucified, is a great argument for the humility of us who are his followers. But his being crucified *for our sakes,* is a much greater argument for it. For Christ's being crucified for our sakes, is the greatest testimony of God against our sins that ever was given. It shows more of God's abhorrence of our sins, than any other act or event that God has ever directed or permitted. The measure of God's abhorrence of our sins, is shown by his having them so terribly punished, and his wrath so executed against them, even when imputed to his own Son. So that this is the greatest inducement to our humility that can be presented, and this on two accounts; because it is the greatest manifestation of the vileness of that for which we should be humble, and also the greatest argument for our loving the humble spirit, which the gospel holds forth. The excellency of Christ, and the love of Christ, more appear in his yielding himself to be crucified for us, than in any other of his acts, so that these things, considered together, above all things tend to draw forth on our part, the exercises of humble love. In the application of this subject we may see,

1. *The excellency of a Christian spirit.*— "The righteous," it is said (Proverbs xii. 26), "is more excellent than his neighbor." And much of this excellence in the true Christian, consists in his meek and lowly spirit which makes him so like his Saviour. This spirit the Apostle speaks of (1 Peter iii. 4) as the richest of all ornaments, "even the ornament of a meek and quiet spirit, which is in the sight of God of great price." The subject should lead us,

2. *To examine ourselves, and see if we are indeed of an humble spirit.*—" His soul," says the prophet (Habakkuk ii. 4), "which is lifted

up, is not upright in him;" and the fact that "God resisteth the proud" (James iv. 6), or, as in the original, "sets himself in battle array against him," shows how he abhors a proud spirit. And it is not every show and appearance of humility that will stand the test of the gospel. There are various imitations of it that fall short of the reality. Some put on an affected humility; others have a natural low-spiritedness, and are wanting in manliness of character; others are melancholy or despondent; others under the convictions of conscience by which, for the time, they are depressed, seem broken in spirit; others seem greatly abased while in adversity and affliction, or have a natural melting of the heart under the common illuminations of the truth; to others there is a counterfeit kind of humility, wrought by the delusions of Satan: and all of these may be mistaken for true humility. Examine yourself, then, and see what is the nature of your humility, whether it be of these superficial kinds, or whether it be indeed wrought by the Holy Spirit in your hearts; and do not rest satisfied, till you find that the spirit and behavior of those whom the gospel accounts humble, are yours.

3. *The subject exhorts those who are strangers to the grace of God, to seek that grace, that they may thus attain to this spirit of humility.* —If such be your character, you are now destitute of a Christian spirit, which is a spirit of grace ; and so, wholly destitute of humility. Your spirit is a proud spirit; and though you may not seem to carry yourself very proudly amongst men, yet you are lifting yourself up against God, in refusing to submit your heart and life to him. And in doing this, you are disregarding or defying God's sovereignty, and daring to contend with your maker, though he dreadfully threatens those who do this. You are proudly casting contempt on God's authority, in refusing to obey it, and continuing to live in disobedience; in refusing to be conformed to his will, and to comply with the humbling conditions and way of salvation by Christ, and in trusting to your own strength and righteousness, instead of that which Christ so freely offers. Now as to such a spirit, consider that this is, in an especial sense, the sin of devils. "Not a novice," says the Apostle (1 Timothy iii. 6), "lest being lifted up with pride, he fall into the condemnation of the devil." And consider, too,

how odious and abominable such a spirit is to God, and how terribly he has threatened it; declaring (Proverbs xvi. 5) that "every one that is proud in heart is an abomination to the Lord; though hand join in hand, he shall not go unpunished;" and again (Proverbs vi. 16), "These things doth the Lord hate, a proud look, &c.:" and again (Proverbs xxix. 23), that "a man's pride shall bring him low," and (2 Samuel xxii. 28) that the eyes of the Lord are upon the haughty that he may bring them down; and still again (Isaiah xxiii. 9), that "the Lord of hosts hath purposed it, to stain the pride of all glory, and to bring into contempt all the honorable of the earth." Consider, too, how Pharaoh and Korah, and Haman, and Belshazzar, and Herod, were awfully punished for their pride of heart and conduct; and be admonished, by their example, to cherish an humble spirit, and to walk humbly with God, and toward men. Finally,

4. *Let all be exhorted earnestly to seek much of an humble spirit, and to endeavor to be humble in all their behavior toward God and men.* —Seek for a deep and abiding sense of your comparative meanness before God and man.

Know God. Confess your nothingness and ill-desert before him. Distrust yourself. Rely only on God. Renounce all glory except from him. Yield yourself heartily to his will and service. Avoid an aspiring, ambitious, ostentatious, assuming, arrogant, scornful, stubborn, wilful, levelling, self-justifying behavior; and strive for more and more of the humble spirit that Christ manifested while he was on earth. Consider the many motives to such a spirit. Humility is a most essential and distinguishing trait in all true piety. It is the attendant of every grace, and in a peculiar manner tends to the purity of Christian feeling. It is the ornament of the spirit; the source of some of the sweetest exercises of Christian experience; the most acceptable sacrifice we can offer to God; the subject of the richest of his promises; the spirit with which he will dwell on earth, and which he will crown with glory in heaven hereafter. Earnestly seek then, and diligently, and prayerfully cherish an humble spirit, and God shall walk with you here below, and when a few more days shall have passed, he will receive you to the honors bestowed on his people at Christ's right hand.

LECTURE VIII.

THE SPIRIT OF CHARITY THE OPPOSITE OF A SELFISH SPIRIT.

"Seeketh not her own."—1 Cor. xiii. 5.

Having shown the nature of charity in respect to the good of others, in the two particulars that it is kind to them, and envies not their enjoyments and blessings; and also in respect to our own good, that it is not proud, either in spirit or behavior, I pass to the next point presented by the Apostle, viz.: that charity "*seeketh not her own.*" The doctrine of these words plainly is,

That the spirit of charity, or Christian love, is the opposite of a selfish spirit.—The ruin that the fall brought upon the soul of man, consists very much in his losing the nobler and more benevolent principles of his nature, and falling wholly under the power and government of self-love. Before, and as God created him, he was exalted and noble, and generous; but now he is debased, and ignoble, and selfish. Immediately upon the fall, the mind of man shrank from its primitive greatness and expandedness, to an exceeding smallness and contractedness; and as in other respects, so especially in this. Before his soul was under the government of that noble principle of divine love, whereby it was enlarged to the comprehension of all his fellow-creatures and their welfare. And not only so, but it was not confined within such narrow limits as the bounds of the creation, but went forth in the exercise of holy love to the Creator, and abroad upon the infinite ocean of good, and was, as it were, swallowed up by it, and became one with it. But so soon as he had transgressed against God, these noble principles were immediately lost, and all this excellent enlargedness of man's soul was gone; and thenceforward, he himself shrank, as it were, into a little space, circumscribed and closely shut up within itself to the exclusion of all things else. Sin, like some powerful astringent, contracted his soul to the very small dimensions of selfishness; and God was forsaken, and fellow-creatures forsaken, and man retired within himself, and became totally governed by narrow and selfish principles and feelings. Self-love became absolute master of his soul, and the more noble and spiritual principles of his being, took wings and flew away. But God, in mercy to miserable man, entered on the work of redemption, and by the glorious gospel of his Son, began the work of bringing the soul of man out of its confinement and contractedness, and back again to those noble and divine principles, by which it was animated and governed at first. And it is through the cross of Christ that he is doing this; for our union with Christ gives us participation in his nature. And so Christianity restores an excellent enlargement, and extensiveness, and liberality to the soul, and again possesses it with that divine love or charity that we read of in the text, whereby it again embraces its fellow-creatures, and is devoted to and swallowed up in the Creator. And thus charity, which is the sum of the Christian spirit, so partakes of the glorious fulness of the divine nature, that she "secketh not her own," or is *contrary to a selfish spirit.* In dwelling on this thought, I would first, show the nature of that selfishness of which charity is the opposite; then how charity is opposed to it; and then some of the evidence in support of the doctrine stated.

I. *I would show the nature of that selfishness of which charity is the opposite.*—And here I would observe,

1. *Negatively: That charity, or the spirit of Christian love, is not contrary to all self-love.*— It is not a thing contrary to Christianity that a man should love himself, or which is the same thing, should love his own happiness. If Christianity did indeed tend to destroy a man's love to himself, and to his own happiness, it would therein tend to destroy the very spirit of humanity; but the very announcement of the gospel, as a system of "peace on earth and good-will toward men" (Luke ii. 14), shows that it is not only not destructive of humanity, but in the highest degree promotive of its spirit. That a man should love his own happiness, is as necessary to his nature as the faculty of the will is; and it is impossible that such a love should be destroyed in any other way than by destroying his being. The saints love their own happiness. Yea, those that are perfect in happiness, the saints and an-

gels in heaven, love their own happiness; otherwise that happiness which God hath given them, would be no happiness to them; for that which any one does not love, he cannot enjoy any happiness in.

That to love ourselves is not unlawful, is evident, also, from the fact, that the law of God makes self-love a rule and measure by which our love to others should be regulated. Thus Christ commands (Matthew xix. 19), "Thou shalt love thy neighbor as thyself," which certainly supposes that we may, and must love ourselves. It is not said *more* than thyself, but *as* thyself. But we are commanded to love our neighbor next to God; and therefore we are to love ourselves with a love, next to that which we should exercise toward God himself. And the same appears, also, from the fact that the Scriptures, from one end of the Bible to the other, are full of motives that are set forth for the very purpose of working on the principle of self-love Such are all the promises and threatenings of the word of God, its calls and invitations, its counsels to seek our own good, and its warnings to beware of misery. These things can have no influence on us in any other way, than as they tend to work upon our hopes or fears. For to what purpose would it be to make any promise of happiness, or hold forth any threatening of misery, to him that has no love for the former or dread of the latter? Or what reason can there be in counselling him to seek the one, or warning him to avoid the other? Thus it is plain, negatively, that charity, or the spirit of Christian love, is not contrary to *all* self-love. But I remark still further,

2. *Affirmatively: That the selfishness which charity, or a Christian spirit, is contrary to, is only an inordinate self-love.*—Here, however, the question arises, in what does this inordinateness consist? This is a point that needs to be well stated, and clearly settled; for the refutation of many scruples and doubts that persons often have, depends upon it. And therefore, I answer,

First, That the inordinateness of self-love, does not consist in our love of our own happiness being, absolutely considered, too great in degree. I do not suppose it can be said of any, that their love to their own happiness, if we consider that love absolutely and not comparatively, *can* be in too high a degree, or that it is a thing that is liable either to increase or diminution. For I apprehend that self-love, in this sense, is not a result of the fall, but is necessary, and what belongs to the nature of all intelligent beings, and that God has made it alike in all; and that saints, and sinners, and all alike, love happiness, and have the same unalterable and instinctive inclination to desire and seek it. The change that takes place in a man when he is converted and sanctified, is not that his love for happiness is diminished, but only that it is regulated with respect to its exercises and influence, and the courses and objects it leads to. Who will say that the happy souls in heaven do not love happiness, as truly as the miserable spirits in hell? If their *love* of happiness is diminished by their being made holy, then that will diminish their *happiness* itself, for the less any one loves happiness, the less he relishes it, and consequently is the less happy.

When God brings a soul out of a miserable state and condition, into a happy state, by conversion, he gives him happiness that before he had not, but he does not at the same time take away some of his love of happiness. And so when a saint increases in grace, he is made still more happy than he was before; but his love of happiness, and his relish of it, do not grow less, as his happiness itself increases, for that would be to increase his happiness one way, and to diminish it another. But in every case in which God makes a miserable soul happy, or a happy soul still more happy, he continues the same love of happiness that existed before. And so, doubtless, the saints ought to have as much of a principle of love to their own happiness, or love to themselves, which is the same thing, as the wicked have. So that if we consider men's love of themselves, or of their own happiness absolutely, it is plain that the inordinateness of self-love does not consist in its being in too great a degree, because it is alike in all. But I remark,

Secondly, That the inordinateness of self-love wherein a corrupt selfishness does consist, lies in two things; *in its being too great comparatively, and in placing our happiness in that which is confined to self.* In the first place, the degree of self-love may be too great *comparatively*, and so the degree of its influence be inordinate. Though the degree of men's love of their own happiness, taken absolutely, may in all be the same, yet the proportion that their love of self bears to their love for others, may not be the same. If we compare a man's love of himself with his love for others, it may be said that he loves himself too much; that is, in proportion too much. And though this may be owing to a defect of love to others, rather than to an excess of love to himself, yet self-love, by this excess in its proportion, itself becomes inordinate in this respect, viz.: that it becomes inordinate in its influence and government of the man. For though the principle of self-love, in itself considered, is not at all greater than if there was a due proportion of love to God and to fellow-creatures with it, yet the proportion being greater, its influence and government of the man becomes greater; and so its influence becomes inordinate by reason of the weakness or absence of other love that should restrain or regulate that influence.

To illustrate this, we may suppose the case of a servant in a family, who was formerly kept in the place of a servant, and whose influence in family affairs was not inordinate while his master's strength was greater than his; and yet if afterward the master grows weaker and loses his strength, and the rest of the family lose their former power, though the servant's strength be not at all increased, yet the proportion of his strength being increased, his influence may become inordinate; and from being in subjection and a servant, he may become master in that house. And so self-love becomes inordinate. Before the fall, man loved himself, or his own happiness, as much as after the fall; but then a superior principle of divine love had the throne, and was of such strength that it wholly regulated and directed self-love. But since the fall, the principle of divine love has lost its strength, or rather is dead, so that self-love continuing in its former strength, and having no superior principle to regulate it, becomes inordinate in its influence, and governs where it should be subject, and only a servant. Self-love, then, may become inordinate in its influence by being comparatively too great; either by love to God and to fellow-creatures being too small, as it is in the saints, who in this world have great remaining corruption; or by its being none at all, as is the case with those who have no divine love in their hearts. Thus the inordinateness of self-love, with respect to the degree of it, is not as it is considered absolutely, but comparatively or with respect to the degree of its influence. In some respects wicked men do not love themselves enough—not so much as the godly do; for they do not love the way of their own welfare and happiness, and in this sense it is sometimes said of the wicked, that they hate themselves, though in another sense, they love self too much.

It is further true, in the second place, that self-love, or a man's love to his own happiness may be inordinate, *in placing that happiness in things that are confined to himself.* In this case, the error is not so much in the degree of his love to himself, as it is in the channel in which it flows. It is not in the degree in which he loves his own happiness, but in his placing his happiness where he ought not, and in limiting and confining his love. Some, although they love their own happiness, do not place that happiness in their own confined good, or in that good which is limited to themselves, but more in the common good; in that which is the good of others, or in the good to be enjoyed in and by others. A man's love of his own happiness, when it runs in this last channel, is not what is called selfishness, but is the very opposite of it. But there are others, who in their love to their own happiness, place that happiness in good things that are confined or limited to themselves to the exclusion of others. And this is selfishness. This is the thing most clearly and directly intended by that self-love which the Scripture condemns. And when it is said, that charity seeketh not her own, we are to understand it of her own private good—good limited to herself. The expression "her own," is a phrase of appropriation, and properly carries in its signification the idea of limitation to self. And so the like phrase in Philippians ii. 21, that "all seek their own," carries the idea of confined and self-appropriated good, or the good that a man has singly and to himself, and in which he has no communion or partnership with another, but which he has so circumscribed and limited to himself as to exclude others. And so the expression is to be understood, in 2 Timothy iii. 2, "For men shall be lovers of their own selves;" for the phrase is of the most confined signification, limited to self alone, and excluding all others.

A man may love himself as much as one can, and may be in the exercise of a high degree of love to his own happiness, ceaselessly longing for it, and yet he may so place that happiness, that in the very act of seeking it he may be in the high exercise of love to God; as for example, when the happiness that he longs for, is, to enjoy God, or to behold his glory, or to hold communion with him. Or a man may place his happiness in glorifying God. It may seem to him the greatest happiness that he can conceive of, to give God glory as he may do, and he may long for this happiness. And in longing for it, he loves that which he looks on as his happiness; for if he did not love what in this case he esteemed his happiness, he would not long for it, and to love his happiness, is to love himself. And yet, in the same act, he loves God, because he places his happiness in God; for nothing can more properly be called love to any being or thing, than to place our happiness in it. And so persons may place their happiness considerably in the good of others, their neighbors for instance; and desiring the happiness that consists in seeking their good, they may, in seeking it, love themselves, and their own happiness. And yet this is not selfishness, because it is not a confined self-love, but the individual's self-love flows out in such a channel as to take in others with himself. The self that he loves, is, as it were, enlarged and multiplied, so that in the very acts in which he loves himself, he loves others also. And this is the Christian spirit, the excellent and noble spirit of the gospel of Jesus Christ. This is the nature of that divine love, or Christian charity, that is spoken of in the text. And a Christian spirit is contrary to that selfish spirit which consists in the self-love that goes out after such objects as are confined and limited—such as a man's worldly wealth, or the honor that consists in a man's being set up higher in the world than his neighbors, or his own worldly ease and convenience, or his pleasing and gratifying his own bodily appetites and lusts. Having thus stated what that selfishness is that a Christian spirit is contrary to, I pass, as proposed, to show,

II. *How the spirit of charity, or Christian love, is contrary to such a spirit.*—And this may be shown in these two particulars, that the spirit of charity, or Christian love, leads us to seek not only our own things, but those of others; and that it disposes us, in many cases, to forego, or part with our own things for the sake of others. And,

1. *The spirit of charity or love leads those who possess it, to seek not only their own things, but the things of others.*

First, Such a spirit seeks *to please and glorify God.* The things that are well pleasing to God and Christ, and that tend to the divine glory, are called the things of Christ, in opposition to our own things, as, where it is said (Philippians ii. 21), "All seek their own, not the things which are Jesus Christ's." Christianity requires that we should make God and Christ our main end; and all Christians, so far as they live like Christians, live so, that "for them to live is Christ." Christians are required to live so as to please God, and so as to "prove what is that good and acceptable and perfect will of God" (Romans xii. 2). We should be such servants of Christ as do, in all things, seek to please our master, as says the Apostle (Ephesians vi. 6), "Not with eye-service, as men-pleasers; but as the servants of Christ, doing the will of God from the heart." And so we are required in all things (1 Corinthians x. 31), "Whether we eat, or drink, or whatsoever we do, to do all to the glory of God." And this, surely, is a spirit, which is the opposite of self-seeking.

Secondly, They that have the spirit of charity, or Christian love, have a spirit to seek *the good of their fellow-creatures*. Thus the Apostle commands (Philippians ii. 4), "Look not every man on his own things, but every man, also, on the things of others." We ought to seek the spiritual good of others, and if we have a Christian spirit, we shall desire and seek their spiritual welfare and happiness, their salvation from hell, and that they may glorify and enjoy God forever. And the same spirit will dispose us to desire and seek the temporal prosperity of others, as says the Apostle (1 Corinthians x. 24), "Let no man seek his own, but every man another's wealth." And we should so seek their pleasure, that therein we can, at the same time, seek their profit, as again it is said by the Apostle (1 Corinthians x. 33), "Even as I please all men in all things, not seeking mine own profit, but the profit of many, that they may be saved;" and again (Romans xv. 2), "Let every one of us please his neighbor, for his good, to edification." But more particularly under this head, I would remark, that a spirit of charity, or Christian love, as exercised toward our fellow-creatures, is opposite to a selfish spirit, *as it is a sympathizing and merciful spirit.* It disposes persons to consider not only their own difficulties, but also the burdens and afflictions of others, and the difficulties of their circumstances, and to esteem the case of those who are in straits and necessities, as their own. A person of selfish spirit, is ready to make much of the afflictions that he himself is under, as if his privations or sufferings were greater than those of anybody else; and if he is not in suffering, he is ready to think he is not called to spare what he has in possession, for the sake of helping others. A selfish man is not apt to discern the wants of others, but rather to overlook them, and can hardly be persuaded to see or feel them. But a man of charitable spirit, is apt to see the afflictions of others, and to take notice of their aggravation, and to be filled with concern for them, as he would be for himself if under difficulties. And he is ready, also, to help them, and take delight in supplying their necessities, and relieving their difficulties. He rejoices to obey that injunction of the Apostle (Colossians iii. 2), "Put on, therefore, as the elect of God, holy and beloved, bowels of mercies, kindness;" and to cherish the spirit of "wisdom (James iii. 17) that is from above," which is "full of mercy;" and like the good man spoken of by the Psalmist (Psalm xxxvii. 26), to be "merciful," that is, full of mercy.

And as it is a sympathizing and merciful spirit, so the spirit of charity as exercised toward our fellow-creatures, is the opposite of a selfish, inasmuch *as it is a liberal spirit.* It not only seeks the good of others that are in affliction, but it is ready to communicate to all, and forward to promote their good, as there may be opportunity. "To do good, and to communicate, it forgets not" (Hebrews xiii. 16); but obeys the exhortation (Galatians vi. 10), "As we have opportunity, let us do good unto all men." But on this point, I need not enlarge, having already dwelt upon it at length, in the Lecture on "Charity is Kind."

And as the spirit of charity, or Christian love, is opposed to a selfish spirit, in that it is merciful and liberal, so it is in this, also, that it *disposes a person to be public-spirited.* A man of a right spirit, is not a man of narrow and private views, but is greatly interested and concerned for the good of the community to which he belongs, and particularly of the city or village in which he resides, and for the true welfare of the society of which he is a member. God commanded the Jews that were carried away captive to Babylon, to seek the good of that city, though it was not their native place, but only the city of their captivity. His injunction was (Jeremiah xxix. 7), "Seek the peace of the city whither I have caused you to be carried away captives, and pray unto the Lord for it." And a man of truly Christian spirit, will be earnest for the good of his country, and of the place of his residence, and will be disposed to lay himself out for its improvement. A man was recommended to Christ by the Jews (Luke vii. 5), as one that loved their nation and had built them a synagogue; and it is spoken of as a very provoking thing to God, with respect to some in Israel (Amos vi. 6), that they "were not grieved for the affliction of Joseph." And it is recorded, to the everlasting honor of Esther (Esther xiv. 16), that she herself fasted and prayed, and stirred up others to fast and pray for the welfare of her people. And the

Apostle Paul (Romans ix. 1, 2, 3), expresses the deepest concern for the welfare of his countrymen. And those that are possessed of the spirit of Christian charity, are of a more enlarged spirit still, for they are concerned, not only for the thrift of the community, but for the welfare of the church of God, and of all the people of God individually. Of such a spirit was Moses, the man of God, and therefore he earnestly interceded for God's visible people, and declared himself ready to die that they might be spared (Exodus xxxii. 11, and 32). And of such a spirit was Paul, who was so concerned for the welfare of all, both Jews and Gentiles, that he was willing to become as they were (1 Corinthians ix. 19–23) if possibly he might save some of them.

Especially will the spirit of Christian love dispose those that stand in a public capacity, such as that of ministers, and magistrates, and all public officers, to seek the public good. It will dispose magistrates to act as the fathers of the commonwealth, with that care and concern for the public good, which the father of a family has for his household. It will make them watchful against public dangers, and forward to use their powers for the promotion of the public benefit; not being governed by selfish motives in their administration; not seeking only, or mainly, to enrich themselves, or to become great, and to advance themselves on the spoils of others, as wicked rulers very often do, but striving to act for the true welfare of all to whom their authority extends. And the same spirit will dispose ministers not to seek their own, and endeavor to get all they can out of their people to enrich themselves and their families, but to seek the good of the flock over which the great Shepherd has placed them; to feed, and watch over them, and lead them to good pastures, and defend them from wolves and wild beasts that would devour them. And so whatever the post of honor or influence, we may be placed in, we should show that, in it, we are solicitous for the good of the public, so that the world may be better for our living in it, and that when we are gone, it may be said of us, as it was so nobly said of David (Acts xiii. 36), that we "served our generation by the will of God." But,

2. *The spirit of charity or love, also disposes us, in many cases, to forego, and part*

with our own things, for the sake of others.—It disposes us to part with our own private temporal interest, and totally and freely to renounce it, for the sake of the honor of God, and the advancement of the kingdom of Christ. Such was the spirit of the Apostle Paul, when he exclaimed (Acts xxi. 13), "I am ready not to be bound only, but also to die at Jerusalem for the name of the Lord Jesus." And the same spirit will dispose us often to forego or part with our own private interest for the good of our neighbors. It will make us ready on every occasion to aid or help them, leading us willingly to part with a lesser good of our own, for the sake of a greater good to them. And the case may even be such (1 John iii. 16), that "we ought to lay down our lives for the brethren." But I will not dwell longer on this point now, as I shall probably have occasion to speak more to it under some other part of the context. I pass then, as proposed,

III. *To notice some of the evidence sustaining the doctrine which has been stated.*—And the truth of the doctrine, that the spirit of charity of Christian love is the opposite of a selfish spirit, will appear, if we consider the nature of love in general, the peculiar nature of Christian or divine love, and the nature of Christian love to God and to man in particular. And,

1. *The nature of love in general.*—This, so far as it is real and truly sincere, is of a diffusive nature, and espouses the interest of others. It is so with the love of natural affection, and earthly friendship. So far as there is any real affection or friendship, the parties between which it subsists do not seek only their own particular interests, but do espouse and seek the interests of each other. They seek not only their own things, but the things of their friends. Selfishness is a principle that contracts the heart, and confines it to self, while love enlarges it and extends it to others. By love, a man's self is so extended and enlarged, that others, so far as they are beloved, do, as it were, become parts of himself, so that wherein their interest is promoted, he believes his own is promoted, and wherein theirs is injured, his also is injured. And still further will this appear, if we consider,

2. *The peculiar nature of Christian or divine love.*—Of charity, or Christian love, it is peculiarly true, that it is above the selfish

principle. Though all real love to others seeks the good, and espouses the interests of those who are beloved, yet all other love, excepting this, has its foundation, in one sense, in the selfish principle. So it is with the natural affection which parents feel for their children, and with the love which relatives have one to another. If we except the impulses of instinct, self-love is the main spring of it. It is because men love themselves, that they love those persons and things that are their own, or that they are nearly related to, and which they look upon as belonging to themselves, and which, by the constitution of society, have their interest and honor linked with their own. And so it is in the closest friendships that exist among men. Self-love is the spring whence they proceed. Sometimes natural gratitude, for good turns that have been done them by others, or for benefits received from them, disposes men, through self-love, to a similar respect to those that have shown them kindness, or by whom their self-interest has been promoted. And sometimes natural men are led into a friendship to others, from qualifications that they see or find in them, whence they hope for the promotion of their own temporal good. If they see that others are disposed to be respectful to them, and to give them honor, then love to their own honor will lead them to friendship with such; or if they see them generously disposed to them, then love to their own profit will dispose them to friendship to them on this account; or if they find in them a great agreement with themselves in disposition and manners, self-love may dispose them to amity with them on account of the enjoyment they hope in their society, or because this agreement with them in their temper and ways, carries with it the approbation of their own temper and ways. And so there are many other ways, in which self-love is the source of that love and friendship that often arises between natural men. Most of the love that there is in the world, arises from this principle, and therefore it does not go beyond nature. And nature cannot go beyond self-love, but all that men do, is, some way or other, from this root.

But divine love, or the charity that is spoken of in the text, is something above self-love, as it is something supernatural, or above and beyond all that is natural. It is not a branch that springs out of the root of self-love, as natural affection, and worldly friendships, and the love that men may have to one another, as such, do. But as self-love is the offspring of natural principles, so divine love is the offspring of supernatural principles. The latter is something of a higher and nobler kind, than any plant that grows naturally in such a soil as the heart of man. It is a plant transplanted into the soul out of the garden of heaven, by the holy and blessed spirit of God; and so has its life in God, and not in self. And therefore there is no other love so much above the selfish principle, as Christian love is; no love that is so free and disinterested, and in the exercise of which God is so loved for himself and his own sake, and men are loved not because of their relation to self, but because of their relation to God as his children, and as those who are the creatures of his power, or under the influence of his spirit. And therefore divine love, or charity, above all love in the world, is contrary to a selfish spirit. Other, or natural love may, in some respects, be contrary to selfishness, inasmuch as it may, and often does, move men to much liberality and generosity to those they love; and yet, in other respects, it agrees with a selfish spirit, because if we follow it up to its original, it arises from the same root, viz.: a principle of self-love. But divine love has its spring, where its root is, in Jesus Christ; and so it is not of this world, but of a higher; and it tends thither whence it came. And as it does not spring out of self, so neither does it tend to self. It delights in the honor and glory of God, for his own sake, and not merely for the sake of self; and it seeks and delights in the good of men, for their sake, and for God's sake. And that divine love is, indeed, a principle far above and contrary to a selfish spirit, appears further from this, viz.: that it goes out even to enemies; and that it is its nature and tendency, to go out to the unthankful and evil, and to those that injure and hate us, which is directly contrary to the tendency of a selfish principle, and entirely above nature —less man-like than God-like. That Christian love, or charity, is contrary to a selfish spirit, is further plain,

3. *From the nature of this love to God and to man in particular.* And,

First, From the nature of this *love to God*. If we consider what the Scriptures tell us of the nature of love to God, we find that they teach that those who truly love God, love him so as wholly to devote themselves to him and his service. This we are taught is the sum of the ten commandments, " Thou shalt love the Lord thy God with all thy heart, and with all thy soul, and with all thy mind, and with all thy strength" (Mark xii. 30). In these words is contained a description of a right love to God; and they teach us, that those who love him aright, do devote themselves wholly to him. They devote all to him: all their heart, and all their soul, and all their mind, and all their strength, or all their powers and faculties. Surely a man who gives all this wholly to God, keeps nothing back, but devotes himself wholly and entirely to him, making no reserve; and all who have true love to God, have a spirit to do this. This shows how much a principle of true love to God, is above the selfish principle. For if self be devoted wholly to God, then there is something, above self, that overcomes it; something superior to self, that takes self, and makes an offering of it to God. A selfish principle never devotes itself to another. The nature of it is, to devote all others to self. They that have true love to God, love him as

God, and as the Supreme Good, whereas it is the nature of selfishness to set up self in the place of God, and to make an idol of self. That being whom men regard supremely, they devote all to. They that idolize self, devote all to self; but they that love God as God, devote all to him.

That Christian love, or charity, is contrary to a selfish spirit, will further appear, if we consider what the Scriptures teach,

Secondly, Of the nature of this love *to man*. And there are two chief and most remarkable descriptions that the Bible gives us of a truly gracious love to our neighbors, each of which should be noticed.

The *first* of these, is the requirement that we love our neighbor as ourselves. This we have in the Old Testament (Leviticus xix. 18); "Thou shalt love thy neighbor as thyself;" and this Christ cites (Matthew xxii. 39), as the sum of all the duties of the second table of the law. Now this is contrary to selfishness, for love is not of such a nature as confines the heart to self, but leads it forth to others as well as self, and in like manner as to self. It disposes us to look upon our neighbors, as being, as it were, one with ourselves; and not only to consider our own circumstances and interests, but to consider the wants of our neighbors, as we do our own; not only to have regard to our own desires, but to the desires of others, and to do to them as we would have them do to us.

And the *second* remarkable description which the Scriptures give us of Christian charity, which shows how contrary it is to selfishness, is, that of loving others, as Christ hath loved us. "A new commandment," says Christ (John xiii. 34), "I give unto you, that ye love one another: as I have loved you, that ye also love one another." It is called a new commandment, as contradistinguished from that old one (Leviticus xix. 18), "Thou shalt love thy neighbor as thyself." Not that the duty of love to others, which is the matter of the commandment, was new, for the same kind of love was required of old, under the Old Testament, which is required now. But it is called a new commandment, in this respect, that the rule and motive annexed which we are now more especially to have an eye to, in these days of the gospel, are new. The rule and motive more especially set in view of old, was, our love to ourselves, that we should love our neighbor *as ourselves*. But the motive and rule more especially set in view now, in these days of the gospel, and since the love of Christ has been so wonderfully manifested, is, the love of Christ to us, that we should love our neighbor *as Christ hath loved us*. It is here called a *new* commandment; and so, in John xv. 12, Christ calls it *his* commandment, saying emphatically, "This is my commandment, that ye love one another as I have loved you." That we should love one another as we love ourselves, is Moses' commandment; but that we should love one another as Christ hath loved us, is the commandment of God our Saviour. It is the same commandment, as to the substance of it, that was given of old, but with new light shining upon it from the love of Jesus Christ, and a new enforcement annexed to it, by him, beyond what Moses annexed. So that this rule of loving others as Christ has loved us, does more clearly, and in a further degree, show us our duty and obligation with respect to loving our neighbors, than as Moses stated it.

But to return from this digression, let us consider how this description that Christ gives of Christian love to others, shows it to be the contrary of selfishness, by considering in what manner Christ has expressed love to us, and how much there is in the example of his love, to enforce the contrary of a selfish spirit. And this we may see in *four* things:—

First, Christ has set his love on *those that were his enemies*. There was not only no love to himself in those on whom he set his love, but they were full of enmity, and of a principle of actual hatred to him. "God commendeth his love toward us, in that, while we were yet sinners," or as in the next verse but one, "enemies," "Christ died for us" (Romans v. 8, 10).

Second, Such was Christ's love to us, that he was pleased, *in some respects, to look on us as himself*. By his love to us, if we will but accept his love, he has so espoused us, and united his heart to us, that he is pleased to speak of us, and regard us as himself. His elect were, from all eternity, dear to him as the apple of his eye. He looked upon them so much as himself, that he regarded their concerns as his, and their interests as his own; and he has even made their guilt as his, by a gracious assumption of it to himself, that it might be looked upon as his own, through that divine imputation, in virtue of which they are treated as innocent, while he suffers for them. And his love has sought to unite them to himself, so as to make them, as it were, members of his body, so that they are his flesh and his bones, as he himself seems to say in Matt. xxv. 40, when he declares, "Inasmuch as ye have done it unto one of the least of these my brethren, ye have done it unto me."

Third; Such was the love of Christ to us, that he did, as it were, *spend himself for our sakes*. His love did not rest in mere feeling, or in light efforts and small sacrifices, but though we were enemies, yet he so loved us, that he had a heart to deny himself, and undertake the greatest efforts, and undergo the greatest sufferings for our sakes. He gave up his own ease, and comfort, and interest, and honor, and wealth, and became poor, and outcast, and despised, and had not where to lay his head, and all for us! And not only so, but he shed his own blood for us, and offered himself a sacrifice to God's justice, that we might be forgiven, and accepted, and saved! And,

Fourth, Christ thus loved us, *without any expectation of ever being requited by us for his love.* He did not stand in need of anything we could do for him, and well knew that we should never be able to requite him for his kindness to us, or even to do anything toward it. He knew that we were poor, miserable, and empty-handed outcasts, who might receive from him, but could render nothing to him in return. He knew that we had no money or price with which to purchase anything, and that he must freely give us all things that we needed, or else we should be eternally without them. And shall not we be far from a selfish spirit and utterly contrary to it, if we love one another after such a manner as this, or if we have the same spirit of love toward others that was in Christ toward ourselves? If this is our spirit, our love to others will not depend on their love to us, but we shall do as Christ did to us, love them even though they are enemies. We shall not only seek our own things, but we shall in our hearts be so united to others, that we shall look on their things as our own. We shall endeavor to be interested in their good, as Christ was in ours; and shall be ready to forego and part with our own things, in many cases, for the things of others, as Christ did toward us. And these things we shall be willing and ready to do for others, without any expectation of being repaid by them, as Christ did such great things for us without any expectation of requital or return. If such be our spirit, we shall not be under the influence of a selfish spirit, but shall be unselfish in principle, and heart, and life.

In the application of this subject, the great use I would make of it, is, *to dissuade all from a selfish spirit and practice, and to exhort all to seek that spirit, and live that life, which shall be contrary to it.* Seek, that by divine love, your heart may be devoted to God and to his glory, and to loving your neighbor as yourself, or rather as Christ has loved you. Do not seek, every one your own things, but every one, also, the things of others. And that you may be stirred up to this, in addition to the motives already presented, consider three things,

First, That you are not your own.—As you have not made yourself, so you were not made *for* yourself. You are neither the *author*, nor the *end* of your own being. Nor is it you that uphold yourself in being; or that provide for yourself; or that are dependent on yourself. There is another that hath made you, and preserves you, and provides for you, and on whom you are dependent: and He hath made you for himself, and for the good of your fellow-creatures, and not only for yourself. He has placed before you higher and nobler ends than self, even the welfare of your fellow-men, and of society, and the interests of his kingdom; and for these you ought to labor and live, not only in time, but for eternity.

And if you are Christians, as many of you profess to be, then, in a peculiar sense, "ye are not your own, for ye are bought with a price," even "with the precious blood of Christ," 1 Cor. vi. 19, 20; and 1 Peter i. 19. And this is urged as an argument why Christians should not seek themselves, but the glory of God; for the apostle adds, "Therefore glorify God in your body, and in your spirit, which are God's." By nature you were in a miserable, lost condition, a captive in the hands of divine justice, and a miserable slave in the bondage of sin and Satan. And Christ has redeemed you, and so you are his by purchase. By a most just title you belong to him, and not to yourself. And, therefore, you must not, henceforth, treat yourself as your own, by seeking your own interests or pleasure, only, or even chiefly; for if you do so, you will be guilty of robbing Christ. And as you are not your own, so nothing that you have is your own. Your abilities of body and mind, your outward possessions, your time, talents, influence, comforts, none of them are your own; nor have you any right to use them as if you had an absolute property in them, as you will be likely to do if you imagine them only for your own private benefit, and not for the honor of Christ, and for the good of your fellow-men. Consider,

Second, How you, by your very profession as a Christian, are united to Christ, and to your fellow-Christians.—Christ, and all Christians, are so united together, that they all make but one body; and of this body, Christ is the head, and Christians are the members. "We being many," says the apostle, "are one body in Christ, and every one members, one of another," Rom. xii. 5; and again, "By one spirit, are we all baptized into one body, whether we be Jews or Gentiles, whether we be bond or free," 1 Cor. xii. 13. How unbecoming, then, is it in Christians to be selfish, and concerned only for their own private interests. In the natural body, the hand is ready to serve the head, and all the members are ready to serve one another. Is what the hands do, done only for their own advantage? Are they not continually employed as much for the other parts of the body, as for themselves? Is not the work they are doing from day to day, for the common good of the whole body? And so it may be said as to the eye, the teeth, the feet, that they are all employed, not for themselves, or for their own limited and partial welfare, but for the common comfort and good of the whole body. And if the head be dishonored, are not all the members of the body at once employed and active to remove the dishonor, and to put honor upon the head? And if any members of the body are wounded, and languishing, and in pain, are not all the members of the body at once engaged to screen that weak or suffering member? Are not the eyes employed in looking about for it, and the ears in attending to the directions of physicians, and the feet in going where relief is to be sought, and the hands in applying the remedies provided? So it should be with the Christian body. All its members should be helpers, and comforts to each other, and thus promote their mutual welfare and happiness, and the glory of Christ, the head. Once more, consider,

Third, That in seeking the glory of God and the good of your fellow-creatures, you take the surest way to have God seek your interests, and promote your welfare.—If you will devote yourself to God, as making a sacrifice of all your own interests to him, you will not throw yourself away. Though you seem to neglect yourself, and to deny yourself, and to overlook self in imitating the divine benevolence, *God will take care of you;* and he will see to it that your interest is provided for, and your welfare made sure! You shall be no loser by all the sacrifices you have made for him. To his glory be it said, he will not be your debtor, but will requite you an hundred-fold even in this life, beside the eternal rewards that he will bestow upon you hereafter. His own declaration is, "Every one that hath forsaken houses, or brethren, or sisters, or father, or mother, or wife, or children, or lands for my name's sake, shall receive an hundred-fold" (the other evangelist adds, "in this present time"), "and shall inherit everlasting life," Matt. xix. 29; and the spirit of this declaration applies to all sacrifices made for Christ, or for our fellow-men for his sake. The greatness of the reward for this life, Christ expresses by a definite number; but he does not make use of numbers, however great, to set forth the reward promised them hereafter. He only says, they shall receive everlasting life, because the reward is so great, and so much exceeds all the expense and self-denial persons can be at for Christ's sake, that no numbers are sufficient to describe it.

If you are selfish, and make yourself and your own private interests your idol, God will leave you to yourself, and let you promote your own interests as well as you can. But if you do not selfishly seek your own, but do seek the things that are Jesus Christ's, and the things of your fellow-beings, then God will make your interest and happiness his own charge, and he is infinitely more able to provide for, and promote it, than you are. The resources of the universe move at his bidding, and he can easily command them all to subserve your welfare. So that not to seek your own, in the selfish sense, is the best way of seeking your own in a better sense. It is the directest course you can take to secure your highest happiness. When you are required not to be selfish, you are not required, as has been observed, not to love and seek your own happiness, but only not to seek mainly your own private and confined interests. But if you place your happiness in God, in glorifying him, and in serving him by doing good, in this way, above all others, will you promote your wealth, and honor, and pleasure here below, and obtain hereafter a crown of unfading glory, and pleasures for evermore at God's right hand. If you seek, in the spirit of selfishness, to grasp all as your own, you shall lose all, and be driven out of the world, at last, naked and forlorn, to everlasting poverty and contempt. But if you seek not your own, but the things of Christ, and the good of your fellow-men, God himself will be yours, and Christ yours, and the Holy Spirit yours, and all things yours. Yes, " all things" shall be yours, whether Paul, or Apollos, or Cephas, or the world, or life, or death, or things present, or things to come ; all are yours ; and ye are

Christ's; and Christ is God's, 1 Cor. iii. 21, 22.

Let these things, then, incline us all to be less selfish than we are, and to seek more of the contrary most excellent spirit. Selfishness is a principle native to us, and, indeed, all the corruption of our nature does radically consist in it; but considering the knowledge that we have of Christianity, and how numerous and powerful the motives it presents, we ought to be far less selfish than we are, and less ready to seek our own interests and these only. How much is there of this evil spirit, and how little of that excellent, noble, diffusive spirit which has now been set before us. But whatever the cause of this, whether it arise from our having too narrow notions of Christianity, and from our not having learned Christ as we ought to have done, or from the habits of selfishness handed down to us from our fathers, whatever the cause be, let us strive to overcome it, that we may grow in the grace of an unselfish spirit, and thus glorify God, and do good to men.

LECTURE IX.

THE SPIRIT OF CHARITY THE OPPOSITE OF AN ANGRY OR WRATHFUL SPIRIT.

"Is not easily provoked."—1 Corinthians xiii. 5.

Having declared that charity is contrary to the two great cardinal vices of pride and selfishness, those deep and ever-flowing fountains of sin and wickedness in the heart, the Apostle next proceeds to show, that it is also contrary to two things that are commonly the fruits of this pride and selfishness, viz.: an angry spirit, and a censorious spirit. To the first of these points, I would now turn your attention, viz.: that charity "*is not easily provoked.*" The doctrine here set before us, is,

That the spirit of charity, or Christian love, is the opposite of an angry or wrathful spirit or disposition.—In speaking to this doctrine, I would inquire, first, in what consists that angry spirit or temper to which a Christian spirit is contrary; and next, give the reason why a Christian spirit is contrary to it.

I. *What is that angry or wrathful spirit, to which charity, or a Christian spirit, is contrary.*—It is not all manner of anger that Christianity is opposite and contrary to. It is said in Ephesians iv. 26, "Be ye angry, and sin not," which seems to suppose that there is such a thing as anger without sin, or that it is possible to be angry in some cases, and yet not offend God. And therefore it may be answered, in a single word, that a Christian spirit, or the spirit of charity, is opposite to all undue and unsuitable anger. But anger may be undue or unsuitable in four respects; in its nature, its occasion, its end, and its measure. And,

1. *Anger may be undue and unsuitable in respect to its nature.*—Anger may be defined to be, an earnest, and more or less violent opposition of spirit against any real or supposed evil, or in view of any fault or offence of another. All anger is opposition of the mind against real or supposed evil; but it is not all opposition of the mind against evil, that is properly

called anger. There is an opposition of the judgment, that is not anger; for anger is the opposition, not of the cool judgment, but of the spirit of the man, that is, of his disposition or heart. But here, again, it is not all opposition of the spirit against evil, that can be called anger. There is an opposition of the spirit against *natural* evil that we suffer, as in grief and sorrow for instance, which is a very different thing from anger; and in distinction from this, anger is opposition to *moral* evil, or evil real or supposed in voluntary agents, or at least in agents that are conceived to be voluntary, or acting by their own will, and against such evil as is supposed to be their fault. But yet again, it is not all opposition of spirit against evil or faultiness in voluntary agents, that is anger; for there may be a dislike, without the spirit being excited and angry; and such dislike is an opposition of the will and judgment, and not always of the feelings, and in order to anger, the latter must be moved. In all anger there must be earnestness and opposition of feeling, and the spirit must be moved and stirred within us. Anger is one of the passions or affections of the soul, though when called an affection, it is, for the most part, to be regarded as an evil affection.

Such being the nature of anger in general, it may now be shown wherein anger is undue or unsuitable in its nature. And this is the case with all anger that contains ill-will, or a desire of revenge. Some have defined anger to be a desire of revenge. But this cannot be considered a just definition of anger in general; for if so, there would be no anger that would not imply ill-will, and the desire that some other might be injured. But doubtless there is such a thing as anger that is consistent with good-will; for a father may be angry with his child, that is, he may find in himself an earnestness and opposition of spirit to the bad conduct of his child, and his spirit may be engaged and stirred in opposition to that conduct, and to his child while continuing in it; and yet, at the same time, he will not have any proper ill-will to the child, but on the contrary, a real good-will; and so far from desiring its injury, he may have the very highest desire for its true welfare, and his very anger be but his opposition to that which he thinks will be of injury to it. And this shows, that anger, in its general nature, rather consists in the opposition of the spirit to evil, than in a desire of revenge.

If the nature of anger in general consisted in ill-will and a desire of revenge, no anger would be lawful in any case whatever; for we are not allowed to entertain ill-will toward others in any case, but are to have good-will to all. We are required by Christ to wish well to, and pray for the prosperity of all, even our enemies, and those that despitefully use us and persecute us, Matt. v. 44; and the rule given by the Apostle is, "Bless them which persecute you: bless and curse not," Rom. xii. 14; that is, we are only to wish good, and pray for good to others, and in no case to wish evil. And so all revenge is forbidden, if we except the vengeance which public justice takes on the transgressor, in inflicting which men act not for themselves, but for God. The rule is, "Thou shalt not avenge, nor bear any grudge against the children of thy people, but thou shalt love thy neighbor as thyself. I am the Lord," Leviticus xix. 18; and says the Apostle, "Dearly beloved, avenge not yourselves, but rather give place unto wrath; for it is written, Vengeance is mine, I will repay, saith the Lord," Romans

xii. 19. So that all the anger that contains ill-will or a desire of revenge, is what Christianity is contrary to, and by the most fearful sanctions forbids. Sometimes anger, as it is spoken of in the Scripture, is meant only in the worst sense, or in that sense of it which implies ill-will, and the desire of revenge; and in this sense, all anger is forbidden, as in Ephesians iv. 31, "Let all bitterness, and wrath, and anger, and clamor, and evil-speaking, be put away from you, with all malice;" and again in Colossians iii. 8, "But now ye, also, put off all these; anger, wrath, malice, blasphemy, filthy communication out of your mouth." Thus anger may be irregular and sinful with respect to its nature. And so,

2. *Anger may be unsuitable and unchristian in respect to its occasion.*—And such unsuitableness consists in its being without any just cause. Of this Christ speaks when he says, "Whosoever is angry with his brother, without a cause, shall be in danger of the judgment," Matt. v. 22. And this may be the case in three ways:—

First, When the occasion of anger is that, which *is no fault at all in the person that is its object*. This is not unfrequently the case.

Many persons are of such a proud and peevish disposition, that they will be angry at anything that is in any respect against them, or troublesome to them, or contrary to their wishes, whether anybody be to blame for it or not. And so, sometimes, men are angry with others for those things that are not from their fault, but which happen merely through their involuntary ignorance, or through their impotence. They are angry that they have not done better, when the only cause was, that the circumstances were such that they could not do otherwise than they did. And oftentimes persons are angry with others, not only for that which is no fault in them, but for that which is really good, and for which they ought to be praised. So it always is when men are angry at God, and fret at his providence and its dispensations toward them. Thus to be fretful, and impatient, and to murmur against God's dealings, is a most horribly wicked kind of anger. And yet this very often is the case in this wicked world. This is what the wicked Israelites were so often guilty of, and for which so many of them were overthrown in the wilderness; and this was what Jonah, though a good man, was guilty of when he was angry with God without a cause—angry for that for which he should have praised God, viz. : his great mercy to the Ninevites. Oftentimes, also, persons' spirits are kept very much in a fret, by reason of things going contrary to them, and their meeting with crosses, and disappointments, and entanglements in their business, when they will not own that it is God they fret at and are angry with, and do not even seem to be convinced of it themselves. But, indeed, such fretfulness can be interpreted no other way; and whatever they may pretend, it is ultimately aimed against the author of providence—against the God who orders these cross events, so that it is a murmuring and fretting against Him.

And it is a common thing, again, for persons to be angry with others, for their doing well, and that which is only their duty. There never was so much bitterness and fierceness of anger among men, one to another, and so much hostility and malice, for any one thing, as there has been for well-doing. History gives no accounts of any such cruelties as those practised toward God's people on account of their profession and practice of religion. And how annoyed were the scribes and Pharisees with Christ, for doing the will of his Father in what he did and said while on earth! When men are angry with others, or with civil or ecclesiastical authorities, for proceeding regularly against them for their errors or sins, they are angry with them for well-doing. And this is the case when they are angry with their neighbors or brethren in the church for bearing a due testimony against them, and endeavoring to bring them to justice when the case requires it. Often men are angry with others not only for well-doing, but for doing those things that are acts of friendship to them, as when we are angry with others for administering Christian reproof for anything they observe in us that is wrong. This the Psalmist said he should accept as a kindness, "Let the righteous smite me, it shall be a kindness;" but such as are angry with it, foolishly and sinfully take it as an injury. In all these things, our anger is undue and unreasonable with regard to its occasion, when that occasion is no fault of the one with whom we are angry. And so,

Second, Anger is unsuitable and unchristian as to its occasion, *when persons are angry*

upon small and trivial occasions, and when though there be something of blame, yet the fault is very small, and such as is not worth our being stirred and engaged about. God does not call us to have our spirits ceaselessly engaged in opposition, and stirred up in anger, unless it be on some important occasions. He that is angry at every little fault he may see in others, is certainly one with whom it is otherwise than is expressed in the text. Of him that is provoked at every little, trifling thing, it surely cannot be said, that he is "not easily provoked." Some are of such an angry, fretful spirit, that they are put out of humor by every little thing, and by things in others, in the family, or in society, or in business, that are no greater faults than they themselves are guilty of every day. Those that will thus be angry at every fault they see in others, will be sure to be always kept in a fret, and their minds will never be composed; for it cannot be expected in this world but that we shall continually be seeing faults in others, as there are continually faults in ourselves. And therefore it is, that Christians are directed to be "slow to speak and slow to wrath," James i. 19; and that it is said, that "He that is soon angry, dealeth foolishly." He that diligently guards his own spirit, will not be very frequently or easily angry. He wisely keeps his mind in a calm, clear frame, and does not suffer it to be stirred with anger, except on extraordinary occasions, and those that do especially call for it. And again,

Third, Anger may be unsuitable and unchristian in its occasion, *when our spirits are stirred at the faults of others chiefly as they affect ourselves, and not as they are against God*. We should never be angry but at sin, and this should always be that which we oppose in our anger. And when our spirits are stirred to oppose this evil, it should be *as* sin, or chiefly as it is against God. If there be no sin and no fault, then we have no cause to be angry; and if there be a fault or sin, then it is infinitely worse as against God, than it is as against us, and therefore it requires the most opposition on that account. Persons sin in their anger, when they are selfish in it, for we are not to act as if we were our own, or for ourselves simply, since we belong to God, and not to ourselves. When a fault is committed wherein God is sinned against, and persons are injured by it, they should be chiefly concerned, and their spirits chiefly moved against it because it is against God; for they should be more solicitous for God's honor, than for their own temporal interests. All anger, as to occasion, is either a virtue or a vice, for there is no middle sort that is neither good nor bad; but there is no virtue or goodness in opposing sin, unless it be opposed as sin. The anger that is virtuous, is the same thing which, in one form, is called zeal. Our anger should be like Christ's anger. He was like a lamb under the greatest personal injuries, and we never read of his being angry but in the cause of God against sin as sin. And this should be the case with us. And as anger may, in these three ways, be unsuitable and unchristian with respect to the occasion or cause of it, so,

3. *It may be undue and sinful with respect to its end.*—And this in two particulars:—

First, When we are angry *without considerately proposing any end* to be gained by it. In this way it is, that anger is rash and inconsiderate, and that it is suffered to rise, and be continued, without any consideration or motive. Reason has no hand in the matter;

but the passions go before the reason, and anger is suffered to rise before even a thought has been given to the question, "of what advantage or benefit will it be, either to me or others?" Such anger is not the anger of men, but the blind passion of beasts: it is a kind of beastly fury, rather than the affection of a rational creature. All things in the soul of man should be under the government of reason, which is the highest faculty of our being; and every other faculty and principle in the soul should be governed and directed by that to its proper end. And, therefore, when our anger is of this kind, it is unchristian and sinful. And so it is,

Second, When we allow ourselves to be angry *for any wrong end*. Though reason would tell us with regard to our anger, that it cannot be for the glory of God, or of any real benefit to ourselves, but on the other hand, much to the mischief of ourselves or others, yet because we have in view the gratification of our own pride, or the extension of our influence, or getting in some way superiority to others, we allow anger as aiding to gain these or other ends, and thus indulge a sinful spirit. And lastly,

4. *Anger may be unsuitable and unchristian with respect to its measure.*—And this, again, in two particulars, as to the measure of its degree, and the measure of its continuance. And,

First, When it is immoderate *in degree*. Anger may be far beyond what the case requires. And often it is so great as to put persons beyond the control of themselves, their passions being so violent that, for the time, they know not what they do, and seem to be unable to direct and regulate either their feelings or conduct. Sometimes men's passions rise so high that they are, as it were, drunk with them, so that their reason is gone, and they act as if beside themselves. But the degree of anger ought always to be regulated by the end of it, and it should never be suffered to rise any higher than so far as tends to the obtaining of the good ends which reason has proposed. And anger is, also, beyond measure, and thus sinful,

Second, When it is immoderate *in its continuance*. It is a very sinful thing for persons to be long angry. The wise man not only gives us the injunction, "Be not hasty in thy spirit to be angry," but he adds, that "Anger resteth in the bosom of fools," Ecc. vii. 9; and says the Apostle, "Be ye angry, and sin not; let not the sun go down upon your wrath," Eph. iv. 26. If anger be long continued, it soon degenerates into malice, for the leaven of evil spreads faster than the leaven of good. If a person allows himself long to hold anger towards another, he will quickly come to hate him. And so we find that it actually is among those that retain a grudge in their hearts against others for week after week, and month after month, and year after year. They do, in the end, truly hate the persons against whom they thus lay up anger, whether they own it or not. And this is a most dreadful sin in the sight of God. All, therefore, should be exceedingly careful how they suffer anger long to continue in their hearts.

Having thus shown what is that angry or wrathful spirit, to which charity or a Christian spirit is contrary, I pass, as proposed, to show,

II. *How charity, or a Christian spirit, is contrary to it.* And this I would do by showing, first, that charity or love, which is the sum of the Christian spirit, is directly, and in itself, contrary to the anger that is sinful and secondly, that the fruits of charity which are mentioned in the context, are all contrary to it. And,

1. *Christian charity or love, is directly, and in itself, contrary to all undue anger.*—Christian love is contrary to anger which is undue in its nature, and that tends to revenge, and so implies ill-will, for the nature of love is good-will. It tends to prevent persons from being angry without just cause, and will be far from disposing any one to be angry for but little faults. Love is backward to anger, and will not yield to it on trivial occasions, much less where there is no cause for being angry. It is a malignant and evil, and not a loving spirit, that disposes persons to be angry without cause. Love to God is opposite to a disposition in men to be angry at other's faults, chiefly as they themselves are offended and injured by them: it rather disposes them to look at them chiefly as committed against God. If love be in exercise, it will tend to keep down the irascible passions, and hold them in subjection, so that reason and the spirit of love may regulate them and keep them from being immoderate in degree or of long continuance. And not only is charity,

or Christian love, directly, and in itself, contrary to all undue anger, but,

2. *All the fruits of this charity which are mentioned in the context, are also contrary to it.*—And I shall mention only two of these fruits, as they may stand for all, viz.: those virtues that are contrary to pride and selfishness. And,

First, Love or charity is contrary to all undue and sinful anger, as, *in its fruits, it is contrary to pride.* Pride is one chief cause of undue anger. It is because men are proud, and exalt themselves in their own hearts, that they are revengeful, and are apt to be excited, and to make great things out of little ones that may be against themselves. Yea, they even treat as vices things that are in themselves virtues, when they think their honor is touched, or when their will is crossed. And it is pride that makes men so unreasonable and rash in their anger, and raises it to such a high degree, and continues it so long, and often keeps it up in the form of habitual malice. But, as we have already seen, love or Christian charity is utterly opposed to pride. And so,

Secondly, Love or charity is contrary to all

sinful anger, as, *in its fruits, it is contrary to selfishness.* It is because men are selfish and seek their own, that they are malicious and revengeful against all that oppose or interfere with their own interests. If men sought not chiefly their own private and selfish interests, but the glory of God and the common good, then their spirit would be a great deal more stirred up in God's cause, than in their own; and they would not be prone to hasty, rash, inconsiderate, immoderate, and long-continued wrath, with any who might have injured or provoked them, but they would, in a great measure, forget themselves for God's sake, and from their zeal for the honor of Christ. The end they would aim at, would be, not making themselves great, or getting their own will, but the glory of God, and the good of their fellow-beings. But love, as we have seen, is opposed to all selfishness.

In the application of this subject, let us use it,

1. *In the way of self-examination.*—Our own consciences, if faithfully searched and imperatively inquired of, can best tell us whether we are, or have been persons of such an angry spirit and wrathful disposition as has been

described; whether we are frequently angry, or indulge in ill-will, or allow the continuance of anger. Have we not often been angry? And if so, is there not reason to think that that anger has been undue, and without just cause, and thus sinful? God does not call Christians into his kingdom, that they may indulge greatly in fretfulness, and to have their minds commonly stirred up and ruffled with anger. And has not most of the anger you have cherished been chiefly, if not entirely on your own account? Men are often wont to plead zeal for religion, and for duty, and for the honor of God, as the cause of their indignation, when it is only their own private interest that is concerned and affected. It is remarkable how forward men are to appear as if they were zealous for God and righteousness, in cases wherein their honor, or will, or interest has been touched, and to make pretence of this in injuring others or complaining of them; and what a great difference there is in their conduct in other cases, wherein God's honor is as much, or a great deal more hurt, and their own interest is not specially concerned. In the latter case, there is no such appearance of zeal and engagedness of spirit, and no forwardness to reprove, and complain, and be angry, but often a readiness to excuse, and leave reproof to others, and to be cold and backward in anything like opposition to the sin.

And ask, still further, what good has been obtained by your anger, and what have you aimed at in it; or have you even thought of these things? There has been a great deal of anger and bitterness in things passing in this town on public occasions, and many of you have been present on such occasions; and such anger has been manifest in your conduct; and I fear rested in your bosoms. Examine yourselves as to this matter, and ask what has been the nature of your anger. Has not most, if not all of it, been of that undue and unchristian kind that has been spoken of? Has it not been of the nature of ill-will, and malice, and bitterness of heart; an anger arising from proud and selfish principles, because your interest, or your opinion, or your party was touched? Has not your anger been far from that Christian zeal that does not disturb charity, or embitter the feelings, or lead to unkindness or revenge in the conduct? And how has it been with respect to your holding anger? Has not the sun more than once gone down upon your wrath, while God and your neighbor knew it? Nay more, has it not gone down again and again, through month after month, and year after year, while winter's cold hath not chilled the heat of your wrath, and the summer's sun hath not melted you to kindness? And are there not some here present, that are sitting before God with anger laid up in their hearts, and burning there? Or if their anger is for a time concealed from human eyes, is it not like an old sore not thoroughly healed, but so that the least touch renews the smart; or like a smothered fire in the heaps of autumn leaves, which the least breeze will kindle into a flame? And how is it in your families? Families are societies the most closely united of all; and their members are in the nearest relation, and under the greatest obligations to peace and harmony and love. And yet what has been your spirit in the family? Many a time have you not been fretful, and angry, and impatient, and peevish, and unkind to those whom God has made in so great a measure dependent on you, and who are so easily made happy or unhappy by what you do or say—

by your kindness or unkindness? And what kind of anger have you indulged in the family? Has it not often been unreasonable and sinful, not only in its nature, but in its occasions, where those with whom you were angry were not in fault, or when the fault was trifling or unintended, or where, perhaps, you were yourself in part to blame for it; and even where there might have been just cause, has not your wrath been continued, and led you to be sullen, or severe, to an extent that your own conscience disapproved? And have you not been angry with your neighbors who live by you, and with whom you have to do daily; and on trifling occasions, and for little things, have you not allowed yourself in anger toward them? In all these points it becomes us to examine ourselves, and know what manner of spirit we are of, and wherein we come short of the spirit of Christ.

2. *The subject dissuades from, and warns against, all undue and sinful anger.*—The heart of man is exceeding prone to undue and sinful anger, being naturally full of pride and selfishness; and we live in a world that is full of occasions that tend to stir up this corruption that is within us, so that we cannot

expect to live in any tolerable measure as Christians should do, in this respect, without constant watchfulness and prayer. And we should not only watch against the exercises, but fight against the principle of anger, and seek earnestly to have *that* mortified in our hearts, by the establishment and increase of the spirit of divine love and humility in our souls. And to this end, several things may be considered. And,

First, Consider frequently *your own failings, by which you have given both God and man occasion to be displeased with you.* All your life-time you have come short of God's requirements, and thus justly incurred his dreadful wrath; and constantly you have occasion to pray God that he will not be angry with you, but will show you mercy. And your failings have also been numerous toward your fellow-men, and have often given them occasion to be angry with you. Your faults are as great perhaps as theirs; and this thought should lead you not to spend so much of your time in fretting at the motes in their eyes, but rather to occupy it in pulling the beams out of your own. Very often those that are most ready to be angry with others, and to carry their resentments highest for their faults, are equally, or still more guilty of the same faults. And so those that are most apt to be angry with others for speaking evil of them, are often most frequent in speaking evil of others, and even in their anger to vilify and abuse them. If others then provoke us, instead of being angry with them, let our first thoughts be turned to ourselves, and let it put us on self-reflection, and lead us to inquire whether we have not been guilty of the very same things that excite our anger, or even of worse. Thus thinking of our own failings and errors, would tend to keep us from undue anger with others. And consider, also,

Second, How such undue anger *destroys the comfort of him that indulges it.* It troubles the soul in which it is, as a storm troubles the ocean. Such anger is inconsistent with a man's enjoying himself, or having any true peace, or self-respect in his own spirit. Men of an angry and wrathful temper, whose minds are always in a fret, are the most miserable sort of men, and live a most miserable life; so that a regard to our own happiness should lead us to shun all undue and sinful anger. Consider, again,

Third, How much such a spirit *unfits persons for the duties of religion*. All undue anger indisposes us for the pious exercises, and the active duties of religion. It puts the soul far from that sweet and excellent frame of spirit, in which we most enjoy communion with God, and which makes truth and ordinances most profitable to us. And hence it is, that God commands us not to approach his altars while we are at enmity with others, but "first to be reconciled to our brother, and then come and offer our gift," Matt. v. 24; and that by the Apostle it is said, "I will, therefore, that men pray everywhere, lifting up holy hands, without wrath and doubting;" 1 Timothy ii. 8. And, once more, consider,

Fourth, That *angry men are spoken of in the Bible, as unfit for human society*. The express direction of God is, "Make no friendship with an angry man, and with a furious man thou shalt not go, lest thou learn his ways, and get a snare to thy soul," Proverbs xxii. 24, 25. Such a man is accursed as a pest of society, who disturbs and disquiets it, and puts everything into confusion. "An angry man stirreth up strife, and a furious man aboundeth in transgression," Proverbs xxix.

22. Every one is uncomfortable about him; his example is evil; and his conduct disapproved alike by God and men. Let these considerations, then, prevail with all, and lead them to avoid an angry spirit and temper, and to cultivate the spirit of gentleness, and kindness, and love, which is the spirit of heaven.

LECTURE X.

THE SPIRIT OF CHARITY THE OPPOSITE OF A CENSORIOUS SPIRIT.

"Thinketh no evil."—1 Cor. xiii. 5.

Having remarked how charity, or Christian love, is opposed not only to pride and selfishness, but to the ordinary fruits of these evil dispositions, viz.: an angry spirit, and a censorious spirit, and having already spoken as to the former, I come now to the latter. And in respect to this, the Apostle declares, that charity "*thinketh no evil.*" The doctrine set forth in these words, is clearly this:—

That the spirit of charity, or Christian love, is the opposite of a censorious spirit.— Or in other words, it is contrary to a disposition to think or judge uncharitably of others. Charity, in one of the common uses of the expression, signifies a disposition to think the best of others that the case will allow. This, however, as I have shown before, is not the scriptural meaning of the word charity, but only one way of its exercise, or one of its many and rich fruits. Charity is of vastly larger extent than this. It signifies, as we have already seen, the same as Christian or divine love, and so is the same as the Christian spirit. And in accordance with this view, we here find the spirit of charitable judging mentioned among many other good fruits of charity, and here expressed, as the other fruits of charity are in the context, *negatively*, or by denying the contrary fruit, viz.: censoriousness, or a disposition uncharitably to judge or censure others. And in speaking to this point, I would, first, show the nature of censoriousness, or wherein it consists; and then mention some things wherein it appears to be contrary to a Christian spirit. I would show,

I. *The nature of censoriousness, or wherein a censorious spirit, or a disposition uncharitably to judge others, consists.*—It consists in a disposition to think evil of others, or to judge evil of them, with respect to three things: their state; their qualities; their actions. And,

1. A censorious spirit appears *in a forwardness to judge evil of the state of others.* It often shows itself in a disposition to think the worst of those about us, whether they are men of the world, or professing Christians. In respect to the latter class, it often leads persons to pass censure on those who are professors of religion, and to condemn them as being hypocrites. Here, however, extremes are to be avoided. Some persons are very apt to be positive, from little things that they observe in others, in determining that they are godly men; and others are forward, from just as little things, to be positive in condemning others as not having the least degree of grace in their hearts, and as being strangers to vital and experimental religion. But all positiveness in an affair of this nature, seems to be without warrant from the word of God. God seems there to have reserved the positive determination of men's state to himself, as a thing to be kept in his own hands, as the great and only searcher of the hearts of the children of men.

Persons are guilty of censoriousness in condemning the state of others, when they will do it from things that are no evidence of their being in a bad estate; or when they will condemn others as hypocrites because of God's providential dealings with them, as Job's three friends condemned him as a hypocrite on account of his uncommon and severe afflictions. And the same is true, when they condemn them for the failings they may see in them, and which are no greater than are often incident to God's children, and it may be no greater, or not so great as their own, though notwithstanding just such things they think well of themselves as Christians. And so persons are censorious, when they condemn others as being unconverted and carnal men, because they differ from them in opinion on some points that are not fundamental; or when they judge ill of their state from what they observe in them, for want of making due allowances for their natural temperament, or for their manner or want of education, or other peculiar disadvantages under which they labor,—or when they are ready to reject all as irreligious and unconverted men, because their experiences do not, in everything, quadrate with their own; setting up themselves, and their own experience, as a standard and rule to all others; not being sensible of that vast variety and liberty which the Spirit of God permits and uses in his saving work on the hearts of men, and how mysterious and inscrutable his ways often are, and especially in this great work of making men new creatures in Christ Jesus. In all these ways, men often act, not only censoriously, but as unreasonably, in not allowing any to be Christians who have not their own experiences, as if they would not allow any to be men, who had not just their own stature, and the same strength, or temperament of body, and the very same features of countenance with themselves. In the next place,

2. A censorious spirit appears in *a forwardness to judge evil of the qualities of others.* It appears in a disposition to overlook their good qualities, or to think them destitute of such qualities when they are not, or to make very little of them; or to magnify their ill qualities, and make more of them than is just; or to charge them with those ill qualities that they have not. Some are very apt to charge others with ignorance and folly, and other contemptible qualities, when they in no sense deserve to be esteemed thus by them. Some seem very apt to entertain a very low

and despicable opinion of others, and so to represent them to their associates and friends, when a charitable disposition would discern many good things in them, to balance or more than balance the evil, and would frankly own them to be persons not to be despised. And some are ready to charge others with those morally evil qualities that they are free from, or to charge them with such qualities in a much higher degree than they at all deserve. Thus some have such a prejudice against some of their neighbors, that they regard them as a great deal more proud sort of persons, more selfish, or spiteful, or malicious, than they really are. Through some deep prejudice they have imbibed against them, they are ready to conceive that they have all manner of bad qualities, and no good ones. They seem to them to be an exceeding proud, or covetous, or selfish, or, in some way, bad sort of men, when it may be that to others they appear well. Others see their many good qualities, and see perhaps many palliations of the qualities that are not good; but the censorious see only that which is evil, and speak only that which is unjust and disparaging as to the qualities of others. And,

3. A censorious spirit appears *in a forwardness to judge evil of the actions of others.* By actions, here, I would be understood to mean, all the external voluntary acts of men, whether consisting in words or deeds. And a censorious spirit in judging evil of others' actions, discovers itself in two things:—

First, In judging them to be guilty of evil actions, *without any evidence that constrains them to such a judgment.* A suspicious spirit, which leads persons to be jealous of others, and ready to suspect them of being guilty of evil things when they have no evidence of it whatever, is an uncharitable spirit, and contrary to Christianity. Some persons are very free in passing their censures on others with respect to those things that they suppose they do out of their sight. They are ready to believe that they commit this, and that, and the other evil deed, in secret, and away from the eyes of men, or that they have done or said thus and so among their associates, and in the circle of their friends, and that, from some design or motive, they keep these things hid from others that are not in the same interest with themselves. These are the persons chargeable with the "evil surmisings," spoken of and condemned by the Apostle, 1 Timothy vi. 4, and which are connected with "envy, strife and railings." Very often, again, persons show an uncharitable and censorious spirit with respect to the actions of others, by being forward to take up, and circulate evil reports about them. Merely hearing a flying and evil rumor about an individual, in such a thoughtless and lying world as this is, is far from being sufficient evidence against any one, to make us believe he has been guilty of that which is reported; for the devil, who is called "the god of this world," is said to be "a liar, and the father of it," and too many, alas! of his children are like him in their speaking of falsehoods. And yet it is a very common thing for persons to pass a judgment on others, on no better ground or foundation, than that they have heard that somebody has said this, or that, or the other thing, though they have no evidence that what is said is true. When they hear that another has done or said so and so, they seem at once to conclude that it is so, without making any further inquiry, though nothing is more uncertain, or more likely to prove false, than the mutterings or whispers of common fame. And some are always so ready to catch up all ill-report, that it seems to be pleasing to them to hear evil of others. Their spirit seems greedy of it; and it is, as it were, food to the hunger of their depraved hearts, and they feed on it, as carrion birds do on the worst of flesh. They easily and greedily take it in as true, without examination, thus showing how contrary they are in character and conduct to him of whom the Psalmist speaks, Psalm xv. 1-3, as dwelling in God's tabernacle and abiding in his holy hill, and of whom he declares, that "he taketh not up a reproach against his neighbor;" and showing, also, that they are rather like "the wicked doer," that "giveth heed to false lips," and as the "liar," who "giveth ear to a naughty tongue," Proverbs xvii. 4. A censorious spirit in judging evil of the actions of others, also, discovers itself,

Second, In a disposition *to put the worst constructions on their actions*. The censorious are not only apt to judge others guilty of evil actions without sufficient evidence, but they are also prone to put a bad construction on their actions, when they will just us well, and perhaps better admit of a good construction. Very often the moving design and end in the action, is secret, confined to the recesses of the actor's own bosom; and yet persons are commonly very forward to pass their censure upon the act, without reference to these: and this is a kind of censoriousness and uncharitable judging, as common, or more common than any other. Thus it is very common with men, when they are prejudiced against others, to put bad constructions on their actions or words that are seemingly good, as though they were performed in hypocrisy; and this is especially true in reference to public offices and affairs. If anything be said or done by persons, wherein there is a show of concern for the public good, or the good of a neighbor, or the honor of God, or the interest of religion, some will always be ready to say, that all this is in hypocrisy, and that the design really is, only to promote their own interest, and to advance themselves; and that they are only flattering and deluding others, having all the time some evil design in their hearts.

But here it may be inquired, "Wherein lies the evil of judging ill of others, since it is not true that all judging ill of others is unlawful?

And where are the lines to be drawn?" To this, I reply,

First, There are some persons *that are appointed on purpose to be judges,* in civil societies, and in churches, who are impartially to judge of others that properly fall under their cognizance, whether good or bad, and to pass sentence according to what they are; to approve the good, and condemn the bad, according to the evidence, and the nature of the act done, and its agreement or disagreement with the law which is the judges' rule.

Second, Particular persons in their private judgments of others, *are not obliged to divest themselves of reason,* that they may thus judge well of all. This would be plainly against reason; for Christian charity is not a thing founded on the ruins of reason, but there is the most sweet harmony between reason and charity. And therefore we are not forbidden to judge all persons when there is plain and clear evidence that they are justly chargeable with evil. We are not to blame, when we judge those to be wicked men, and poor Christless wretches, who give flagrant proof that they are so by a course of wicked action. "Some men's sins." says the Apostle, "are open beforehand, going before to judgment, and some men they follow after." That is, some men's sins are such plain testimony against them, that they are sufficient to condemn them as wicked men in full sight of the world, even before the coming of that final day of judgment that shall disclose the secrets of the heart to all. And so some men's actions give such clear evidence of the evil of their intentions, that it is no judging the secrets of the heart, to judge that their designs and ends are wicked. And therefore it is plain, that all judging as to others' state, or qualifications, or actions, is not an uncharitable censoriousness. But the evil of that judging wherein censoriousness consists, lies in two things:—

It lies, *first*, in judging evil of others when evidence does not oblige to it, or in thinking ill of them when the case very well allows of thinking well of them; when those things that seem to be in their favor are overlooked, and only those that are against them are regarded, and when the latter are magnified, and too great stress laid on them. And the same is the case, when persons are hasty and rash in judging and condemning others, though both prudence and charity oblige them to suspend their judgment till they know more of the matter, and all the circumstances are plain before them. Persons may often show a great deal of uncharitableness and rashness, in freely censuring others before they have heard what they have to say in their defence. And hence it is said, " He that answereth a matter before he heareth it, it is folly and shame unto him," Proverbs xviii. 13.

And the evil of that judging which is censorious, lies, in the *second* place, in a well-pleasedness in judging ill of others. Persons may judge ill of others, from clear and plain evidence that compels them to it, and yet it may be to their grief that they are obliged to judge as they do; just as when a tender parent hears of some great crime of a child with such evidence that he cannot but think it true. But very often judgment is passed against others, in such a manner as shows that the individual is well pleased in passing it. He is so forward in judging evil, and judges on such slight evidence, and carries his judgment to such extremes, as shows that his inclination is in it, and that he loves to think the worst of others. Such a well-pleasedness in judging ill of others, is also manifested in our being forward to declare our judgment, and to speak, as well as think evil of others. It may be in speaking of them with ridicule, or an air of contempt, or in bitterness, or maliciousness of spirit, or with manifest pleasure in their deficiencies or errors. When to judge ill of others, is against the inclination of persons, they will be very cautious in doing it, and will go no further in it than evidence obliges them, and will think the best that the nature of the case will admit, and will put the best possible construction on the words and actions of others. And when they are obliged, against their inclination, to think evil of another, it will be no pleasure to declare it, but they will be backward to speak of it to any, and will only do so when a sense of duty leads them to it. Having thus shown the nature of censoriousness, I pass, as proposed,

II. *To show how a censorious spirit is contrary to the spirit of charity or Christian love.* And,

1. *It is contrary to love to our neighbor.* And this appears by three things.

First, We see that persons are *very back-*

ward to judge evil of themselves. They are very ready to think well of their own qualifications. And so they are forward to think the best of their own state. If there be anything in them that resembles grace, they are exceeding apt to think that their state is good. And so they are ready to think well of their own words and deeds, and very backward to think evil of themselves in any of these respects. And the reason is, that they have a great love to themselves. And, therefore, if they loved their neighbor as themselves, love would have the same tendency with respect to him.

Second, We see that persons *are very backward to judge evil of those they love.* Thus we see it is in men toward those that are their personal friends, and thus it is in parents toward their children. They are very ready to think well of them, and to think the best of their qualifications, whether natural or moral. They are much more backward than others, to take up evil reports of them, and slow to believe what is said against them. They are forward to put the most favorable constructions on their actions. And the reason is, because they love them.

Third, We see, also, that it is universally

the case, *that where hatred and ill-will toward others most prevail, there a censorious spirit does most prevail also.* When persons fall out, and there is a difficulty between them, and anger and prejudice arise, and ill-will is contracted, there is always a forwardness to judge the worst of each other; an aptness to think meanly of each other's qualifications, and to imagine they discover in each other a great many evil qualities, and some that are very evil indeed. And each is apt to entertain jealousies of what the other may do when absent and out of sight; and is forward to listen to evil reports respecting him, and to believe every word of them, and apt to put the worst construction on all that he may say or do. And very commonly there is a forwardness to think ill of the condition he is in, and to censure him as a graceless person. And as it is in cases like this, of difficulty between particular persons, so it is apt to be the like in cases of difference between two parties. And these things show plainly, that it is want of Christian love to our neighbor, and the indulgence of a contrary spirit, from which censoriousness arises. I will only add,

2. *That a censorious spirit manifests a*

proud spirit.—And this, the context declares, is contrary to the spirit of charity, or Christian love. A forwardness to judge and censure others, shows a proud disposition, as though the censorious person thought himself free from such faults and blemishes, and therefore felt justified in being busy and bitter in charging others with them, and censuring and condemning them for them. This is implied in the language of the Saviour, in the seventh chapter of Matthew, "Judge not that ye be not judged," and "why beholdest thou the mote that is in thy brother's eye, but considerest not the beam that is in thine own eye? Or how wilt thou say to thy brother, let me pull out the mote out of thine eye, and behold a beam is in thine own eye? *Thou hypocrite!*" And the same is implied in the declaration of the apostle, "Therefore thou art inexcusable, O man, whosoever thou art that judgest: for wherein thou judgest another, thou condemnest thyself; for thou that judgest, doest the same things," Rom. ii. 1. If men were humbly sensible of their own failings, they would not be very forward or pleased in judging others, for the censure passed upon others would but rest on themselves. There are the same kinds of corruption in one man's heart, as in another's; and if those persons that are most busy in censuring others would but look within, and seriously examine their own hearts and lives, they might generally see the same dispositions and behavior in themselves, at one time or another, which they see and judge in others, or at least something as much deserving of censure. And a disposition to judge and condemn, shows a conceited and arrogant disposition. It has the appearance of a person's setting himself up above others, as though he was fit to be the lord and judge of his fellow-servants, and he supposed they were to stand or fall according to his sentence. This seems implied in the language of the Apostle, "He that speaketh evil of his brother, and judgeth his brother, speaketh evil of the law, and judgeth the law; but if thou judge the law, thou art not a doer of the law, but a judge," James iv. 11. That is, you do not act as a fellow-servant to him that you judge, or as one that is under the same law with him, but as the giver of the law, and the judge whose province it is to pass sentence under it. And therefore it is added, in the next verse, "There is one lawgiver, who is able to save and to destroy. Who art thou that judgest another?" And so, in Romans xiv. 4, "Who art thou that judgest another man's servant? To his own master he standeth or falleth." God is the only rightful judge, and the thought of his sovereignty and dominion should hold us back from daring to judge or censure our fellow-beings.

In the application of this subject, I remark,

1. *It sternly reproves those who commonly take to themselves the liberty of speaking evil of others.*—If to think evil be so much to be condemned, surely they are still more to be condemned who not only allow themselves in thinking, but also in speaking evil of others, and backbiting them with their tongues. The evil-speaking that is against neighbors behind their backs, does very much consist in censuring them, or in the expression of uncharitable thoughts and judgments of their persons and behavior. And, therefore, speaking evil of others, and judging others, are sometimes put for the same thing in the Bible, as in the passage just quoted from the Apostle James. How often does the Scripture condemn backbiting and evil-speaking! The Psalmist declares of the wicked, "Thou givest thy mouth

to evil, and thy tongue frameth deceit. Thou sittest and speakest against thy brother; thou slanderest thine own mother's son," Psalm l. 19, 20. And, says the Apostle, to Titus, "Put them in mind to speak evil of no man, to be no brawlers, but gentle, showing all meekness unto all men," Titus iii. 1, 2; and again it is written, "Wherefore laying aside all malice, and all guile, and hypocrisies, and envies, and all evil-speakings," 1 Peter ii. 1. And it is mentioned, as part of the character of every one that is a citizen of Zion, and that shall stand on God's holy hill, "that he backbiteth not with his tongue," Psalm xv. 3. Inquire, therefore, whether you have not been often guilty of this; whether you have not frequently censured others, and expressed your hard thoughts of them, especially of those with whom you may have had some difficulty, or that have been of a different party from yourself? And is it not a practice in which you more or less allow yourself now, from day to day? And if so, consider how contrary it is to the spirit of Christianity, and to the solemn profession which, it may be, you have made as Christians; and be admonished entirely and at once to forsake it. The subject,

2. *Warns all against censoriousness either by thinking or speaking evil of others, as they would be worthy of the name of Christians.*— And here in addition to the thoughts already suggested, let two or three things be considered. And,

First, How often, *when the truth comes fully out, do things appear far better concerning others, than at first we were ready to judge.* There are many instances in the Scriptures to this point. When the children of Reuben, and of Gad, and the half tribe of Manasseh had built an altar by Jordan, the rest of Israel heard of it, and presently concluded that they had turned away from the Lord, and rashly resolved to go to war against them. But when the truth came to light, it appeared, on the contrary, that they had erected their altar for a good end, even for the worship of God, as may be seen in the twenty-second chapter of Joshua. Eli thought Hannah was drunk, when she came up to the temple; but when the truth came to light, he was satisfied that she was full of grief, and was praying and pouring out her soul before God, 1 Samuel i, 12–16. David concluded, from what Ziba told him, that Mephibosheth had manifested a rebellious and treasonable spirit against his crown, and so acted on his censorious judgment, greatly to the injury of the latter; but when the truth came to appear, he saw it was quite otherwise. Elijah judged ill of the state of Israel, that none were true worshippers of God but himself; but when God told him the truth, it appeared that there were seven thousand who had not bowed the knee to Baal. And how commonly are things very much the same now-a-days! How often, on thorough examination, have we found things better of others than we have heard, and than at first we were ready to judge! There are always two sides to every story, and it is generally wise, and safe, and charitable to take the best; and yet there is probably no one way in which persons are so liable to be wrong, as in presuming the worst is true, and in forming and expressing their judgment of others, and of their actions, without waiting till all the truth is known.

Second, How *little occasion is there for us to pass our sentence on others* with respect to their state, qualifications, or actions that do not concern us. Our great concern is with ourselves. It is of infinite consequence to us, that we have a good estate before God; that we are possessed of good qualities and principles; and that we behave ourselves well, and act with right aims, and for right ends. But it is a minor matter to us how it is with others. And there is little need of our censure being passed, even if it were deserved, which we cannot be sure of; for the business is in the hands of God, who is infinitely more fit to see to it than we can be. And there is a day appointed for his decision. So that if we assume to judge others, we shall not only take upon ourselves a work that does not belong to us, but we shall be doing it before the time. "Therefore," says the Apostle, "judge nothing before the time, until the Lord come, who both will bring to light the hidden things of darkness, and will make manifest the counsels of the hearts; and then shall every man have praise of God," 1 Corinthians iv. 5.

Third, God has threatened, that *if we are found censoriously judging and condemning others, we shall be condemned ourselves.* "Judge not," he says, "that ye be not judged; for with what judgment ye judge, ye shall be judged." And, again, the Apostle asks, "And thinkest thou this, O man, that judgest them which do such things, and doest the same, that thou shalt escape the just judgment of God?" Romans ii. 3. These are awful threatenings, from the lips of that great being who is to be our judge at the final day, by whom it infinitely concerns us to be acquitted, and from whom a sentence of condemnation will be unspeakably dreadful to us, if at last we sink forever under it. Therefore as we would not ourselves receive condemnation from him, let us not mete out such measure to others.

LECTURE XI.

ALL TRUE GRACE IN THE HEART TENDS TO HOLY PRACTICE IN THE LIFE.

"Rejoiceth not in iniquity, but rejoiceth in the truth."—
1 CORINTHIANS xiii. 6.

HAVING mentioned in the two preceding verses, many of the good fruits of charity, and shown how it tends to an excellent behavior in many particulars, the Apostle now sums up these, and all other good tendencies of charity in respect to active conduct, by saying, "It rejoiceth not in iniquity, but rejoiceth in the truth." As if he had said, "I have mentioned many excellent things that charity has a tendency to, and shown how it is contrary to many evil things. But I need not go on to multiply particulars, for, in a word, charity is contrary to everything in the life and practice that is evil, and tends to everything that is good. It rejoiceth not in iniquity, but rejoiceth in the truth."

By "iniquity," seems to be intended here, everything that is sinful in the life and practice; and by "the truth," everything that is good in the life, or all that is included in Christian and holy practice. The word truth is, indeed, variously used in the Bible. Sometimes it means the true doctrines of religion; sometimes the knowledge of these doctrines; sometimes, veracity or faithfulness; and sometimes, it signifies all virtue and holiness, including both the knowledge and reception of all the great truths of the Scriptures, and conformity to these in the life and conduct. In this last sense the word is used by the Apostle John, when he says, "I rejoiced greatly when the brethren came and testified of the truth that is in thee, even as thou walkest in the truth," 3 John 3. Taking the word in this sense, and generalizing the proposition, we have, as suggested by the text, the doctrine,

THAT ALL TRUE CHRISTIAN GRACE IN THE HEART, TENDS TO HOLY PRACTICE IN THE LIFE.— *Negatively*, the Apostle declares that charity is opposed to all wickedness, or evil practice;

and *positively*, that it tends to all righteousness, or holy practice. And as the principle may be generalized, and also as charity has been shown to be the sum of all true and saving grace, the doctrine that has been stated seems clearly contained in the words of the text, viz.: the doctrine, that *all true Christian grace tends to holy practice.* If any have the notion of grace, that it is something put into the heart, there to be confined and dormant, and that its influence does not govern the man, throughout, *as an active being;* or if they suppose that the change made by grace, though it indeed betters the heart itself, yet has no tendency to a corresponding improvement of the outward life, they have a very wrong notion. And that this is so, I would endeavor to make plain, first, by some arguments in favor of the doctrine that has been stated; and, second, by showing its truth with respect to particular graces. And,

I. *I would state some arguments in support of the doctrine, that all true grace in the heart, tends to holy practice in the life.* And,

1. *Holy practice is the aim of that eternal election, which is the first ground of the bestowment of all true grace*—Holy practice is not

the ground and reason of election, as is supposed by the Arminians, who imagine that God elects men to everlasting life upon a foresight of their good works; but it is the aim and end of election. God does not elect men because he foresees they will be holy, but that he may make them, and that they may be holy. Thus, in election, God ordained that men should walk in good works, as says the Apostle, "For we are his workmanship, created in Christ Jesus unto good works, which God hath before ordained that we should walk in them," Ephesians ii. 10. And again it is said, that the elect are chosen to this very end, "He hath chosen us, in him, before the foundation of the world, that we should be holy, and without blame before him in love," Ephesians i. 4. And so Christ tells his disciples, "I have chosen you, and ordained you, that ye should go, and bring forth fruit, and that your fruit should remain," John xv. 16. Now God's eternal election is the first ground of the bestowment of saving grace. And some have such saving grace, and others do not have it, because some are from eternity chosen of God, and others are not chosen. And seeing that holy practice is the scope and aim of that which is the first ground of the bestowment of grace, this same holy practice is doubtless the tendency of grace itself. Otherwise it would follow, that God makes use of a certain means to attain an end which is not fitted to attain that end, and has no tendency to it. It is further true,

2. *That redemption, by which grace is purchased, is to the same end.*—The redemption made by Christ is the next ground of the bestowment of grace on all who possess it. Christ, by his merits, in the great things that he did and suffered in the world, has purchased grace and holiness for his own people. "For their sakes," he says, "I sanctify myself, that they also might be sanctified through the truth," John xvii. 19. And Christ thus redeemed the elect, and purchased grace for them, to the end that they might walk in holy practice. He has reconciled them to God by his death, to save them from wicked works, that they might be holy and unblamable in their lives, says the Apostle, "And you, that were sometime alienated, and enemies in your mind by wicked works, yet now hath he reconciled, in the body of his flesh, through

death, to present you holy, and unblamable, and unreprovable in his sight," Colossians i. 21, 22. When the angel appeared to Joseph, he told him that the child that should be born of Mary should be called Jesus, that is, Saviour, because he should save his people from their sins, Matt. i. 21. And holiness of life is declared to be the end of redemption, when it is said of Christ, that " he gave himself for us, that he might redeem us from all iniquity, and purify unto himself a peculiar people, zealous of good works," Titus ii. 14. And so we are told that Christ " died for all, that they which live should not henceforth live unto themselves, but unto him which died for them and rose again," 1 Corinthians v. 15. And for this end, he is said to have offered himself, through the eternal Spirit, without spot to God, that his blood might purge our conscience from dead works to serve the living God, Hebrews ix. 15.

The most remarkable type of the work of redemption by divine love in all the Old Testament history, was the redemption of the children of Israel out of Egypt. But the holy living of his people, was the end God had in view in that redemption, as he often signified to Pharaoh, when from time to time he said to him by Moses and Aaron, "Let my people go that they may serve me." And we have a like expression concerning Christ's redemption in the New Testament, where it is said, "Blessed be the Lord God of Israel, for he hath visited and redeemed his people, to perform the mercy promised to our fathers, and to remember his holy covenant, the oath which he sware to our father Abraham, that he would grant unto us, that we, being delivered out of the hand of our enemies, might serve him without fear, in holiness and righteousness before him, all the days of our life," Luke i. 68–75. All these things make it very plain that the end of redemption is, that we might be holy. Still further it is true,

3. *That effectual calling, or that saving conversion in which grace is commenced in the soul, is to the same end.*—God, by his Spirit, and through his truth, calls, awakens, convicts, converts and leads to the exercise of grace, all those who are made willing in the day of his power, to the end that they might exercise themselves in holy practice. "We are his workmanship," says the Apostle, "created in Christ Jesus unto good works, which God

hath before ordained that we should live in them," Ephesians ii. 10. And the Apostle tells the Christian Thessalonians, that God had not called them unto uncleanness, but unto holiness, 1 Thes. iv. 7; and again it is written, "As he which hath called you is holy, so be ye holy in all manner of conversation," 1 Peter i. 15. It is also true,

4. *That spiritual knowledge and understanding, which are the inward attendants of all true grace in the heart, tend to holy practice.*—A true knowledge of God and divine things, is a practical knowledge. As to a mere speculative knowledge of the things of religion, many wicked men have attained to great measures of it. Men may possess vast learning, and their learning may consist very much of their knowledge in divinity, and of the Bible, and of the things pertaining to religion, and they may be able to reason very strongly about the attributes of God, and the doctrines of Christianity, and yet herein their knowledge fails of being a saving knowledge, that it is only speculative and not practical. He that has a right and saving acquaintance with divine things, sees the excellency of holiness, and of all the ways of holiness, for he sees the

beauty and excellency of God, which consist in his holiness; and for the same reason he sees the hatefulness of sin, and of all the ways of sin. And if a man knows the hatefulness of the ways of sin, certainly this tends to his avoiding these ways; and if he sees the loveliness of the ways of holiness, this tends to incline him to walk in them.

He that knows God, sees that he is worthy to be obeyed. Pharaoh did not see why he should obey God, because he did not know who he was, and therefore he says, "Who is the Lord, that I should obey his voice? I know not the Lord, neither will I let Israel go," Exodus v. 2. This is signified to be the reason why wicked men work or practise iniquity, and carry themselves so wickedly, that they have no spiritual knowledge, as says the Psalmist, "Have all the workers of iniquity no knowledge? who eat up my people as they eat bread, and call not upon the Lord," Psalm xiv. 4. And when God would describe the true knowledge of himself to the people of Israel, he does it by this fruit of it, that it led to holy practice, "He judged the cause of the poor and needy; then it was well with him. Was not this to know me? saith the

Lord," Jeremiah xxii. 16. And so the Apostle John informs us, that the keeping of Christ's commands is an infallible fruit of our knowing him; and he stigmatizes him as a gross hypocrite and liar, who pretends that he knows Christ, and does not keep his commandments, 1 John ii. 3 and 4. If a man has spiritual knowledge and understanding, it tends to make him to be of an excellent spirit. "A man of understanding is of an excellent spirit," Prov. xvii. 27. And such an excellent spirit, will lead to a corresponding behavior. And the same appears, also,

5. *From the more immediate consideration of the principle of grace itself, from which it will be seen, that the tendency of all Christian grace is to practice.* And here,

First, It appears that all true Christian grace tends to practice, because *the faculty which is the immediate seat of it, is the faculty of the will, which is the faculty that commands all a man's actions and practice.* The immediate seat of grace, is in the will or disposition. And this shows that all true grace tends to practice; for there is not one of man's acts that can properly be said to belong to, or to be any part of his practice, in any respect but that it is at the command of the will. When we speak of a man's practice, we have respect to those things that he does as a free and voluntary agent, or which is the same thing, to those things that he does by an act of his will; so that the whole of a man's practice is directed by the faculty of the will. All the executive powers of the man, whether of body or mind, are subject to the faculty of the will by the constitution of him who hath made man, and who is the great author of our being. The will is the fountain of the practice, as truly as the head of a spring is the fountain of the stream that flows from it. And therefore if a principle of true grace be seated in this faculty it must necessarily tend to practice; as much as the flowing of water in the fountain, tends to its flowing in the stream.

Second, It is the definition of grace, that it is a principle of holy action.—What is grace but a principle of holiness, or a holy principle in the heart? But the word "*principle*" is relative to something, of which it is a principle. And if grace be a principle, what is it a principle of, but of action? Principles and actions are correlates, that necessarily have respect one to the other. Thus the very idea of a principle of life, is, a principle that acts in the life. And so when we speak of a principle of understanding, we mean a principle whence flow acts of understanding. And so by a principle of sin, is meant a principle whence flow acts of sin. And in the same manner when we speak of a principle of grace, we mean a principle whence flow acts of grace, or gracious actions. A principle of grace has as much a relation to practice, as a root has to the plant that it is the root of. If there be a root, it is a root of something; either the root of something that actually grows from it, or that tends to bring forth some plant. It is absurd to speak of a root, that is the root of nothing; and so it is absurd to speak of a principle of grace, that does not tend to grace in the practice.

Third, One more thing, by which that which is real and substantial, is distinguished from that which is only a shadow or appearance, is, *that it is effectual*. A shadow or picture of a man, though it be ever so distinct or well drawn, or give ever so lively a representation, and though it be the picture of a very strong man, or even of a mighty giant, can do nothing. There is nothing accom plished and brought to pass by it, because it is not real, but only a shadow or image. The substance or reality, however, is something that is effectual. And so it is with what is in the heart of man. That which is only an appearance or image of grace, though it looks like grace, is not effectual, because it wants reality and substance. But that which is real and substantial is effectual, and does indeed bring something to pass in the life. In other words, it acts itself out in practice. And so, again,

Fourth, The nature of a principle of grace, *is to be a principle of life, or a vital principle.* This we are everywhere taught in the Scriptures. There, natural men who have no principle of grace in the heart, are represented as dead men, while those that have grace are represented as being alive, or having the principle of life in them. But it is the nature of a principle of life, to be a principle of action and operation. A dead man does not act, or move, or bring anything to pass; but in living persons, the life appears by a continued course of action from day to day. They move, and walk, and work, and fill up their time with actions that are the fruits of life.

Fifth, True Christian grace, is not only a principle of life, *but an exceedingly powerful principle.* Hence we read of "the power of godliness," as in 2 Timothy iii. 5; and are taught that there is in it a divine power, such as wrought in Christ when he was raised from the dead. But the more powerful any principle is, the more effectual it is to produce those operations, and that practice, to which it tends. Having thus shown, in general, that all true grace in the heart tends to holy practice in the life, I proceed, as was proposed,

II. *To show the same with respect to the particular Christian graces.*—And here, I remark that this is the case,

1. *With respect to a true and saving faith in the Lord Jesus Christ.*—This is one thing that very much distinguishes that faith which is saving, from that which is only common. A true faith, is a faith that works; whereas a false faith, is a barren and inoperative faith. And therefore the Apostle describes a saving faith, as a "faith that worketh by love," Galatians v. 6. And the Apostle James tells us, "A man may say, Thou hast faith, and I have works: show me thy faith without thy

works, and I will show thee my faith by my works," James ii. 18. But more particularly,

First, The *conviction of the understandtng and judgment*, which is implied in saving faith, *tends to holy practice*. He that has true faith, is convinced of the reality and certainty of the great things of religion; and he that is convinced of the reality of these things, will be influenced by them, and they will govern his actions and behavior. If men are told of great things, which if true, do most intimately concern them, and do not believe what they are told, they will not be much moved by them, nor will they alter their conduct for what they hear. But if they do really believe what they are told, and regard it as certain, they will be influenced by it in their actions, and in view of it will alter their conduct, and will do very differently from what they would if they had heard nothing. We see that this is so in all things of great concern that appear real to men. If a man hears important news that concerns himself, and we do not see that he alters at all for it in his practice, we at once conclude that he does not give heed to it as true; for we know the nature of man is such, that he will govern his actions by what he believes, and is convinced of. And so if men are really convinced of the truth of the things they are told in the gospel, about an eternal world, and the everlasting salvation that Christ has purchased for all that will accept it, it will influence their practice. They will regulate their behavior according to such a belief, and will act in such a manner as will tend to their obtaining this eternal salvation. If men are convinced of the certain truth of the promises of the gospel, which promise eternal riches, and honors, and pleasures, and if they really believe that those are immensely more valuable than all the riches, and honors, and pleasures of the world, they will, for these, forsake the things of the world, and if need be, sell all and follow Christ. If they are fully convinced of the truth of the promise, that Christ will indeed bestow all these things upon his people, and if all this appears real to them, it will have influence on their practice, and it will induce them to live accordingly. Their practice will be according to their convictions. The very nature of man forbids that it should be otherwise. If a man be promised by another, that if he will part with one pound, he will give him a thousand, and if he is fully convinced of the truth of this promise, he will readily part with the former in the assurance of obtaining the latter. And so he that is convinced of the sufficiency of Christ to deliver him from all evil, and to bring him to the possession of all good that he needs, will be influenced in his practice by the promise which offers him all this. Such a man, while he actually has such a conviction, will not be afraid to believe Christ in things wherein he otherwise would seem greatly to expose himself to calamity, for he is convinced that Christ is able to deliver him. And so he will not be afraid to forego other ways of securing earthly happiness, because he is convinced that Christ alone is sufficient to bestow all needed happiness upon him. And so,

Second, That *act of the will*, which there is in saving faith, *tends to holy practice*. He that by the act of his will, does truly accept of Christ as a Saviour, accepts of him as a Saviour from *sin*, and not merely as a Saviour from the *punishment* of sin. But it is impossible that any one should heartily receive Christ as a Saviour from sin, and from the ways of sin, if he has not willed and does not aim, sincerely, in heart and life, to turn from all the ways of sin ; for he that has not willed that sin and he should part, cannot have willed to receive Christ as his Saviour to part them. And so he, again, that receives Christ by a living faith, closes with him as a Lord and King to rule over and reign in him, and not merely as a priest to make atonement for him. But to choose Christ, and close with him as a King, is the same as to yield in submission to his law and in obedience to his authority and commands ; and he that does this, lives a life of holy practice.

Third, All *the true trust in God*, that is implied in saving faith, *tends to holy practice*. And herein a true trust differs from all false trust. A trust in God in the way of negligence, is what in Scripture is called tempting God ; and a trust in him in the way of sin, is what is called presumption, which is a thing terribly threatened in his word. But he that truly and rightly trusts in God, trusts in him in the way of diligence and holiness ; or, which is the same thing, in the way of holy practice. The very idea of our trusting in another, is, resting or living in acquiescence of mind and heart in the full persuasion of his sufficiency and faithfulness, so as to be ready fully to venture on him in our actions. But they that do not practise and act upon the persuasion of another's sufficiency and faithfulness, do not thus venture. They do not enter on any action or course of action in such a confidence, and so venture nothing, and therefore cannot be said truly to trust. He that really trusts in another, ventures on his confidence. And so it is with those that truly trust in God. They rest in the full persuasion that God is sufficient and faithful, so as to proceed in this confidence to follow God, and if need be, to undergo difficulties and hardships for him, because he has promised that they shall be no losers by such a course; and they have such a confidence of this, that they can, and do venture upon his promise, while those who are not willing thus to venture, show that they do not trust in him. They that have the full trust in God which is implied in a living faith, will not be afraid to trust God with their estates. It is so with respect to trust in men, that if those we have full confidence in, desire to borrow anything of us, and promise to pay us again, and to pay us an hundred fold, we are not afraid to venture, and do actually venture it. And so those that feel full confidence in God, are not afraid to lend to the Lord. And so if we trust in God, we shall not be afraid to venture labor, and fighting, and watching, and suffering, and all things for him, since he has so abundantly promised to reward these things with that which will infinitely more than make up for all the losses or difficulties or sorrows we may experience in the way of duty. If our faith be saving, it will lead us thus actually to venture on God, in the fullest trust in his character and promises. And as faith in itself, and in all that is implied in it, tends to holy practice, so the same is the case,

2. *With respect to all true love to God.*—Love is an active principle; a principle that we always find is active in things of this world. Love to our fellow-creatures, always influences us in our actions and practice. The whole world of mankind are chiefly kept in action from day to day, and from year to year, by love of some kind or another. He that loves money, is influenced in his practice by that love, and kept by it in the continual pursuit of wealth. He that loves honor, is

governed in his practice by that love, and his actions through the whole of life are regulated by his desire for it. And how diligently do they that love carnal pleasures, pursue after them in their practice! And so he that truly loves God, is also influenced by that love in his practice. He constantly seeks after God, in the course of his life: seeks his grace, and acceptance, and glory.

Reason teaches, that a man's actions are the most proper test and evidence of his love. Thus if a man professes a great deal of love and friendship to another, reason, in such a case, teaches all mankind that the most proper evidence of his being a real and hearty friend, as he professes to be, is his appearing a friend in his deeds, and not only in his words; and that he shall be willing, if need be, to deny himself for his friend, and to suffer in his own private interest for the sake of doing him a kindness. If a man professes ever so much kindness, or friendship, a wise man will not trust the profession, except as he sees the trial and proof of it in the behavior; unless in his actions he has found him a faithful and constant friend, ready to do and suffer for him. He will trust to such evidence of his love, more than he will to the greatest professions, or even the most solemn oaths without it. And so if we see a man, who by his constant behavior, shows himself ready to take pains and lay himself out for God, reason teaches, that in this he gives an evidence of love to God, more to be depended on, than if he only professes that he feels great love to God in his heart. And so if we see a man, who by what we behold of the course of his life, seems to follow and imitate Christ, and greatly lay himself out for Christ's honor, and the advancement of his kingdom in the world, reason teaches that he gives greater evidence of the sincerity and strength of his love to the Saviour, than if he only declares that he loves him, and tells how his heart at such and such a time was drawn out in love to him, while at the same time he is backward to do any great matter for Christ, or to put himself out of the way for the promotion of his kingdom, and is ready to excuse himself when called to active effort or self-denial for his Saviour's sake.

There are various ways for the exercise of sincere love to God, and they all tend to holy practice. One is in having a high *esteem* for

God, for that which we love we have the highest esteem for, and naturally show this esteem in our behavior. Another way of showing our love to God, is, in making *choice* of him above all other things; and if we do sincerely choose him above all other things, then we shall actually leave other things for him when it comes to the trial in our practice: and when in the course of our life it comes to pass, that God and our honor, or God and our money, or God and our ease, are at the same time set before us, so that we must cleave to the one and forsake the other, then if we really choose God above these other things, we shall in our practice cleave to God and let these things go. Another way of the exercise of love to God is, in our *desires* after him; and these, also, tend to practice. He that really has earnest desires after God, with be stirred up actively to seek after him. He will apply himself to it as a business, just as men do for this world, when they have earnest desires for a good which they believe is attainable. And still another way of the exercise of love to God, is, in *delighting* in him, and finding satisfaction and happiness in him; and this also tends to practice. He that really and sincerely delights more in God than in other things, and finds his satisfaction in God, will not forsake God for other things; and thus, by his conduct, he shows that he indeed is satisfied in him as his portion. And so it is in all cases. If we have had enjoyment in any possession whatever, and then afterward forsake it for something else, this is an evidence that we were not fully satisfied with it, and that we did not delight in it above all other things. In all these cases, the feelings and choices will be seen in the practice.

3. *All true and saving repentance tends to holy practice.*—In the original of the New Testament, the word commonly rendered "repentance," signifies *a change of the mind;* and men are said to repent of sin, when they change their minds with respect to it, so that though formerly they esteemed and approved of it, they now utterly disapprove and dislike it. But such a change of the mind, must and does tend to a corresponding change of the practice. We see it to be so universally in other things. If a man has heretofore been engaged in any pursuit or business whatever, and then changes his mind upon it, he will change his practice also, and will cease from

that business, or pursuit, or way of life, and turn his hand to some other. Sorrow for sin is one thing belonging to saving repentance. But sorrow for sin, if it be thorough and sincere, will tend, in practice, to the forsaking of sin. And so it is in everything. If a man has long gone on in any one way or manner of behavior, and afterwards is convinced of the foolishness and sinfulness of it, and is heartily sorry and grieved for it, the natural and necessary effect of this will be, that he will avoid it for the future. And if he goes on in it just as he did before, no one will believe that he is heartily sorry for having gone on in time past. Again,

4. *All true humility tends to holy practice.*—This is a grace abundantly recommended and insisted on in the Bible, and which is often spoken of as distinguishing a true Christian experience from that which is counterfeit. But this grace in the heart, has a direct tendency to holy practice in the life. A humble heart tends to a humble behavior. He that is sensible of his own littleness, and nothingness, and exceeding unworthiness, will be disposed, by a sense of it, to carry himself accordingly both before God and man. He that once was

of a proud heart, and under the dominion of pride in his conduct, if afterward he has his heart changed to a humble heart, will necessarily have a corresponding change in his behavior. He will no longer appear in his demeanor as proud, and scornful, and ambitious as once he was, affecting, as much as ever, to appear above others, and striving as much after it, and as apt to condemn others, and to be dissatisfied or even enraged with those that seem to stand in the way of his earthly glory. For that which such a behavior in him rose from, before he was changed, was pride of heart; and therefore if now there be a great alteration with respect to this pride of heart, and it be mortified and banished from the soul, and humility implanted in its place, surely there will be an alteration, also, in the demeanor and practice; for humility of heart is a principle that has as strong a tendency to practice as pride of heart has, and therefore if the latter be mortified, and the former take its place, then the proud practice that proceeded from the former will proportionably cease, and the humble practice which is the natural fruit of the latter, will be manifest.

True Christian humility of heart tends, also, to make persons resigned to the will of God, and to lead them to be patient and submissive to his holy hand under the afflictions he may send, and to be filled with deep reverence toward the Deity, and to treat divine things with the highest respect. It leads, also, to a meek behavior toward men, making us condescending to inferiors, respectful to superiors, and toward all gentle, peaceful, easy to be entreated, not self-willed, not envious of others but contented with our own condition, of a calm and quiet spirit, not disposed to resent injuries, but apt to forgive. And surely these are traits that belong to holy practice. And so again,

5. *All true fear of God tends to holy practice.*—The principal thing meant in the Scriptures by the fear of God, is a holy solicitude or dread lest we should offend God by sinning against him. Now if a man do truly fear to offend God, and if he habitually dreads the thought of sinning against him, this will surely tend to his avoiding sin against him. That which men are afraid of they will shun. If a man professes that he is afraid and has a dread of a poisonous serpent, for example, but

at the same time is seen to take no care to shun him, but is very bold to keep near to him, who will believe his profession? Fearing God and observing to do all his commandments, are joined together as necessarily arising the one from the other, as in Deuteronomy xxviii. 58. "If thou wilt not observe to do all the words of this law, that are written in this book, that thou mayest fear this glorious and fearful name, the Lord, thy God." And Joseph gives as a reason of his righteous and merciful conduct towards his brethren, that he feared God, as may be seen in Genesis xlii. 18. And in Proverbs viii. 13, it is said, that "the fear of the Lord is to hate evil." Job gives it as a reason why he avoided sin, that "destruction from God was a terror to him," Job xxxi. 23. And God himself, when he speaks of Job as "eschewing evil," mentions his fear of God as the ground and reason of it, Job i. 8. And in any person whatever, just so far as the fear of God reigns, just so far will it lead its possessor to avoid sin, and to aim to be holy. Again,

6. *The spirit of thankfulness and praise tends to holy practice.*—Sincere thankfulness to God leads us to render again according to

the benefits received. This we look upon as a sure evidence of true gratitude or thankfulness toward our fellow-men. If any one does his neighbor any remarkable kindness, and he is really thankful for it, he will be ready, when an occasion offers, to do him a good in return. And though we cannot requite God's kindness to us by doing anything that shall be profitable to him, yet a spirit of thankfulness will dispose us to do what we can which is well-pleasing or acceptable to him, or which may tend to his declarative glory. If one man should take pity on another who was in some great distress, or in danger of some terrible death, and moved by this pity should greatly lay himself out for his defence and deliverance, and should undergo great hardships and sufferings in order to it, and by these means should actually deliver him, and if the latter should express great thankfulness toward his deliverer, and yet in his actions and course of conduct should oppose and dishonor and cast contempt upon him, and do him great injury, no one would give much heed to all his professions of thankfulness. If he is truly thankful, he will never act thus wickedly toward his benefactor. And so no man can be truly thankful to God for the dying love of Christ, and for the infinite mercy and love of God toward himself, and yet lead a wicked life. His gratitude, if sincere, will lead him to be holy. The same is true, again,

7. *Of a Christian weanedness from the world, and of heavenly-mindedness, that they tend to holy practice.*—And I speak of the two together, for they are very much the same thing expressed negatively and positively. Not to be weaned from the world, is the same thing as to be worldly-minded; and on the other hand, to have a truly Christian weanedness from the world, is to be not worldly, but heavenly-minded. And this grace, like all the others mentioned, tends to holy practice. If the heart be taken off from the world, it will tend to take off the pursuits from the world; and if the heart be set on heavenly things, which are things not of the world, it will tend to lead us to pursue the things that are heavenly. He that has his heart loose from the world, will not practically keep the world close in his grasp, as being exceeding loth to part with any of it. If a man speaking of his experience, tells how at some given time he felt his heart weaned from the world,

so that the world seemed as nothing and vanity to him, and yet if in practice he seems as violent after the world as ever, and a great deal more earnest after it than he is after heavenly things, such as growth in grace, and in the knowledge of God, and in duty, then his profession will have but little weight in comparison with his practice. And so if his conduct shows that he thinks more of treasure on earth than of treasure in heaven, and if when he has got the world, or some part of it, he hugs it close, and appears exceedingly reluctant to let even a little of it go for pious and charitable uses, though God promises him a thousand-fold more in heaven for it, he gives not the least evidence of his being weaned from the world, or that he prefers heavenly things to the things of the world. Judging by his practice, there is sad reason to believe that his profession is in vain. The same is true, also,

8. *Of the spirit of Christian love to men, that this also tends to holy practice.*—If the spirit of love to man be sincere, it will tend to the practice and deeds of love. That is a hypocritical, and not a sincere love, that appears only in word and tongue, and not in

deed; but that love which is sincere, and really a true love, will be manifest in the deeds, as says the Apostle, "My little children, let us not love in word, neither in tongue, but in deed and in truth. And hereby we know that we are of the truth, and shall assure our hearts before him," 1 John iii. 18, 19. No other love to brethren, except that which shows itself in deeds of love, will profit any man. "If a brother or sister be naked, and destitute of daily food, and one of you say unto them, Depart in peace, be ye warmed and filled, notwithstanding ye give them not those things which are needful to the body, what doth it profit?" James ii. 15, 16.

Experience shows, that those who cherish a sincere love toward others, are ready both to do and suffer for them. We are very ready to believe that parents love their own children, because this is natural; and such a love generally prevails throughout the world. But incredible as it is that a man should not love his own children, yet if there was a father that beheld his child in suffering circumstances, and would not put himself out of the way to relieve him, or that did not ordinarily treat his children with consideration and kindness, but acted from day to day as though he were utterly careless of their comfort, or as to what became of them, we should scarcely believe that he had anything of a father's love in his heart. Love to our children, will dispose us to loving deeds to our children. And so love to our neighbor, will dispose us to all manner of good practice toward our neighbor. So the Apostle declares, when after summing up the several commandments of the second table of the law, he says, "And if there be any other commandment, it is briefly comprehended in this saying, namely, Thou shalt love thy neighbor as thyself," and then adds, " Love worketh no ill to his neighbor: therefore love is the fulfilling of the law," Romans xiii. 9, 10. Once more, and lastly, the same remark applies,

9. *To a true and gracious hope, that this also tends to holy practice.*—A false hope has a tendency just the reverse of this. It tends to licentiousness; to encourage men in their sinful desires and lusts, and to flatter and embolden them even when they are in the way of evil. But a true hope, so far from hardening men in sin, and making them careless of their duty, tends to stir them up to holiness of life,

to awaken them to duty, and to make them more careful to avoid sin, and more diligent in serving God. "Every man that hath this hope in him, purifieth himself even as he is pure," 1 John iii. 3. A gracious hope has this tendency from the nature of the happiness hoped for, which is a holy happiness; a happiness that the more a man seeks and hopes for, the more he is quickened and enlivened in the disposition to be holy. And it also has this tendency from the respect it has to the author of the happiness hoped for; for it hopes for it from God, as the fruit of his undeserved and infinite mercy, and therefore by every motive of gratitude the heart is engaged and stirred up to seek that which is well-pleasing to him. And it has the same tendency from a regard to the means by which it hopes to obtain this happiness; for a true hope looks forward to the obtaining of happiness in no other way but the way of the gospel, which is by a holy Saviour, and in a way of cleaving to and following him. And it has, lastly, the same tendency by the influence of that which is the immediate source of all gracious hope, which is faith in Christ, and such faith always works, and works by love, and purifies the heart, and brings forth holy fruits in the life.

Thus it has been shown, first by general arguments, and then by an induction of particulars wherein all the principal Christian graces have been mentioned, that all true grace in the heart tends to holy practice in the life, just as truly as the root of the plant tends to growth in the plant itself, or as light has a tendency to shine, or the principle of life to manifest itself in the actions of the living person. In the application of the subject,

1. *We may see one main reason why Christian practice and good works, are so abundantly insisted on in the Scriptures as an evidence of sincerity in grace.* Christ has given it as a rule to us, that we are to judge men by their fruits, Matthew vii. 16–20; and he insists on it, in a very emphatic manner, that the one that keeps his commandments, is the one that truly loves him, John xiv. 21; and declares that the man that loves him, will keep them, and the man that does not love him, will not keep them, John xiv. 23, 24. Hence we may see the reason why the Apostle Paul so much insisted on this point, declar-

ing to those to whom he wrote, that if any pretended to belong to the kingdom of God, and yet did not keep God's commandments, they were either hypocrites or self-deceivers. His language is, "For this ye know, that no whoremonger, nor unclean person, nor covetous man, who is an idolater, hath any inheritance in the kingdom of Christ and of God. Let no man deceive you with vain words; for because of these things cometh the wrath of God upon the children of disobedience," Ephesians v. 5, 6. "Know ye not that the unrighteous shall not inherit the kingdom of God? Be not deceived; neither fornicators, nor idolaters, nor adulterers, nor effeminate, nor abusers of themselves with mankind, nor thieves, nor covetous, nor drunkards, nor revilers, nor extortioners, shall inherit the kingdom of God," 1 Corinthians vi. 9, 10. "They that are Christ's, have crucified the flesh, with the affections and lusts," Galatians v. 24. "If ye live after the flesh, ye shall die," Romans viii. 13. And all this teaches us the reason, why the same thing is so much insisted on by the Apostle James, in various places with which you are familiar, and by the Apostle John, more than almost any other subject. It is because God would have it deeply impressed on all, that good works are the only satisfying evidence that we are truly possessed of grace in the soul. It is by our practice that God judges us here on earth, and it is by our practice that he will judge us all at the great and final day

2. *In view of this subject let all examine themselves, whether their grace is real and sincere.*—Let every one diligently and prayerfully ask, whether their graces all tend to practice, and are seen from day to day in the life and conduct. But here even some truly godly persons may be ready to say, that if they judge themselves by their practice, they must condemn themselves, for they fail so much and so frequently, and are so often wandering out of the way, that at times it scarcely seems that they can be the children of God. But to such I answer, that persons who try themselves by their practice, may find that they greatly fail every day, and are often wandering out of the way, and yet they may really see no just cause in their practice to condemn themselves. For when we speak of a life of Christian practice, and when the Scriptures speak of the course of life as

Christian, the meaning is not, that the life is a perfect and sinless life. On the contrary, a Christian's life may be attended with many and exceeding great imperfections, and yet be a holy life, or a truly Christian life. It may be such a life as to clearly, and even necessarily show, that the grace which the individual has, is of the kind which has a tendency to holy practice. His fruits may be such as to be good evidence of the good nature of the tree, and his works such as to show his faith. And if you ask for still further light, then I would say, whatever your imperfections and failings may be, examine yourself whether you find the following evidences of your grace being of that kind which tends to holy practice.

First, Has your supposed grace such influence, *as to render those things in which you have failed of holy practice, loathsome, grievous and humbling to you?* Has it such influence in your mind as to render your past sinful practices hateful in your eyes, and has it led you to mourn before God for them? And does it render those things in your conduct that since your supposed conversion have been contrary to Christian practice, odious in your eyes? And is it the great burden of your life, that your practice is no better? Is it really grievous to you, that you have fallen, or do fall into sin; and are you ready, after the example of holy Job, to abhor yourself for it, and repent in dust and ashes, and like Paul to lament your wretchedness, and pray to be delivered from sin, as you would from a body of death?

Second, Do you carry about with you, habitually, a dread of sin? Do you not only mourn, and humble yourself for sins that are past, but have you a dread of sin for the future? And do you dread it because in itself it is evil, and so hurtful to your own soul, and offensive to God? Do you dread it as a terrible enemy that you have often suffered by, and feel that it has been a grievous thing to you heretofore? And do you dread it as something that has hurt, and wounded, and stung you, so that you would see it no more? Do you stand on your watch against it, as a man would keep watch against something that he dreads, with such a dread as led Joseph to say, "How can I do this great wickedness, and sin against God?" Genesis xxxix. 9.

Third, Are you sensible of the beauty and

pleasantness of the ways of holy practice? Do you see the beauty of holiness, and the loveliness of the ways of God and Christ? It is said in the text that "charity rejoiceth in the truth;" and it is given as the character of the truly godly, that "he rejoiceth and worketh righteousness," which is the same as saying that "he rejoices to work righteousness." And how often does the Psalmist speak of the law of God as being his delight, and of his love to the divine commandments!

Fourth, Do you find that you do particularly esteem and delight in those practices that may, by way of eminence, be called Christian practices, in distinction from mere worldly morality? And by Christian practices are meant such as are implied in a meek, humble, prayerful, self-denying, self-renouncing, heavenly walk and behavior. Some of the heathen have been eminent for many of the moral virtues, and wrote excellently about them, as for example, of justice, and generosity, and fortitude, &c.; but they were far from a Christian poverty of spirit and lowliness of mind. They sought their own glory, and gloried exceedingly in their outward virtues, and seemed to know nothing of such a walk as the gospel commands, a walk of self-emptiness, and poverty of spirit, and self-distrust, and self-renunciation, and prayerful reliance on God. They were strangers to meekness, and did not allow, or even dream that the forgiveness and love of enemies was a virtue. Such virtues as these, are peculiarly Christian virtues, and Christian by way of distinction and eminence, and of these it is, that I ask, if you hold them in special esteem, for your Saviour's sake, and because they are fraught with his spirit? If you are essentially distinguished and different in your spirit from the mere moralist, or the heathen sage or philosopher, you will have a spirit of special esteem for and delight in these virtues that do especially belong to the gospel.

Fifth, Do you hunger and thirst after a holy practice? Do you long to live a holy life, to be conformed to God, to have your conduct, day by day, better regulated, and more spiritual, more to God's glory, and more such as becometh a Christian? Is this what you love, and pray for, and long for, and live for? This is mentioned by Christ, as belonging to the character of true Christians, that they "hunger and thirst after righteousness.' Does this trait belong to you?

Sixth, Do you make a business of endeavoring to live holily, and as God would have you, in all respects? Not only can you be said to endeavor after holiness, but do you make *a business* of endeavoring after it? Is it a matter that lies with weight upon your mind. A true and faithful Christian does not make holy living a mere incidental thing, but it is his great concern. As the buisness of the soldier is to fight, so the business of the Christian is to be like Christ, to be holy as he is holy. Christian practice is the great work that he is engaged in, just as the race was the great work of the racers. Is this so with you? And is it your great aim and love to keep *all* God's commandments, and so far as known to neglect none? "Then," says the Psalmist, "I shall not be ashamed when I have respect unto all thy commandments." Is this your serious, constant, and prayerful aim, that you may be faithful in every known duty? And once more,

Seventh, Do you greatly desire that you may know all that is your duty? And do you desire to know it that you may do it? With the patriarch Job, can you, and do you pray to the Almighty, "That which I see not, teach thou me," adding, as he added, to the great searcher of hearts, "If I have done iniquity, I will do no more?"

If you can honestly meet these tests, then you have the evidence that your grace is of the kind that tends to holy practice, and to growth in it. And though you may fall, through God's mercy you shall rise again. He that hath begun a good work in you, will carry it on until the day of Jesus Christ. Though you may be, at times, faint, yet if pursuing, you shall be borne on from strength to strength, and kept by the power of God, through faith, unto salvation.

LECTURE XII.

CHARITY OR A CHRISTIAN SPIRIT WILLING TO UNDERGO ALL SUFFERINGS IN THE WAY OF DUTY.

"Beareth all things."—1 Cor. xiii. 7.

Having in the previous verses declared those fruits of charity that consist in *doing*, the Apostle now proceeds to speak of those that have reference to *suffering;* and here he declares that charity, or the spirit of Christian love, tends to dispose men, and make them willing to undergo all sufferings for Christ's sake, and in the way of duty. This I suppose to be the meaning of the expression, "*Beareth all things.*" Some, I know, would understand these words as referring only to the meek bearing of injuries from our fellow-men. But it seems to me that they are rather to be understood in the sense here given, of suffering in the cause of Christ and religion; and that, for the following reasons:—

First, As to bearing injuries from men, *that* the Apostle had mentioned before, in saying that "charity suffereth long," and again, in declaring that it "is not easily provoked," or that it tends to the resisting of the passion of anger; and therefore there is no need to suppose that he would use such tautology as again to mention the same thing a third time.

Second, The Apostle seems evidently to have done with the fruits of charity of a more active nature, and to have summed them all up in the expression of the previous verse, "rejoiceth not in iniquity, but rejoiceth in the truth." He had been rehearsing over the various points of good conduct toward our neighbor which charity tends to, and having summed up these in the above expression, he now seems to proceed to traits of another nature, and not to be repeating the same things over in other words.

Third, It is a frequent thing for the Apostle Paul, to mention suffering in the cause of Christ as a fruit of Christian love; and therefore it is not probable that he would omit so great a fruit of love in this place, where he is professedly reckoning up *all* the important fruits of love or charity. It is common for the Apostle elsewhere to mention suffering in the cause of religion as a fruit of love or charity. So he does in 2 Cor. v, 14, where, after speaking of what he had undergone in the cause of Christ, on account of which others were ready to say he was beside himself, he gives as the reason of it, that the love of Christ constrained him. And so, again, in Rom. v. 3, 5, he gives it as a reason why he was willing to glory in tribulations, that "the love of God was shed abroad in his heart by the Holy Ghost." And still again, he declares, that neither tribulation, nor distress, nor persecution, nor famine, nor nakedness, nor peril, nor sword, should be able to separate him from the love of Christ, Rom. viii. 35. Now since suffering in the cause of Christ is so great a fruit of charity, and so often spoken of elsewhere by the Apostle, it is not likely that he would omit it here, where he is professedly speaking of the various fruits of charity.

Fourth, The following words, "believeth all things, hopeth all things, endureth all things," all show that the Apostle has done with those fruits of charity that have chief reference to our fellow-men, as may be manifest hereafter when these expressions may be more fully considered. The doctrine, then, that I would draw from the text, is,

THAT CHARITY, OR A TRULY CHRISTIAN SPIRIT, WILL MAKE US WILLING, FOR CHRIST'S SAKE, TO UNDERGO ALL SUFFERINGS TO WHICH WE MAY BE EXPOSED IN THE WAY OF DUTY.—And in clearing this doctrine, I would first, briefly explain it, and then give some reason or proof of its truth.

I. *I would explain the doctrine.*—And in so doing, I remark,

1. *That it implies that those that have the true spirit of charity, or Christian love, are willing not only to do, but also to suffer for Christ.*—Hypocrites may, and oftentimes do make a great show of religion in profession, and in words that cost nothing, and in actions that involve no great difficulty or suffering. But they have not *a suffering spirit*, or a spirit that inclines them willingly to suffer for Christ's sake. When they undertook in religion, it was not with any view to suffering, or with any design or expectation of being in-

jured by it in their temporal interests. They closed with Christ, so far as they did, only to serve a turn for themselves. All that they do in religious things, is from a selfish spirit, and commonly very much for their interest, as it was with the Pharisees of old; and therefore they are far from the spirit that is willing to meet suffering, either in their persons or their interests. But those that are truly Christians, have a spirit to suffer for Christ; and they are willing to follow him on that condition which he himself has given : "Whosoever doth not bear his cross and come after me, cannot be my disciple," Luke xiv. 27. And not only are they willing to suffer for Christ, but,

2. *It is also implied in our doctrine, that they have the spirit to undergo all the sufferings to which their duty to Christ may expose them.* And here,

First, They are willing to undergo all sufferings, *of all kinds*, that are in the way of duty. They have the spirit of willingness to suffer in their good name: for Christ's sake to suffer reproach and contempt, and to prefer the honor of Christ before their own. With the Apostle they can say, "Therefore I take pleasure in infirmities, in reproaches, in necessities, in persecutions, in distresses, for Christ's sake," 2 Cor. xii. 10. They have a spirit to suffer the hatred and ill-will of men, as was foretold by Christ when he said, "Ye shall be hated of all men for my name's sake," Matthew x. 22. They have a spirit to suffer losses in their outward possessions; as says the Apostle, "Yea, doubtless, and I count all things but loss for the excellency of the knowledge of Christ Jesus, my Lord, for whom I have suffered the loss of all things," Philippians iii. 8. They have the spirit to suffer in their ease and comfort, and to endure hardships and fatigues; like Paul, to approve themselves faithful, "in much patience, in afflictions, in necessities, in distresses, in stripes, in imprisonments, in tumults, in labors, in watchings, in fastings," 2 Cor. vi. 4, 5. They have the spirit to suffer pain of body, like those "who were tortured, not accepting deliverance, and those who had trial of cruel mockings and scourgings, and of bonds and imprisonment," Hebrews xi. 35, 36. They have a spirit to suffer even death itself. "He that findeth his life shall lose it, and he that loseth his life for my sake shall find it," Matt. x. 39. These, and all other conceivable sufferings *in kind* they are willing to undergo for Christ's sake, and in the way of duty. And so,

Second, They are willing to undergo all sufferings, *of all degrees*, that are in the way of duty. They are like pure gold, that will bear the trial of the hottest furnace. They have the heart to forsake all and follow Christ, and comparatively to "hate" even "father, and mother, and wife, and children, and brethren, and sisters, yea, and their own life, also," for Christ's sake, Luke xiv. 26. They have the spirit to suffer the greatest degrees of reproach and contempt; and to have trial not only of mockings, but of *cruel* mockings; and to bear not only loss, but the loss of *all* things. They have the spirit to suffer death, and not only so, but the most cruel and tormenting forms of death, such as "to be stoned, to be sawn asunder, and to be slain with the sword, and to wander about in sheep-skins and goat-skins, being destitute, afflicted, tormented," Hebrews xi. 37. The fiercest and most cruel sufferings *in degree*, they are willing to undergo for Christ. I proceed,

II. *To give some reason or proof of the doctrine.*—And that it is so, that they who have a truly gracious spirit are willing to undergo all sufferings that they may be exposed to in the way of their duty, will appear from the following considerations:—

1. *If we have not such a spirit, it is an evidence that we have never given ourselves unreservedly to Christ.*—It is necessary to our being Christians, or followers of Christ, that we should give ourselves to him unreservedly, to be his wholly, and his only, and his forever. And therefore the believer's closing with Christ, is, often, in the Scriptures, compared to the act of a bride in giving herself in marriage to her husband; as when God says to his people, "I will betroth thee unto me forever; yea, I will betroth thee unto me in righteousness, and in judgment, and in lovingkindness, and in mercies," Hosea ii. 19. But a woman, in marriage, gives herself to her husband to be his, and his only. True believers are not their own, for they are bought with a price; and they consent to the full right that Christ has in them, and recognize it by their own act, giving themselves to him as a voluntary and living sacrifice, wholly devoted to him. But they that have not a spirit to suffer all things for Christ, show that they do

not give themselves wholly to him, because they make a reserve of such cases of suffering as they are not willing to bear for his sake. In those cases they desire to be excused from being for Christ and his glory, and choose rather that his cause should be set aside for their own ease or interest, and indeed should entirely give way for it. But making such reserves of cases of suffering, is certainly inconsistent with truly devoting themselves to God. It is rather being like Ananias and Sapphira, who gave but part, and kept back part of that which they professed to give to the Lord. To give ourselves wholly to Christ, implies the sacrificing of our own temporal interest wholly to him. But he that wholly sacrifices his temporal interest to Christ, is ready to suffer all things in his worldly interests for him. If God be truly loved, he is loved as God; and to love him as God, is to love him as the supreme good. But he that loves God as the supreme good, is ready to make all other good give place to that; or, which is the same thing, he is willing to suffer all for the sake of this good.

2. *They that are truly Christians, so fear God, that his displeasure is far more terrible*

than all earthly afflictions and sufferings.—
When Christ is telling his disciples what sufferings they should be exposed to for his sake, he says to them, "Be not afraid of them that kill the body, and after that have no more that they can do; but I will forewarn you whom ye shall fear; fear him, which after he hath killed, hath power to cast into hell; yea, I say unto you, fear him," Luke xii. 4, 5. And so, again, it is said by the prophet, "Sanctify the Lord of hosts himself, and let him be your fear, and let him be your dread," Isaiah viii. 13. Now they that are truly Christians, see and know him who is so great and dreadful a God, and they know that his displeasure and wrath are far more dreadful than all the temporal sufferings that can be in the way of their duty, and more dreadful than the wrath and cruelty of men, or the worst torments that they can inflict. And therefore they have a spirit to suffer all that can be inflicted, rather than forsake God, and sin against him who can inflict upon them eternal wrath.

3. *They that are truly Christians, have that faith whereby they see that which is more than sufficient to make up for the greatest sufferings they can endure in the cause of Christ.*

--They see that excellency in God and Christ, whom they have chosen for their portion, which far outweighs all possible sufferings. And they see, too, that glory which God has promised to them that suffer for his sake—that far more exceeding and eternal weight of glory, which their sufferings for Christ's sake work out for them, and in comparison with which, the heaviest sorrows and most enduring trials, are but "light afflictions, enduring but for a moment," 2 Cor. iv. 17. Moses' faith is given as a reason why he was willing to suffer affliction with the people of God, and to endure reproach for Christ's sake, because, in the exercise of that faith, he saw something better than the throne and riches of Egypt laid up for him in heaven, Heb. xi. 24-26.

4. *If we are not willing to close with religion, notwithstanding all the difficulties attending it, we shall be overwhelmed with shame at last.*—So Christ expressly teaches us. His language is, "For which of you intending to build a tower, sitteth not down first and counteth the cost, whether he have sufficient to finish it; lest, haply, after he hath laid the foundation, and is not able to finish it, all that behold it begin to mock him, saying, this man

began to build and was not able to finish; or what king, going to make war against another king, sitteth not down first, and consulteth whether he be able, with ten thousand, to meet him that cometh against him with twenty thousand? Or else, while the other is yet a great way off, he sendeth an embassage, and desireth conditions of peace. So likewise whosoever he be of you, that forsaketh not all that he hath, he cannot be my disciple," Luke xiv. 28–33. The sufferings that are in the way of our duty, are among the difficulties that attend religion. They are part of the cost of being religious. He, therefore, that is not willing to meet this cost, never complies with the terms of religion. He is like the man that wishes his house was built, but is not willing to meet the cost of building it; and so, in effect, refuses to build it. He that does not receive the gospel with all its difficulties; does not receive it as it is proposed to him. He that does not receive Christ with his cross as well as his crown, does not truly receive him at all. It is true that Christ invites us to come to him to find rest, and to buy wine and milk, but then he also invites us to come and take up the cross, and that daily that we may follow him; and if we come only to accept the former, we do not in truth accept the offer of the gospel, for both go together, the rest and the yoke, the cross and the crown: and it will signify nothing that in accepting only the one, we accept what God never offered to us. They that receive only the easy part of Christianity, and not the difficult, at best are but almost Christians; while they that are wholly Christians, receive the whole of Christianity, and thus shall be accepted and honored, and not cast out with shame at the last day.

5. *Without this spirit which the text implies, we cannot be said to forsake all for Christ.*—If there be any one kind or degree of temporal suffering that we have not a spirit to undergo for Christ, then there is something that we do not forsake for him. For example, if we are not willing to suffer reproach for Christ, then we are not willing to forsake honor for him. And so if we are not willing to suffer poverty, pain, and death for his sake, then we are not willing to forsake wealth, ease, and life for him. But Christ is abundant in teaching us, that we must be willing to forsake all that we have for him, if duty

requires it, or we cannot be his disciples, Luke xiv. 26, &c.

6. *Without this spirit, we cannot be said to deny ourselves in the sense in which the Scriptures require us to do it.*—The Scriptures teach us, that it is absolutely necessary to deny ourselves in order to our being the disciples of Christ. "Then said Jesus unto his disciples, If any man will come after me, let him deny himself, and take up his cross, and follow me; for whosoever will save his life shall lose it, and whosoever will lose his life for my sake, shall find it," Matt. xvi. 24, 25. These expressions, as here used, signify as much as a man's renouncing himself. And the one who acts according to them in his practice, lives as though he disowned himself for Christ. He puts himself to difficulty or suffering, as though he did not own himself. As the children of Levi were said not to know or acknowledge their own relatives and friends, when they put them to the sword for their sin in making the golden calf, so Christians are said not to acknowledge, but to deny themselves, when they crucify the flesh, and undergo great sufferings for Christ as though they had no mercy on themselves. Those that will do

contrary to the will of Christ and his glory, for the sake of avoiding suffering, deny Christ instead of denying themselves. Those that dare not confess Christ before persecutors, do in fact deny him before men, and are of the number of whom Christ says, that "he will deny them before his father in heaven," Matt. x. 33; and as to whom the Apostle says, "If we suffer, we shall also reign with him; if we deny him, he also will deny us," 2 Timothy ii. 12.

7. *It is the character of all the true followers of Christ, that they follow him in all things.* "These are they," says the beloved disciple, alluding to those about the throne of God, "these are they which follow the Lamb whithersoever he goeth," Rev. xiv. 4. Those that are willing to follow Christ only in prosperity and not in adversity, or only in some sufferings and not in all, cannot be said to follow him whithersoever he goeth. We read of one who said to Christ, while he was on earth, "Master, I will follow thee whithersoever thou goest;" and that Christ said to him, "The foxes have holes, and the birds of the air have nests, but the Son of man hath not where to lay his head," Matt. viii. 19, 20. And by this

he signified to him, that if he would follow him wherever he went, he must follow him through great difficulties and sufferings. They that are true followers of Christ, are of the same spirit toward Christ, that Ittai the Gittite manifested toward David, in not only clinging to him in prosperity, but also in his adversity, even when David would have excused him from going with him. He said, "As the Lord liveth, and as my lord the king liveth, surely in what place my lord the king shall be, whether in death or life, even there also will thy servant be," 2 Samuel xv. 21. Of such a spirit are true Christians toward Christ, the spiritual David.

8. *It is the character of true Christians, that they overcome the world.*—"Whatsoever is born of God, overcometh the world," 1 John v. 4. But to overcome the world, implies that we overcome alike its flatteries and frowns, its sufferings and difficulties. These are the weapons of the world, by which it seeks to conquer us; and if there be any of these that we have not a spirit to encounter for Christ's sake, then by such weapons the world will have us in subjection, and gain the victory over us. But Christ gives his servants the

victory over the world in *all* its forms. They are conquerors, and more than conquerors, through him that hath loved them. Once more,

9. *The sufferings in the way of duty, are often, in the Bible, called temptations or trials, because by them God tries the sincerity of our character as Christians.*—By placing such sufferings in our way, God tries whether we have a spirit to undergo suffering, and so tries our sincerity by suffering, as gold is tried by the fire, to know whether it is pure gold or not. And as by the fire the pure gold may be known from all baser metals, and from all imitations of it; so by observing whether we are willing to undergo trials and sufferings for Christ's sake, God sees whether we are indeed his people, or whether we are ready to forsake him and his service when any difficulty or danger is in the way. It seems to be with this view that the Apostle Peter says to those to whom he wrote, "Though now for a season, if need be, ye are in heaviness through manifold temptations, that the trial of your faith, being much more precious than of gold that perisheth, though it be tried with fire, might be found unto praise, and honor, and

glory, at the appearing of Jesus Christ," 1 Peter i. 6, 7. And again, "Beloved, think it not strange concerning the fiery trial which is to try you, as though some strange thing happened unto you; but rejoice, inasmuch as ye are partakers of Christ's sufferings, that when his glory shall be revealed, ye may be glad also with exceeding joy," 1 Pet. iv. 12, 13. And so God by his prophet declares, "I will bring the third part through the fire, and will refine them as silver is refined, and will try them as gold is tried: they shall call on my name, and I will hear them; I will say, It is my people; and they shall say, the Lord is my God," Zechariah xiii. 9.

In the application of this subject, let it

1. *Lead those who think themselves Christians, to examine themselves, whether or no they have the spirit to undergo all sufferings for Christ.*—It becomes all persons very strictly to examine themselves, whether they are of a suffering spirit or not, seeing such great importance is attached to such a spirit in the Scriptures. Though you never have had the trial of having such great and extreme sufferings laid in the way of your duty as many others have had, yet you have had enough, in

the course of God's providence, to show what your spirit is, and whether you are of a disposition to suffer, and to renounce your own comfort, and ease, and interest, rather than forsake Christ. It is God's manner in his providence, commonly, to exercise all professors of religion, and especially those that may live in times of trial, with trials of this sort, by laying such difficulties in their way as shall make manifest what their spirit is, and whether it be a spirit of self-renunciation or not. It is often the case with Christians who are exposed to persecutions, that if they will cleave to Christ, and be faithful to him, they must suffer in their good name, and in losing the good-will of others, or in their outward ease and convenience, being exposed to many troubles; or in their estates, being brought into difficulty as to their business; or must do many things that they are exceeding averse to, and that are even dreadful to them. Have you, when you have had such trials, found in yourself a spirit to bear all things that come upon you, rather than in anything be unfaithful to your great Lord and Redeemer? And you have the more need to examine yourselves with respect to this point, for you know not but that before you die you may have such trial of persecutions as other Christians have had. Every true Christian has the spirit of a martyr. And if you have not the suffering spirit in the lesser trials or sufferings that God may have sent upon you, how will it be if he should expose you to bitter persecutions, such as the saints of old sometimes were called to endure? If you cannot bear trials in little things, how can you possess that charity which beareth *all* things? As the prophet says in another case, "If thou hast run with the footmen and they have wearied thee, then how canst thou contend with horses? And if in the land of peace, wherein thou trustedst, they wearied thee, then how wilt thou do in the swelling of Jordan?" Jeremiah xii. 5. Our subject,

2. *Exhorts all professors of religion, to cherish a ready spirit, for Christ's sake, to undergo all sufferings that may be in the way of duty.* And here consider,

First, *How happy those persons are represented in the Scriptures to be, who have a spirit to suffer, and do actually suffer for Christ.*— "Blessed," says Christ, "are they which are persecuted for righteousness' sake, for theirs is the kingdom of heaven. Blessed are ye when men shall revile you, and persecute you, and shall say all manner of evil against you, falsely, for my sake. Rejoice and be exceeding glad, for great is your reward in heaven," Matt. v. 10, 12. And again, "Blessed are ye that hunger now, for ye shall be filled. Blessed are ye that weep now, for ye shall laugh. Blessed are ye when men shall hate you, and shall separate you from their company, and shall reproach you, and cast out your name as evil for the Son of man's sake. Rejoice ye in that day, and leap for joy, for great is your reward in heaven," Luke vi. 21–23. And again, " Unto you it is given, in the behalf of Christ, not only to believe on him, but also to suffer for his sake," Philippians i. 29. And again, " Blessed is the man that endureth temptation, for when he is tried, he shall receive the crown of life, which the Lord hath promised to them that love him," James i. 12. And again, "But and if ye suffer for righteousness' sake, happy are ye," 1 Pet. iii. 14. And the New Testament is full of similar expressions, all of which may encourage us in the way of suffering for Christ. And consider, also,

Second, What glorious rewards God has promised hereafter to bestow on those that do willingly suffer for Christ.—It is said that they shall receive a "crown of life;" and Christ promises, that those that forsake houses, or brethren, or sisters, or father, or mother, or wife, or children, or lands, for his name's sake, shall receive an hundred-fold, and shall inherit everlasting life, Matt. xix. 29. And again we are told, of those who suffer for Christ's sake, that they shall be counted worthy of the kingdom of God, 2 Thes. i. 5; and again, that it is a faithful saying, that if we suffer with Christ, we shall also reign with him, 2 Timothy ii. 11, 12; and still again, that if we suffer with him, we shall also be glorified together with him, Romans viii. 17. And we have, also, the most glorious promises made to those that overcome, and gain the victory over the world. "To him that overcometh," says Christ, "will I give to eat of the tree of life, which is in the midst of the paradise of God," and "he shall not be hurt of the second death;" and "to him will I give to eat of the hidden manna;" and "to him will I give power over the nations;" and "I will give him the morning star;" and "he shall be clothed in white raiment, and I will not blot out his name out of the book of life, but I will confess his name before my Father, and before his angels;" and "him will I make a pillar in the temple of my God, and he shall go no more out, and I will write upon him my new name;" and "to him that overcometh will I grant to sit with me in my throne, even as I also overcame, and am set down with my Father in his throne," Rev. ii. 7, 11, 17, 26, 27, 28, and iii. 5, 12, 21. Surely promises so rich and abundant as these, should make us willing to undergo all sufferings for the sake of Christ, who will so gloriously reward us for them all. Once more, consider,

Third, How the Scriptures abound with blessed examples of those that have suffered for Christ's sake.—The Psalmist, speaking of the reproach and blasphemy he had suffered from the enemy and avenger, says, "All this is come upon us, yet have we not forgotten thee, neither have we dealt falsely in thy covenant," Psalm xliv. 17, 18; and again, "The proud have had me greatly in derision, yet have I not declined from thy law; many are my persecutors and mine enemies, yet do I not decline from thy testimonies; princes have persecuted me without a cause, but my heart standeth in awe of thy word," Psalm cxix. 51, 157, 161. And the prophet Jeremiah spake boldly for God, though he was threatened with death for so doing, Jer. xxvi. 11, 15. And Shadrach, Meshach, and Abednego refused to bow down and worship the golden image that the king of Babylon had set up, though they knew they would be cast into the fiery furnace, Daniel iii.; and Daniel himself would still faithfully pray to his God, though he expected for it to be shut up in the den of lions, Daniel vi. But the time would fail me to tell of Apostles, and prophets, and martyrs, and saints, and of Christ himself, who were faithful alike through good report and evil report, and in sufferings and trials, and who counted not their lives dear, so that they might be faithful to the end. "Wherefore seeing we, also, are compassed about with so great a cloud of witnesses, let us lay aside every weight, and the sin which doth so easily beset us, and let us run with patience the race that is set before us, looking unto Jesus, the author and finisher of our faith, who for the joy that was set before him, endured the cross, despising the shame, and is set down at the right hand of the throne of God," Heb. xii. 1, 2. "Fear none of those things which thou shalt suffer. Be thou faithful unto death, and I will give thee a crown of life."

LECTURE XIII.

ALL THE GRACES OF CHRISTIANITY CONNECTED.

"Believeth all things, hopeth all things."—1 Cor. xiii. 7.

In these words, the Apostle is commonly understood to mean, that charity disposes us to believe the best, and hope the best concerning our neighbors, in all cases. But it appears to me that this is not his meaning in this place; but rather that he intends to say, that charity is a grace which cherishes and promotes the exercise of all other graces, as particularly of the graces of faith and hope. Mentioning the graces of believing and hoping, or of faith and hope, the Apostle here shows how the exercise of these is promoted by charity. My reasons for understanding the Apostle in this sense, are the following:—

First, He had just before mentioned that fruit of charity whereby it leads us to think the best of our neighbors, in saying that it "*thinketh no evil;*" and we have no reason to think he would repeat the same thing over again in these words.

Second, It seems plain that the Apostle had finished speaking of the fruits of charity toward our neighbors, when he summed them all up, as we have seen, in saying, that it "*rejoiceth not in iniquity, but rejoiceth in the truth;*" that is, that it tends to prevent all evil behavior, and to promote all good behavior. So that in this verse we might expect him to proceed to mention some fruits of charity of another kind, such for example, as its tendency to promote the graces of faith and hope, which are such great graces of the gospel.

Third, We find that the Apostle does, in this chapter, more than once mention the three graces of faith, hope, and charity, together. And it is but reasonable to suppose, that each time he does so, he means the same three graces. In the last verse of the chapter, we find these three mentioned and compared together; and there, by "faith" and "hope," the Apostle plainly does not mean believing or hoping the best respecting our neighbors, but he does intend those great graces of the gospel that have God and Christ for their main and immediate object. And so when, in this place, he mentions the same three graces as in the last verse of the chapter, why should we not believe that he means the same three things in the former place as in the latter, since it is in the same chapter, and the same discourse, and in the course of the same argument. And, again,

Fourth, This view is agreeable to the drift and aim of the Apostle throughout the chapter, which is to show the relation of charity to the other graces, and particularly to faith and hope. This is what the Apostle is aiming at in all that he says; and therefore when he comes to the conclusion of the matter in the last verse, and says that of faith, hope, and charity, the last is the greatest, he seems to have reference to what he had said in the words of the text, viz.: that charity "believeth all things, and hopeth all things," meaning that charity is greater than the other two, as it has the most effectual influence in producing them, and is that by which they are cherished and promoted in the soul. For these reasons, the doctrine I would draw from the text, is this:—

That the graces of Christianity are all connected together and mutually dependent on each other.—That is, they are all linked together, and united one to another and within another, as the links of a chain are; and one does, as it were, hang on another, from one end of the chain to the other, so that if one link be broken, all fall to the ground, and the whole ceases to be of any effect. And in unfolding this thought, I would, first, briefly explain how the graces of Christianity are all connected, and then give some reasons why they are so. And I would,

I. *Briefly explain the manner in which the graces of Christianity are connected.* And this may be shown in three things:—

1. *All the graces of Christianity always go together.*—They so go together, that where there is one, there are all, and where one is wanting, all are wanting. Where there is faith, there are love, and hope, and humility; and where there is love, there is also trust; and where there is a holy trust in God, there is love to God; and where there is a gracious hope, there also is a holy fear of God. "The Lord taketh pleasure in them that fear him; in those that hope in his mercy," Psalm cxlvii

11. Where there is love to God, there is a gracious love to man; and where there is a Christian love to man, there is love to God. Hence we find that the Apostle John, at one time gives love to the brethren as a sign of love to God, saying, "If a man say, I love God, and hateth his brother, he is a liar," 1 John iv. 20; and then, again, speaks of love to God, as a sign of love to the brethren, saying, "By this we know that we love the children of God, when we love God and keep his commandments," 1 John v. 2. It is, also, true,

2. *That the graces of Christianity depend upon one another.*—There is not only a connection, whereby they are always joined together, but there is also a mutual dependence between them, so that one cannot be without the others. To deny one, would in effect be, to deny another, and so all; just as to deny the cause, would be to deny the effect, or to deny the effect, would be to deny the cause. Faith promotes love, and love is the most effectual ingredient in a living faith. Love is dependent on faith; for a being cannot be truly loved, and especially loved above all other beings, who is not looked upon as a real

being. And then love, again, enlarges and promotes faith, because we are more apt to believe and give credit to, and more disposed to trust in those we love, than in those we do not. So faith begets hope, for faith sees and trusts in God's sufficiency to bestow blessings, and in his faithfulness to his promises, that he will do what he has said. All gracious hope, is hope resting on faith; and hope encourages, and draws forth acts of faith. And so love tends to hope, for the spirit of love is the spirit of a child, and the more any one feels in himself this spirit toward God, the more natural it will be to him to look to God, and go to God as his father. This childlike spirit casts out the spirit of bondage and fear, and gives the spirit of adoption, which is the spirit of confidence and hope. "Ye have not received the spirit of bondage again, to fear; but ye have received the spirit of adoption, whereby we cry, Abba, Father," Rom. viii. 15; and the Apostle John tells us, "There is no fear in love, but perfect love casteth out fear," 1 John iv. 18. And so, again, a true and genuine hope tends greatly to promote love. When a Christian has most of a right hope of his interest in God's favor, and in those eternal blessings that are its fruits, this tends to draw forth the exercise of love, and oftentimes does draw it forth; as says the Apostle Paul, "Tribulation worketh patience, and patience experience, and experience hope, and hope maketh not ashamed, because the love of God is shed abroad in our hearts," Rom. v. 3–5.

Faith, too, promotes humility; for the more entirely any one depends on God's sufficiency, the more will it tend to a low sense of his own sufficiency. And so humility tends to promote faith; for the more any one has an humble sense of his own insufficiency, the more will his heart be disposed to trust only on God, and to depend entirely on Christ. So love promotes humility; for the more the heart is ravished with God's loveliness, the more will it abhor itself, and abase and humble itself for its own unloveliness and vileness. Humility promotes love; for the more any one has an humble sense of his own unworthiness, the more will he admire God's goodness to him, and the more will his heart be drawn out in love to him for his glorious grace. Love tends to repentance; for he that truly repents of sin, repents of it because it is committed against a being that he loves. And repentance tends to humility; for no one can be truly sorry for sin, and self-condemned in view of it, without being humbled in heart for it. So repentance, faith, and love, all tend to thankfulness. He that, by faith, trusts to Christ for salvation, will be thankful to him for salvation. He that loves God, will be disposed thankfully to acknowledge his kindness. And he that repents of his sins, will be disposed heartily to thank God for the grace that is sufficient to deliver him from their guilt and power. A true love to God, tends to love to men, who bear the image of God; and a spirit of love and peace toward men, cherishes a spirit of love to God, as love to the image cherishes love to the original. And so it might be shown how all the graces depend one upon another, by mentioning many other particulars. Humility cherishes all other graces, and all other graces promote humility; and so faith promotes all other graces, and all other graces cherish and promote faith. And the like is true of every one of the graces of the gospel.

3. *The different graces of Christianity, are, in some respects, implied, one in another.—*

They are not only mutually connected and dependent, and each promotive of the others, but are in some respects implied in the nature of each other. In respect to several of them it is true, that one is essential to another, or belongs to its very essence. Thus, for example, humility is implied in the nature of a true faith, so as to be of the essence of it. It is essential to a true faith, that it be an humble faith; and essential to a true trust, that it be an humble trust. And so humility belongs to the nature and essence of many other true graces. It is essential to Christian love, that it be an humble love; to submission, that it be an humble submission; to repentance, that it be an humble repentance; to thankfulness, that it be an humble thankfulness; and to reverence, that it be an humble reverence.

And so love is implied in a gracious faith. It is an ingredient in it, and belongs to its essence, and is, as it were, the very soul of it, or its working, operative nature. As the working, operative nature of man is his soul, so the working and operative nature of faith is love; for the Apostle Paul tells us, that "faith worketh by love," Galatians v. 6;

and the Apostle James tells us, that faith without its working nature is dead, as the body is without the spirit, James ii. 26. And so faith is, in some respects, implied in love; for it is essential to a true Christian love, that it be a believing love. So saving repentance and faith are implied in each other. They are both one and the same conversion of the soul from sin to God, through Christ. The act of the soul in turning from sin to God through Christ, as it respects the thing from which the turning is, viz.: sin, is called repentance; and as it respects the thing to which, and the mediation by which it turns, is called faith. But it is the same motion of the soul; just as when a man turns, or flees from darkness to the light, it is the same act and motion, though it may be called by different names, according as it respects the darkness fled from, or the light fled to; in the one case, being called avoiding, or turning from, and in the other, receiving or embracing.

And so there is love implied in thankfulness. True thankfulness is no other than the exercise of love to God on occasion of his goodness to us. So there is love in a true and childlike fear of God; for a childlike fear differs from a slavish, for a slavish fear has no love in it. And all these three graces of love, humility and repentance, are implied in gracious childlike submission to the will of God. And so weanedness from the world, and heavenly mindedness do consist mainly in the three graces of faith, hope, and love. And so a Christian love to man, is a kind of mediate or indirect love to Christ; and that justice and truth towards men that are truly Christian graces, have love in them, and essential to them. Love and humility, again, are the graces wherein consists meekness toward men. And so it is love to God, and faith, and humility, that are the ingredients of Christian patience and contentment with our condition, and with the allotments of providence toward us. Thus it appears, that all the graces of Christianity are concatenated and linked together, so as to be mutually connected and mutually dependent. I proceed, then, as proposed,

II. *To give some reasons of their being thus connected and dependent.* And,

1. *They are all from the same source.*—All the graces of Christianity are from the same spirit; as says the Apostle, "There are diversities of gifts, but the same Spirit; diversities

of operations, but it is the same God which worketh all in all," 1 Cor. xii. 4, 6. The graces of Christianity are all from the same spirit of Christ sent forth into the heart and dwelling there as a holy, and powerful, and divine nature; and therefore all graces are only the different ways of acting on the part of the same divine nature; as there may be different reflections of the light of the sun, and yet all in origin the same kind of light, because it all comes from the same source or body of light. Grace in the soul, is the Holy Spirit acting in the soul, and thus communicating his own holy nature. As it is with water in the fountain, so here it is all one and the same holy nature, only diversified by the variety of streams sent forth from it. These streams must all be of the same nature, seeing they all thus come from the same source; and the difference of many of them, whereby they have different names, is chiefly relative, and more from reference to their various objects and modes of exercise, than from a real difference in their abstract nature. So also,

2. *They are all communicated in the same work of the Spirit, namely in conversion.*— There is not one conversion of the soul to

faith, and another conversion to love to God, and another to humility, and another to repentance, and still another to love to man; but all are produced by one and the same work of the Spirit, and are the result of one and the same conversion, or change of the heart. And this proves that all the graces are united and linked together, as being contained in that one and the same new nature that is given us in regeneration. It is here, as it is in the first generation, that of the body, in which the several faculties are communicated in one and the same generation, the senses of seeing, hearing, feeling, tasting, and smelling, and so the powers of moving, breathing, &c., all being given at the same time, and all being but one human nature, and one human life, though diversified in its modes and forms. It is further true of the Christian graces,

3. *That they all have the same root and foundation, namely, the knowledge of God's excellence.*—The same sight or sense of God's excellency begets faith, and love, and repentance, and all the other graces. One sight of this excellence will beget all these graces, because it shows the ground and reason of all holy dispositions, and of all holy behavior

toward God. They that truly know God's nature will love him, and trust in him, and have a spirit to submit to him, and serve, and obey him. "They that know thy name, will put their trust in thee," Psalm ix. 10. "Whosoever sinneth, hath not seen him, neither known him," 1 John iii. 6. "Every one that loveth, is born of God, and knoweth God," 1 John iv. 7. It is also true of the Christian graces,

4. *That they all have the same rule, namely the law of God.*—And therefore they must be linked together; for seeing they all have respect to this rule, they all tend to confirm the whole of the rule, and to conform the heart and life to it. He that has a true respect to one of God's commands, will have a true respect to all; for they are all established by the same authority, and are all jointly an expression of the same holy nature of God. "Whosoever shall keep the whole law, and yet offend in one point, he is guilty of all; for he that said, Do not commit adultery, said also, Do not kill. Now if thou commit no adultery, yet if thou kill, thou art become a transgressor of the law," James ii. 10, 11.

5. *All the Christian graces have the same*

end, namely God.—He is their end, for they all tend to him. As they are all from the same source, rising from the same fountain; and all stand on the same foundation, growing from the same root; and are all directed by the same rule, the law of God; so they are all directed to the same end, namely God, and his glory, and our happiness in him. And this shows that they must be nearly related, and very much linked together. And once more, it is true,

6. *That all the Christian graces are alike related to one and the same grace, namely charity, or divine love, as the sum of them all.*—As we have before seen, charity or love is the sum of all true Christian graces, however many names we may give them. And however different the modes of their exercise, or the ways of their manifestation, if we do but carefully examine them, we shall find they are all resolved into one. Love, or charity, is the fulfilling of them all, and they are but so many diversifications, and different branches, and relations, and modes of exercise of the same thing. One grace does, in effect, contain them all, just as the one principle of life comprehends all its manifestations.

And hence it is no wonder that they are always together, and are dependent on and implied in one another. In the application of this subject,

1. *It may aid us to understand in what sense old things are said to be done away, and all things become new in conversion.*—This is what the Apostle teaches us is the fact. "If any man be in Christ, he is a new creature; old things are passed away; behold all things are become new," 2 Cor. v. 17. Now the doctrine of the text and what has been said under it, may in some measure show us how this is; for by this we learn, that all the graces of Christianity are at once imparted in conversion, inasmuch as they are all linked together, so that when one is bestowed, all are bestowed, and not a single one merely. A true convert, the moment he is converted, is possessed not of one or two, but of *all* holy principles, and all gracious dispositions. They may be feeble indeed, like the faculties and powers of an infant child, but they are all truly there, and will be seen flowing out progressively in every kind of holy feeling and behavior toward both God and man. In every real convert, there are as many graces as

there were in Jesus Christ himself, which is what the evangelist John means, when he says, "The word was made flesh, and dwelt among us, and we beheld his glory, the glory as of the only begotten of the Father, full of grace and truth; and of his fulness have all we received, and grace for grace," John i. 14, 16. And, indeed, it cannot be otherwise, for all true converts are renewed in Christ's image, as says the Apostle, "And have put on the new man, which is renewed in knowledge, after the image of him that created him," Colos. iii. 10. But that is no true image or picture of another, which has some parts or features wanting. An exact image has a part answerable to each part in that of which it is an image. The copy answers to the original, throughout, in all its parts and features, though it may be obscure in some respects, and not represent any part perfectly, as grace answers to grace. Grace in the soul, is a reflection of Christ's glory, as appears by 2 Cor. iii. 18. It is a reflection of his glory, as the image of a man is reflected from a glass that exhibits part for part.

It is in the new birth, as it is in the birth of the infant child. He has all the parts of a man, though they are as yet in a very imperfect state. Not a part is wanting, but there are as many members as to a man of full stature and strength. And therefore what is wrought in regeneration, is called "the new man;" not only new eyes, or new ears, or new hands, but a new man, possessing all the human faculties and members. But all the graces of the Christian are new. All of them are members of the individual after conversion, and none of them were members before conversion. And because there is, as it were, a new man, with all these members, begotten in conversion, therefore Christians are said to be sanctified wholly, in soul, body and spirit, as in 1 Thes. v. 23. And so old things pass away, and all things become new, because as the new man is put on, the old man is put off, so that the man in a sense becomes new all over.

And if there be all graces alive in this new man, it will follow that all corruptions are mortified; for there is no one corruption but what has a grace opposite to, or to answer it: and the bestowment of the grace, mortifies the opposing corruption. Thus faith tends to mortify unbelief; love, to mortify enmity; humility, to mortify pride ; meekness, to mortify revenge; thankfulness, to mortify a thankless spirit, &c. And as one of these takes its place in the heart, the opposite gives way, just as darkness in a room vanishes when a light is brought in. Thus old things pass away. All old things, in a measure, pass away, though none perfectly on earth; and so all things become new, though also imperfectly. This shows that conversion, whenever and wherever it is wrought, is a great work and a great change. Though grace may be very imperfect, he must needs have a great change wrought in him, who, before, had no corruption mortified, and now has all mortified ; and who, before, had not one grace, and now has all graces. He may well be called a new creature, or, as in the original, a new creation in Christ Jesus.

2. *Hence, also, they that hope they have grace in their hearts, may try one grace by another, for all graces go together.*—If persons think they have faith, and therefore think they have come to Christ, they should inquire whether their faith was accompanied with repentance; whether they came to Christ in a broken-hearted manner, sensible of their

own utter unworthiness and vileness by sin; or whether they did not come in a presumptuous, pharisaical spirit, taking encouragement from their own supposed goodness. They should try their faith, by inquiring whether it was accompanied with humility; whether or no they trusted in Christ in a lowly and humble manner, delighting to renounce themselves, and to give all the glory of their salvation to Him. So they should try their faith, by their love; and if their faith has in it only light, but no warmth, it has not the true light; neither is it genuine faith, if it does not work by love.

And so persons should examine their love, by their faith. If they seem to have an affectionate love towards God and Christ, they should inquire whether or no this be accompanied with a real conviction of soul of the reality of Christ, and of the truth of the gospel that reveals him, and with the full conviction that he is the Son of God, the only, and glorious, and all-sufficient Saviour. Herein is one great difference between false affections and true ones, that the former are not accompanied with this conviction, and they do not withal see the truth and reality of divine things.

And therefore such affections are very little to be depended on. They are very much like the affection which we may have towards a person we are reading of in a romance, and whom we at the same time suppose to be no other than a feigned person. Such affections as are not accompanied with conviction, will never carry men very far in duty, or influence them, to any great extent, either in doing or suffering.

So, again, persons should examine themselves as to that in them which seems to be the grace of hope. They should inquire whether their hope is accompanied with faith, and arises from faith in Jesus Christ, and from a trust in his worthiness, and in his only? Is their hope built on this rock, or is it rather founded on a high opinion of something they think good in themselves? And so they should examine in what way their hope works, and what influence it has upon them, and whether or no it be accompanied with humility? A true hope leads its possessor to see his own unworthiness, and in view of his sins to reflect on himself with shame and brokenness of heart. It lies in the dust before God, and the comfort that arises from it, is a lowly humble joy and peace. On the contrary, a false hope is wont to lift its possessor up with a high conceit of himself, and of his own experience and doings. We should also inquire whether our hope be accompanied with a spirit of obedience, and self-denial, and weanedness from the world? A true hope is accompanied with these other graces, linked to, and dependent upon it, whereas a false hope is without them. It does not engage the heart in obedience, but flatters and hardens it in disobedience. It does not mortify carnal appetites, and wean from the world, but indulges the appetites and passions that are sinful, and chooses them, and makes men easy while living in them.

So, again, persons should examine their weanedness from the world, by inquiring whether it be accompanied with such a principle of love as draws their hearts off from the things of the world to those spiritual and heavenly objects which a true divine love carries the soul out to, more than to the things of the world. They should not only ask if they have something that appears like a true love, but they should hear Christ asking of them, as he did of Peter, "Simon, son of

Jonas, lovest thou me *more than these?*" Herein a true weanedness from the world, differs from a false weanedness. The latter is not from love to God and heavenly things, but commonly either from fear and distress of conscience, or perhaps from some outward affliction, whereby persons have their minds drawn off for a time from the world to something that they are constrained to feel is better, though it is not really sweeter to them; and they are only drawn, or beaten, or torn off from the world, while their hearts would still cleave to it just as much as ever, if they could but enjoy it, free from these terrors and afflictions. But they, on the other hand, that have a true weanedness from the world, are not wedded to worldly things even in their best and most inviting forms, because their hearts are drawn off by the love of something better. They are so in love with God, and with spiritual things, that their affections cannot fasten on the things of the world.

In the same way, persons should try their love to God, by their love to the people of God; and also, their love to their fellow Christians, by their love to God. False grace is like a defective or monstrous picture or image, wherein some essential part is wanting. There is, it may be, an appearance of some good disposition toward God, while at the same time there is a destitution of Christian dispositions toward men. Or if there appears to be a kind, just, generous, good-hearted disposition toward man, there is a want of right feeling toward God. On this account, we find God complains of Ephraim, that "he is a cake not turned," Hosea vii. 8; that is, that his goodness is partial and not consistent; that he is good in one thing, and bad in another, like a cake not turned, which is generally burnt on one side, and raw on the other, and good for nothing on either. Such a character we should studiously avoid, and endeavor that each grace that we have may testify to the genuineness of all our other graces, so that we may be proportioned Christians, growing in the unity of the faith, and of the knowledge of the Son of God, unto perfect men, unto the measure of the stature of the fulness of Christ.

LECTURE XIV.

CHARITY, OR TRUE GRACE, NOT TO BE OVERTHROWN BY OPPOSITION.

"Endureth all things."—1 Cor. xiii. 7.

In these words, and in saying previously that "charity suffereth long," and again, that it "beareth all things," the Apostle is commonly understood as making statements of substantially the same signification, as though the three expressions were synonymous, and all of them only said the same things in different words.

But this idea is doubtless from a misunderstanding of his meaning. For if we closely consider these various expressions, and the manner in which they are used, we shall find that every one of them signifies or points to a different fruit of charity. Two of these expressions have already been considered, viz.: that "charity suffereth long," and that it "beareth all things;" and the former was shown to have reference to the bearing of injuries received from men, and the latter, to the spirit that would lead us to undergo all sufferings to which we might be called for Christ's sake, and rather than to forsake him or our duty. And this expression of the text, that charity "endureth all things," signifies something different from either of the other statements. It expresses *the lasting and abiding nature of the principle of charity, or true grace in the soul*, and declares that it will not fail, but will continue and endure, notwithstanding all the opposition it may meet with, or that may be brought against it. The two expressions, "beareth all things," and "endureth all things," as in our English translation, and as commonly used, are indeed very much of the same import. But the expression of the original, if literally translated, would be, "charity remains under all things;" that is, it still remains, or still remains constant, and persevering, under all opposition that may come against it. Whatever assaults may be made upon it, yet it still remains, and endures, and does not cease, but bears up, and bears onward with constancy, and perseverance, and patience, notwithstanding them all.

According to the explanation that has been given of the four expressions of this verse "beareth," "believeth," "hopeth," and "endureth all things," the meaning of the Apostle appears easy, natural, and agreeable to the context. He is endeavoring to set forth the universal benefit of charity, or a spirit of Christian love. And to show how it is the sum of all good in the heart, he first shows how it disposes to all good behavior towards men, and sums up that matter by saying that charity rejoiceth not in iniquity but rejoiceth in the truth. And then he proceeds, and declares that charity not only disposes to doing and suffering in the cause of Christ, but that it includes a suffering spirit, so that it beareth all things; and that it does this by promoting the two graces of faith and hope, which are mainly occupied in sufferings in the cause of Christ; for such sufferings are the trials of our faith, and what upholds the Christian under them is the hope of a far more exceeding and eternal weight of glory to be given to the faithful in the end; and charity cherishes this faith and hope; and as the fruit of this faith and hope, it endures all things, and perseveres, and holds out, and cannot be conquered by all the opposition made against it, for faith overcomes the world, and hope in God enables the Christian always to triumph in Christ Jesus. The doctrine, then, that I would derive from the text, is, THAT CHARITY, OR TRUE CHRISTIAN GRACE, CANNOT BE OVERTHROWN BY ANYTHING THAT OPPOSES IT.—In speaking to this doctrine, I would, *first*, notice the fact that many things do oppose grace in the heart of the Christian; *second*, advert to the great truth, that it cannot be overthrown; and *third*, state some reasons why it cannot be shaken, but remains firm under all opposition. And,

I. *There are many things that do greatly oppose the grace which is in the heart of the Christian.*—This holy principle has innumerable enemies constantly watching and warring against it. The child of God is encompassed with enemies on every side. He is a pilgrim and stranger passing through an enemy's country, and exposed to attack at any and every moment. There are thousands of devils, artful, intelligent, active, mighty, and implacable, that are bitter enemies to the grace that is in the heart of the Christian, and do all that lies in their power against it. And the world is an enemy to this grace, because it abounds with persons and things that make opposition to it, and with various forms of allurement and temptation, to win or drive us from the path of duty. And the Christian has not only many enemies without, but multitudes within his own breast, that he carries about with him, and from which he cannot get free. Evil thoughts and sinful inclinations cling to him; and many corruptions that still hold their footing in his heart are the worst enemies that grace has, and have the greatest advantage of any in their warfare against it. And these enemies are not only many, but exceeding strong and powerful, and very bitter in their animosity, implacable, irreconcilable, mortal enemies, seeking nothing short of the utter ruin and overthrow of grace. And they are unwearied in their opposition, so that the Christian, while he remains in this world, is represented as being in a state of warfare, and his business is that of the soldier, insomuch that he is often spoken of as a soldier of the cross, and as one whose great duty it is to fight manfully the good fight of faith.

Many are the powerful and violent assaults that the enemies of grace make upon it. They are not only constantly besieging it, but often they assault it, as a city that they would take by storm. They are always lurking and watching for opportunity against it, and sometimes they rise up, in dreadful wrath, and endeavor to carry it by urgent assault. Sometimes one enemy, and sometimes another, and sometimes all together, with one consent, buffeting it on every side, and coming in like a flood, are ready to overwhelm it, and to swallow it up at once. Sometimes grace, in the midst of the most violent opposition of its enemies fighting against it with their united subtilty and strength, is like a spark of fire encompassed with swelling billows and raging waves, that appear as if they would swallow it up and extinguish it in a moment. Or it is like a flake of snow falling into the burning volcano; or rather like a rich jewel of gold in the midst of a fiery furnace, the raging heat of which is enough to consume anything except the pure gold, which is of such a nature that it cannot be consumed by the fire.

It is with grace in the heart of a Christian, very much as it is with the church of God in the world. It is God's post; and it is but small, and great opposition is made against it by innumerable enemies. The powers of earth and hell are engaged against it, if possible to destroy it; and oftentimes they rise with such violence, and come with such great strength against it, that if we were to judge only by what appears, we should think it would be taken and destroyed immediately. It is with it as it was with the children of Israel in Egypt, against whom Pharaoh and the Egyptians united all their craft and power, and set themselves to endeavor to extirpate them as a people. It is with it as it was with David in the wilderness, when he was hunted as a partridge on the mountains, and driven about by those that sought his life from one desert or cave to another, and several times was chased out into a strange land. And it is with it as it has been with the Christian church under the heathen and antichristian persecutions, when all the world, as it were, united their strength and wit to exterminate it from the earth, destroying thousands and millions with the utmost cruelty, and by the most bloody persecutions without respect to sex or age. But,

II. *All the opposition that is, or can be made against true grace in the heart, cannot overthrow it.*—The enemies of grace may, in many respects, gain great advantages against it. They may exceedingly oppress and reduce it, and bring it into such circumstances that it may seem to be brought to the very brink of utter ruin. But yet it will live. The ruin that seemed impending shall be averted. Though the roaring lion sometimes comes with open mouth, and no visible refuge appears, yet the lamb shall escape and be safe. Yea, though it be in the very paw of the lion or the bear, yet it shall be rescued and not devoured. And though it even seems actually swallowed down, as Jonah was by the whale, yet it shall be brought up again and live. It is with grace in the heart in this respect, as it was with the ark upon the waters, however terrible the storm may be, yea, though it be such a deluge as overwhelms all things else, yet it shall not overwhelm that. Though the floods rise ever so high, yet it shall be kept above the waters; and though the mighty waves may rise above the tops of the highest mountains, yet they shall not be able to get above this ark, but it shall still float in safety. Or it is with this grace, as it was with the ship in which Christ was when there arose a great storm, and the waves ran high, inasmuch that it seemed as if the ship would instantly sink; and yet it did not sink, though it was actually covered with waters, for Christ was in it.

And so, again, grace in the heart, is like the children of Israel in Egypt, and at the Red Sea, and in the wilderness. Though Pharaoh strove ever so much to destroy them, they yet grew and prospered. And when, at last, he pursued them with all his army, and with chariots and horsemen, and they were pent up by the Red Sea, and saw no way of escape, but seemed to themselves to be on the very brink of ruin, yet they did escape, and were not delivered a prey to their foes. Yea, they were preserved in passing through the very sea itself, for the waters opened before them, and when they had safely passed over, rolled back and overwhelmed their foes. And they were preserved for a long time in the desolate wilderness, in the midst of pits, and drought, and fiery flying-serpents. Thus as the gates of hell can never prevail against the church of Christ, so neither can they prevail against grace in the heart of the Christian. The seed remaineth, and none can root it out. The fire is kept alive even in the midst of the floods of water; and though it often appears dim, or as if it were just going out, so that there is no flame, but only a little smoke, yet the smoking flax shall not be quenched.

And grace shall not only remain, but at last shall have the victory. Though it may pass through a long time of sore conflicts, and may suffer many disadvantages and depressions, yet it shall live; and not only live, but it will finally prosper, and prevail, and triumph, and all its enemies shall be subdued under its feet. As David in the wilderness, though he was long kept in very low and distressed circumstances, pursued by his potent enemies, and many times apparently on the brink of ruin where there seemed but a step between him and death, was yet through all preserved, and at last exalted to the throne of Israel, and to wear the royal crown in great prosperity and with glory, so we see it is with grace, that it can never be overthrown, and its depressions do but prepare the way for its exaltation. Where it does truly exist in the heart, all its enemies cannot destroy it, and all the opposition made against it cannot crush it. It endures all things, and stands all shocks, and remains notwithstanding all opposers. And the reason of this may be seen in these two things:

1. *That there is so much more in the nature of true grace that tends to perseverance, than in false grace.*—False grace is a superficial thing, consisting in mere outward show, or in superficial affections, and not in any change of nature. But true grace reaches to the very bottom of the heart. It consists in a new nature, and therefore it is lasting and enduring. Where there is nothing but counterfeit grace, corruption is unmortified, and whatever wounds may seem to be given it, they are but slight wounds, that do not at all reach its life or diminish the strength of its principle, but leave sin in its full strength in the soul, so that it is no wonder that it ultimately prevails, and bears down all before it. But true grace really mortifies sin in the heart. It strikes at its vitals, and gives it a wound that is mortal, sending its stroke to the very heart. When it first enters the soul, it begins

a never-ceasing conflict with sin, and therefore it is no wonder that it keeps possession, and finally prevails over its enemy. Counterfeit grace never dispossesses sin of the dominion of the soul, or destroys its reigning power there, and therefore it is no wonder that it does not itself remain. But true grace is of such a nature that it is inconsistent with the reigning power of sin, and dispossesses the heart of it as it enters, and takes the throne from it, and therefore is the more likely to keep its seat there, and finally to prevail entirely against it. Counterfeit grace, though it may affect the heart, yet is not founded on any real conviction of the soul. But true grace begins in real and thorough conviction, and having such a foundation, has so much the greater tendency to perseverance. Counterfeit grace is not diligent in prayer; but true grace is prayerful, and thus lays hold on the divine strength to support it, and indeed becomes divine itself, so that the life of God is, as it were, imparted to it. Counterfeit grace is careless whether it perseveres to the end, or not; but true grace naturally causes earnest desires for perseverance, and leads to hungerings and thirstings for it. It also makes men sensible of the dangers they are encompassed with, and has a tendency to excite them to watchfulness, and to care and diligence that they may persevere, and to look to God for help, and trust in him for preservation from the many enemies that oppose it. And,

2. *God will uphold true grace, when he has once implanted it in the heart, against all opposition.*—He will never suffer it to be overthrown by all the force that may be brought against it. Though there be much more in true grace that tends to perseverance than there is in counterfeit grace, yet nothing that is in the nature of grace, considered by itself and apart from God's purpose to uphold it, would be sufficient to make sure its continuance, or effectually to keep it from final overthrow. We are kept from falling, not by the inherent power of grace itself, but as the Apostle Peter tells us (1 Pet. i. 5), "by the power of God through faith." The principle of holiness in the hearts of our first parents, where it had no corruption to contend with, was overthrown; and much more might we expect the seed of grace in the hearts of fallen men, in the midst of so much corruption, and

exposed to such active and constant opposition, would be overthrown did not God uphold it. He has undertaken to defend it from all its enemies, and to give it the victory at last, and therefore it shall never be overthrown. And here I would briefly show how it is evident that God will uphold true grace, and not suffer it to be overthrown, and then show some reasons why he will not suffer it.

First, I would show *how it is evident that God will uphold true grace in the heart.* And in one word it is evident from his promise. God has explicitly and often promised that true grace shall never be overthrown. It is promised in that declaration concerning the good man (Psalm xxxvii. 24), that "though he fall, he shall not be utterly cast down; for the Lord upholdeth him with his hand;" and again in the words (Jer. xxxii. 40), "I will make an everlasting covenant with them, that I will not turn away from them to do them good; but I will put my fear in their hearts, that they shall not depart from me;" and again, in those words of Christ (Matt. xviii. 14), that "it is not the will of your Father which is in heaven, that one of these little ones should perish." And in accordance with these various declarations, Christ has promised concerning grace (John xiv. 14), that it shall be in the soul, " as a well of water, springing up into everlasting life." . And again he says (John vi. 39), " This is the Father's will which hath sent me, that of all which he hath given me, I should lose nothing, but should raise it up again at the last day." And in other places it is said, that Christ's sheep " shall never perish, neither shall any man pluck them out of his hand," John x. 27; that whom God " did foreknow, them he also called ; and whom he called, them he also justified; and whom he justified, them he also glorified," and that nothing "shall separate" Christians " from the love of Christ," Rom. viii. 29, 30, 35 ; and again, "that he which hath begun a good work" in us, "will perform it until the day of Jesus Christ," Phil. i. 6 ; and again, that Christ " shall confirm" his people " unto the end that" they " may be blameless in the day of our Lord Jesus Christ," 1 Cor. i. 8; and still again, that "he is able to keep" them "from falling, and to present" them " faultless before the presence of his glory with exceeding joy," Jude 24. And many other similar promises might be mentioned, all of which declare that God will uphold grace in the heart in which he has once implanted it, and that he will keep to the end those who put their trust in him. But,

Second, I would briefly show *some reasons why God will uphold the principle of grace, and keep it from being overthrown.* And in the *first* place, unless the redemption provided by Christ secured our perseverance through all opposition, it would not be a complete redemption. Christ died to redeem us from the evil we were subject to under the law, and to bring us to glory. But if he brought us no further than the state we were in at first, and left us as liable to fall as before, then all his redemption might be made void, and come to nothing. Man, before the fall, being left to the freedom of his own will, fell from his steadfastness, and lost his grace when he was comparatively strong and not exposed to the enemies that now beset him. What then could he do in his present fallen state, and with such imperfect grace, in the midst of his powerful and manifold enemies, if his perseverance depended on himself alone? He would utterly fall and perish; and the redemption provided by Christ, if it did not secure him from thus falling, would be a very imperfect redemption.

In the *second* place, the covenant of grace was introduced to supply what was wanting in the first covenant, and a sure ground of perseverance was the main thing that was wanting in it. The first covenant had no defect on the part of God who constructed it; in that respect it was most holy and just, and wise and perfect. But the result proved that on our part it was wanting, and needed something more in order to its being effectual for our happiness; and the thing needed was something that should be a sure ground of our perseverance. All the ground we had under the first covenant was the freedom of our own will; and this was found not to be depended on: and therefore God has made another covenant. The first was liable to fail, and therefore another was ordained more enduring than the first, and that could not fail, and which therefore is called "an everlasting covenant." The things that could be shaken are removed, to make way for those that cannot be shaken. The first covenant had a head and surety that was liable to fail, even the father of our race; and therefore God has provided as the head and surety of the new covenant, one that cannot fail, even Christ, with whom, as the head and representative of all his people, the new covenant is made, and ordered in all things and sure.

In the *third* place, it is not fit that in a covenant of mercy and saving grace, the reward of life should be suspended on man's perseverance as depending on the strength and steadfastness of his own will. It is a covenant of works, and not a covenant of grace that suspends eternal life on that which is the fruit of a man's own strength to keep him from falling. If all is of free and sovereign grace, then free grace has undertaken the matter to complete and finish it, and has not left it to men themselves, and to the power of their own wills, as it was under the first covenant. As divine grace has commenced the work, it will finish it; and therefore we shall be kept to the end.

In the *fourth* place, our second surety has already persevered and done what our first surety failed of doing; and therefore we shall surely persevere. Adam, our first surety, did not persevere; and so all fell with him. But if he had persevered, all would have stood with him, and never would have fallen But our second surety has already persevered, and therefore all that have him for their surety will persevere with him. When Adam fell, he was condemned, and all his posterity was condemned with him, and fell with him. But if he had stood, he would have been justified, and so would have partaken of the tree of life, and been confirmed in a state of life, and all his posterity would have been confirmed. And by parity of reason, now that Christ, the second Adam, has stood, and persevered, and is justified, and confirmed in life, all who are in Christ and represented by him, are also accepted, and justified, and confirmed in him. The fact that he, as the covenant head of his people, has fulfilled the terms of that covenant, makes it sure that they shall persevere.

In the *fifth* place, the believer is already actually justified, and thus entitled, through the promise of mercy, to eternal life, and therefore God will not suffer him to fail and come short of it. Justification is the actual acquittal of the sinner. It is a full acquittance from guilt, and freedom from condemnation, and deliverance from hell, and acceptance to a full title to eternal life. And all this is plainly inconsistent with the idea that deliverance from hell, and the attainment of eternal life, are yet suspended on an uncertain perseverance.

In the *sixth* place, the Scriptures teach us, that the believer's grace and spiritual life, are a partaking of the life of Christ in his resurrection, which is an immortal and unfading life. This is plainly taught by the Apostle, when he says (Col. ii. 13), "You hath he quickened together with him," that is, with Christ; and again (Eph. ii. 4, 6), "But God, who is rich in mercy, for his great love wherewith he loved us, even when we were dead in sins, hath quickened us together with Christ, and hath raised us up together, and made us sit together in heavenly places in Christ Jesus;" and still again (Gal. ii. 20), "I live; yet not I, but Christ liveth in me." These expressions show that the believer's spiritual life cannot fail; for Christ says (Rev. i. 18), "I am he that liveth, and was dead; and behold I am alive for evermore;" and the Apostle says (Rom. vi. 9), "Knowing that Christ, being raised from the dead, dieth no more; death hath no more dominion over him." Our spiritual life being his life, as truly as the life of the branch is the life of the tree, cannot but continue.

In the *seventh* place, grace is that which God hath implanted in the heart against the great opposition of enemies, and therefore he will doubtless maintain it there against their continued and combined efforts to root it out. The enemies of God and the soul used their utmost endeavors to prevent grace being implanted in the heart that possesses it. But God manifested his all-conquering and glorious power in introducing it there in spite of them all. And therefore he will not at last suffer himself to be conquered by their expelling that which he by his mighty power has so triumphantly brought in. From all which it is plain, that God will uphold the principle of grace in the heart of the Christian, so that it shall never be overthrown or fail. In the application of this subject,

1. *We may learn one reason why the devil so exceedingly opposes the conversion of sinners.*—It is because if they are once converted, they are forever converted, and thus forever put beyond his reach, so that he can never overthrow and ruin them. If there was such a thing as falling from grace, doubtless the

devil would even then oppose our having grace; but more especially does he oppose it since he knows that if once we have it, he can never expect to overthrow it, but that we, by its very possession, are finally lost to him and forever out of the reach of his destroying power. This may show us something of the reason of that violent opposition that persons who are under awakenings and convictions, and who are seeking conversion, meet with through the many and great temptations they are assailed with by the adversary. He is always active and greatly bestirs himself for the overthrow of such, and heaps mountains in their way, if possible, to hinder the saving work of the Holy Spirit, and prevent their conversion. He labors to the utmost to quench convictions of sin, and if possible to lead persons that are under them to return to the ways of heedlessness and sloth in transgression. Sometimes he endeavors to flatter, and at other times to discourage them, laboring to entangle and perplex their minds, and to his utmost stirring up exercises of corruption, suggesting blasphemous thoughts, and leading them to quarreling with God. By many sub tle temptations he endeavors to make them think that it is in vain to seek salvation. He tempts them from the doctrine of God's decrees; or by their own impotence and helplessness; or by telling them that all they do is sin; or by trying to persuade them that their day of grace is past; or by terrifying them with the idea that they have committed the unpardonable sin. Or it may be he tells them that their pains and trouble are needless, and that there is time enough hereafter; or if possible he will deceive them with false hopes, and flatter them that they are in a safe estate while they are still out of Christ. In these, and innumerable other ways, Satan endeavors to hinder the conversion of men, for he knows the truth of the doctrine we have insisted on, that if ever grace be implanted in the soul, he can never overthrow it, and that the gates of hell cannot prevail against it. Again,

2. *We may see from this subject, that those whose seeming grace fails, and is overthrown, may conclude that they never had any true grace.*—That is not true grace which is like the morning cloud, and the early dew, which passeth away. When persons seem for a while to be awakened and terrified, and have more or less of a sense of their sinfulness and

vileness, and then afterwards seem much affected with the mercy of God, and appear to find comfort in him, and yet after all, when the novelty is over, their impressions decline and pass away, so that there is no abiding change in the heart and life, then it is a sign that they have no true grace. There is nothing in the case of such that answers to the declaration of the Apostle (2 Cor. v. 17), that "if any man be in Christ, he is a new creature." If the individual, after seeming conversion, turns back from God and Christ and spiritual things, and the heart again goes after vanity and the world, and the known duties of religion are neglected, and the person again returns to the ways of sin, and goes on gratifying the selfish or sensual appetites, and leading a carnal and careless life, then all the promise of his apparent conversion is deceptive. It is but like the promise of the blossoms on the trees in the time of spring or early summer, so many of which fall off, and never bring forth fruit. The result proves that all these seeming appearances of grace are only appearances, and that those who trust to them are awfully deluded. The grace that does not hold out and persevere, is not real grace. Once more,

3. *The subject affords matter of great joy and comfort to all who have good evidence that they indeed have true grace in their hearts.*— Those with whom it is thus, are possessed of an inestimable jewel, which is worth more than all the jewels and precious stones, and all the crowns and costly treasures in the universe. And this may be a matter of great comfort to them, that they never shall lose this jewel, but that he that gave it will keep it for them; and that as he has brought them into a most happy state, so he will uphold them in it, and that his mighty power by which he is able to subdue all things to himself, is on their side, and pledged for their protection, so that none of their enemies shall be able to destroy them. They may rejoice that they have a strong city unto which God has appointed salvation for walls and bulwarks. And whatever bitterness their enemies manifest against them, and however subtle and violent they may be in their attacks upon them, they may still stand on high on their munitions of rocks on which God has set them, and laugh their foes to scorn, and glory in the Most High as their sure refuge and defence. The everlasting arms are underneath them.

Jehovah, who rides upon the heavens, is their help. And all their foes he will subdue under his feet; so that they may well rejoice in the Lord, and joy in the rock of their salvation. Finally,

4. *The subject also affords matter of great encouragement to the saints in carrying on the warfare against the enemies of their souls.*— It is the greatest of all disadvantages to a soldier to have to go forth to battle without the hope of being able to conquer, but with the prevailing expectation of being overcome. As hope in the one case might be half the victory, so despondency in the other would be likely to ensure defeat. The latter would debilitate and weaken, while the former would co-operate with and increase strength. You that have good evidence that you have grace in your hearts, have, then, all that you can need to encourage you. The captain of your salvation will assuredly conduct you to victory in the end. He who is able to uphold you has promised that you shall overcome, and his promise shall never fail. Resting on that promise, be faithful to your part, and ere long the song of victory shall be yours, and the crown of victory he will place, with his own hands, upon your head.

LECTURE XV.

THE HOLY SPIRIT FOREVER TO BE COMMUNICATED TO THE SAINTS, IN THE GRACE OF CHARITY, OR DIVINE LOVE.

"Charity never faileth. But whether there be prophecies, they shall fail; whether there be tongues, they shall cease; whether there be knowledge, it shall vanish away."
—1 COR. xiii. 8.

IN the entire context, the drift of the Apostle is, to show the superiority of charity over all the other graces of the Spirit. And in this chapter he sets forth its excellence by three things: *first*, by showing that it is the most essential thing, and that all other gifts are nothing without it; *second*, by showing that from it all good dispositions and behavior do arise; and *third*, by showing that it is the most durable of all gifts, and shall remain when the church of God shall be in its most perfect state, and when the other gifts of the

Spirit shall have vanished away. And in the text may be observed two things:—

First, That one property of charity by which its excellence is set forth, is, that it is unfailing and everlasting. "Charity never faileth." This naturally follows the last words of the preceding verse, that "Charity endureth all things." There the Apostle declares the durableness of charity as it appears in its withstanding the shock of all the opposition that can be made against it in the world. And now he proceeds further, and declares that charity not only endures to the end of *time*, but also throughout *eternity*. "Charity *never* faileth." When all temporal things shall have failed, this shall still abide, and abide forever. We may also observe in the text,

Second, That herein charity is distinguished from all the other gifts of the Spirit, such as prophecies, and the gift of tongues, and the gift of knowledge, &c. "Whether there be prophecies, they shall fail; whether there be tongues, they shall cease; whether there be knowledge, it shall vanish away;" but "charity never faileth." By the knowledge here spoken of, is not meant spiritual and divine knowledge in general; for surely there will be such knowledge hereafter in heaven, as well as now on earth, and vastly more than there is on earth, as the Apostle expressly declares in the following verses. The knowledge that Christians have of God, and Christ, and spiritual things, and in fact all their *knowledge,* as that word is commonly understood, shall not vanish away, but shall be gloriously increased and perfected in heaven which is a world of light as well as love. But by the knowledge which the Apostle says shall vanish away, is meant a particular miraculous gift that was in the church of God in those days. For the Apostle, as we have seen, is here comparing charity with the miraculous gifts of the Spirit, those extraordinary gifts which were common in the church in those days, one of which was the gift of prophecy, and another the gift of tongues, or the power of speaking in languages that had never been learned. Both these gifts are mentioned in the text, and the Apostle says they shall fail and cease. And another gift was the gift of knowledge, or the *word* of knowledge, as it is called in the eighth verse of the previous chapter, where it is so spoken of as to show that it was a different thing both from that speculative knowledge which is obtained from reason and study, and also from that spiritual or divine knowledge that comes from the saving influence of the Holy Spirit in the soul. It was a particular gift of the Spirit with which some persons were endowed, whereby they were enabled by immediate inspiration to understand mysteries, or the mysterious prophecies and types of the Scriptures, which the Apostle speaks of in the second verse of this chapter, saying, "Though I have the gift of prophecy, and understand all mysteries and all knowledge, &c." It is this miraculous gift which the Apostle here says shall vanish away, together with the other miraculous gifts of which he speaks, such as prophecy, and the gift of tongues, &c. All these were extraordinary gifts, bestowed for a season for the introduction and establishment of Christianity in the world, and when this their end was gained, they were all to fail and cease. But charity was never to cease. Thus the Apostle plainly teaches, as the doctrine of the text,

That that great fruit of the Spirit, in which the Holy Ghost shall, not only for a season, but everlastingly be communicated

TO THE CHURCH OF CHRIST, IS CHARITY, OR DIVINE LOVE.

That the meaning and truth of this doctrine may be better understood, I would speak to it in the four following propositions: *first*, The spirit of Christ will be everlastingly given to his church and people, to influence and dwell in them; *second*, There are other fruits of the Spirit besides divine love, wherein the Spirit of God is communicated to his church; *third*, These other fruits are but for a season, and either have already, or will at some time cease; *fourth*, That charity, or divine love, is that great and unfailing fruit of the Spirit, in which his everlasting influence and indwelling in the saints, or in his church, shall appear.

I. *The Spirit of Christ is given to his church and people, everlastingly to influence and dwell in them.*—The Holy Spirit is the great purchase, or purchased gift of Christ. The chief and sum of all the good things in this life and in the life to come, that are purchased for the church, is the Holy Spirit. And as he is the great purchase, so he is the great promise, or the great thing promised by God and Christ to the church, as said the Apostle Peter on the day of Pentecost (Acts ii. 32, 33), "This

Jesus, being by the right hand of God exalted, and having received of the Father the promise of the Holy Ghost, he hath shed forth this which ye now see and hear." And this great purchase and promise of Christ is forever to be given to his church. He has promised that his church shall continue, and expressly declared that the gates of hell shall not prevail against it. And that it may be preserved, he has given his Holy Spirit to every true member of it, and promised the continuance of that Spirit forever. His own language is (John xiv. 16, 17), "And I will pray the Father, and he shall give you another comforter, that he may abide with you forever; even the Spirit of truth, whom the world cannot receive, because it seeth him not, neither knoweth him; but ye know him, for he dwelleth with you, and shall be in you."

Man, in his first estate in Eden, had the Holy Spirit; but he lost it by his disobedience. But a way has been provided by which it may be restored, and now it is given a second time, never more to depart from the saints. The Spirit of God is so given to his own people as to become truly theirs. It was, indeed, given to our first parents in their state of innocence, and dwelt with them, but not in the same sense in which it is given and dwells in believers in Christ. They had no proper right or sure title to the Spirit, and it was not finally and forever given to them, as it is to believers in Christ; for if it had been, they never would have lost it. But the Spirit of Christ is not only communicated to those that are converted, but he is made over to them by a sure covenant, so that he is become their own. Christ is become theirs, and therefore his fulness is theirs, and therefore his Spirit is theirs—their purchased, and promised, and sure possession. But,

II. *There are other fruits of the Spirit besides that which summarily consists in charity, or divine love, wherein the Spirit of God is communicated to his church.* For example,

1. *The Spirit of God has been communicated to his church in extraordinary gifts, such as the gift of miracles, the gift of inspiration, &c.*—The Spirit of God seems to have been communicated to the church in such gifts, formerly to the prophets under the Old Testament, and to the Apostles, and evangelists, and prophets, and to the generality of the

early ministers of the gospel, and also to multitudes of common Christians under the New Testament. To them were given such gifts as the gift of prophecy, and the gift of tongues, and the gift called the gift of knowledge, and others mentioned in the context, and in the foregoing chapter. And besides these,

2. *There are the common and ordinary gifts of the Spirit of God.*—These, in all ages, have more or less been bestowed on many natural, unconverted men, in common convictions of sin, and common illuminations, and common religious affections, which, though they have nothing in them of the nature of divine love, or of true and saving grace, are yet the fruits of the Spirit in the sense that they are the effect of his influences on the hearts of men. And as to faith and hope, if there be nothing of divine love with them, there can be no more of the Spirit of God in them than is common to natural, unregenerate men. This is clearly implied by the Apostle, when he says, in this chapter, "Though I have all faith, so that I could remove mountains, and have not charity, I am nothing." All saving faith and hope have love in them as ingredients, and as their essence; and if this ingre-

dient be taken out, there is nothing left but the body without the spirit. It is nothing saving; but at best, only a common fruit of the Spirit. But,

III. *All these other fruits of the Spirit are but for a season, and either have already ceased, or at some time will cease.*—As to the miraculous gifts of prophecy and tongues, &c., they are but of a temporary use, and cannot be continued in heaven. They were given only as an extraordinary means of grace that God was once pleased to grant to his church in the world. But when the saints that once enjoyed the use of these means went to heaven, such means of grace ceased, for they were no longer needful. There is no occasion for any means of grace in heaven, whether ordinary, such as the stated and common means of God's house, or extraordinary, such as the gifts of tongues, and of knowledge, and of prophecy. I say there is no occasion for any of these means of grace to be continued in heaven, because there the end of all means of grace is already fully obtained in the perfect sanctification and happiness of God's people. The Apostle, speaking in the fourth chapter of Ephesians, of the various means of grace, says that they are given "for the perfecting of the saints, for the work of the ministry, for the edifying of the body of Christ, till we all come, in the unity of the faith and of the knowledge of the Son of God, unto a perfect man." But when this has come to pass, and the saints are perfected, and are already come to the measure of the stature of the fulness of Christ, then there will be no further occasion for any of these means, whether ordinary or extraordinary. It is in this respect, very much as it is with the fruits of the field, which stand in need of tillage, and rain, and sunshine, till they are ripe and gathered in, and then they need them no more.

And as these miraculous gifts of the Spirit were but temporary with regard to those particular persons that enjoyed them, so they are but for a season with regard to the church of God taken as a collective body. These gifts are not fruits of the Spirit that were given to be continued to the church throughout all ages. They were continued in the church, or at least were granted from time to time, though not without some considerable intermissions, from the beginning of the world till the canon of the Scriptures was completed. They were bestowed on the church before the beginning of the sacred canon, that is before the book of Job and the five books of Moses were written. People had the word of God then in another way, viz.: by immediate revelation from time to time given to eminent persons who were, as it were, fathers in the church of God, and this revelation handed down from them to others by oral tradition. It was a very common thing then for the Spirit of God to communicate himself in dreams and visions, as appears by several passages in the book of Job. They had extraordinary gifts of the Spirit before the flood. God immediately and miraculously revealed himself to Adam and Eve, and so to Abel, and to Enoch, who we are informed (Jude 14) had the gift of prophecy. And so Noah had immediate revelations made to him, and he warned the old world from God; and Christ, by his Spirit speaking through him, went and preached to the spirits that are now in prison, who were sometime disobedient when once the long-suffering of God waited while the ark was preparing, 1 Pet. iii. 19, 20. And so Abraham, and Isaac, and Jacob were favored with immediate revelations; and Joseph had extraordinary gifts of the Spirit, and so had Job and his friends. From this time, there seems to have been an intermission of the extraordinary gifts of the Spirit until the time of Moses; and from his time they were continued in a succession of prophets that was kept up, though not again without some interruptions, till the time of Malachi. After that, there seems to have been a long intermission of several hundred years, till the dawn of the gospel day, when the Spirit began again to be given in his extraordinary gifts, as to Anna, and Simeon, and Zacharias, and Elizabeth, and Mary, and Joseph, and John the Baptist.

These communications of the Spirit were given to make way for him who hath the Spirit without measure, the great prophet of God, by whom the Spirit is communicated to all other prophets. And in the days of his flesh, his disciples had a measure of the miraculous gifts of the Spirit, being enabled thus to teach and to work miracles. But after the resurrection and ascension, was the most full and remarkable effusion of the Spirit in his miraculous gifts that ever took place, beginning with the day of Pentecost, after Christ had risen and ascended to heaven. And in consequence of this, not only here and there an extraordinary person was endowed with these extraordinary gifts, but they were common in the church, and so continued during the lifetime of the Apostles, or till the death of the last of them, even the Apostle John, which took place about an hundred years from the birth of Christ; so that the first hundred years of the Christian era, or the first century, was the era of miracles. But soon after that, the canon of Scripture being completed when the Apostle John had written the book of Revelation, which he wrote not long before his death, these miraculous gifts were no longer continued in the church. For there was now completed an established written revelation of the mind and will of God, wherein God had fully recorded a standing and all-sufficient rule for his church in all ages. And the Jewish church and nation being overthrown, and the Christian church and the last dispensation of the church of God being established, the miraculous gifts of the Spirit were no longer needed, and therefore they ceased; for though they had been continued in the church for so many ages, yet then they failed, and God caused them to fail because there was no further occasion for them. And so was fulfilled the saying of the text, "Whether there be prophecies, they shall fail: whether there be tongues, they shall cease; whether there be knowledge, it shall vanish away." And now there seems to be an end to all such fruits of the Spirit as these, and we have no reason to expect them any more. And as to those fruits of the Spirit that are common, such as the conviction, illumination, belief, &c., which are common both to the godly and ungodly, these are given in all ages of the church in the world; and yet with respect to the persons that have these common gifts, they will cease when they come to die; and with respect to the church of God considered collectively, they will cease, and there will be no more of them after the day of judgment. I pass, then, to show, as proposed,

IV. *That charity, or divine love, is that great fruit of the Spirit that never fails, and in which his continued and everlasting influence and indwelling in his church, shall appear and be manifest.*—We have seen that the Spirit of Christ is forever given to the church of Christ, and given that it may dwell in his saints forever, in influences that shall never fail. And therefore however many fruits of the Spirit may be but temporary, and have their limits where they fail, yet it must be that there is some way of the Spirit's influence, and some fruit of that influence, which is unfailing and eternal. And charity, or divine love is that fruit, in communicating, and nourishing, and exercising which, his unfailing and eternal influences appear. This is a fruit of the Spirit that never fails or ceases in the church of Christ, whether we consider it with respect to its particular members, or regard it as a collective body. And,

1. *We may consider the church of Christ with respect to the particular members of which it consists.*—And here it will appear that charity, or Christian love, is an unfailing fruit of the spirit. Every one of the true members of Christ's invisible church, is possessed of this fruit of the spirit in the heart. Divine or Christian love, is implanted, and dwells, and reigns there, as an everlasting fruit of the spirit, and one that never fails. It never fails in this world, but remains through all trials and oppositions, for the Apostle tells us (Romans viii. 38, 39), that nothing " shall be able to separate us from the love of God,

which is in Christ Jesus our Lord." And it ceases not when the saints come to die. When the Apostles and others of their day died and went to heaven, they left all their miraculous gifts behind them with their bodies. But they did not leave the love that was in their hearts behind them, but carried that with them to heaven, where it was gloriously perfected. Though when wicked men die, who have had the common influences of the Spirit, their gifts shall eternally cease, yet death never overthrows Christian love, that great fruit of the Spirit, in any that have it. They that have it, may and shall leave behind them many other fruits of the Spirit which they had in common with wicked men. And though they shall leave all that was common in their faith, and hope, and all that did not pertain to this divine and holy love, yet this love they shall not leave behind, but it shall go with them to eternity, and shall be perfected there, and shall live and reign with perfect and glorious dominion in their souls forever and ever. And so, again,

2. *We may consider the church of Christ collectively, or as a body.*—And here, again, it will appear that charity, or Christian love,

shall never fail. Though other fruits of the Spirit fail in it, this shall never fail. Of old, when there were interruptions of the miraculous gifts of the Spirit in the church, and when there were seasons in which no prophet or inspired person appeared that was possessed of such gifts, still there never was any total interruption of this excellent fruit or influence of the Spirit. Miraculous gifts were intermitted through the long time extending from Malachi to near the birth of Christ; but in all this time, the influence of the Spirit in keeping up divine love in the church, was never suspended. As God always had a church of saints in the world, from the first creation of the church after the fall, so this influence and fruit of his spirit never failed in it. And when after the completion of the canon of the Scriptures, the miraculous gifts of the Spirit seemed finally to have ceased and failed in the church, this influence of the Spirit in causing divine love in the hearts of his saints did not cease, but has been kept up through all ages from that time to this, and so will be to the end of the world. And at the end of the world, when the church of Christ shall be settled in its last, and most complete, and its eternal state, and all common gifts, such as convictions and illuminations, and all miraculous gifts shall be eternally at an end, yet then divine love shall not fail, but shall be brought to its most glorious perfection in every individual member of the ransomed church above. Then, in every heart, that love which now seems as but a spark, shall be kindled to a bright and glowing flame, and every ransomed soul shall be as it were in a blaze of divine and holy love, and shall remain and grow in this glorious perfection and blessedness through all eternity!

I shall give but a single reason for the truth of the doctrine which has thus been presented. And the great reason why it is so, that other fruits of the Spirit fail, and the great fruit of love remains, is, that *love is the great end of all the other fruits and gifts of the Spirit.* The principle and the exercises of divine love in the heart, and the fruits of it in the conduct, and the happiness that consists in and flows from it, these things are the great end of all the fruits of the Spirit that fail. Charity or divine love is the end, to which all the inspiration, and all the miraculous gifts that ever were in the world, are but the means.

They were only *means* of grace, but charity or divine love is *grace itself;* and not only so, but the sum of all grace. Revelation and miracles were never given for any other end, but only to promote holiness, and build up the kingdom of Christ in men's hearts; but Christian love is the sum of all holiness, and its growth is but the growth of Christ's kingdom in the soul. The extraordinary fruits of the Spirit were given for revealing and confirming the word and will of God, that men by believing might be conformed to that will; and they were valuable and good, only so far as they tended to this end. And hence when that end was obtained, and when the canon of the Scriptures, the great and powerful means of grace was completed, and the ordinances of the New Testament and of the last dispensation were fully established, the extraordinary gifts ceased and came to an end as being no further useful. Miraculous gifts being a means to a further end, they are good no further than as they tend to that end. But divine love is that end itself, and therefore remains when the means to it cease. The end is not only a good, but the highest kind of good in itself, and therefore remains for ever. So it is with respect to the common gifts of the Spirit that are given in all ages, such as illumination, conviction, &c. They have no good in themselves, and are no further good than as they tend to promote that grace and holiness which radically and summarily consist in divine love, and therefore when this end is once fully answered, there shall be an end forever of these common gifts, while divine love, which is the end of them all, shall eternally remain.

In the application of this subject, I would remark,

1. *That there seems to be no reason to think, as some have thought, that the extraordinary gifts of the Spirit are to be restored to the church in the future and glorious times of her latter day prosperity and blessedness.*—Many divines have been of the opinion, that when the latter day glory of the church which is spoken of in the word of God shall come, there will again be prophets, and men endowed with the gifts of tongues and of working miracles, as was the case in the times of the Apostles; and some now living seem to be of the same mind.

But from what the Apostle says in the text

and context, it seems as though we had no reason to imagine any such thing from what the Scriptures say of the gloriousness of those times, or because it speaks of the state of the church then as being more glorious than ever before, and as though the Spirit of God would then be poured out in more abundant measure than ever in times past. All these things may be, and yet there be no such extraordinary gifts bestowed on the church. When the Spirit of God is poured out for the purpose of producing and promoting divine love, he is poured out in a more excellent way than when he is manifested in miraculous gifts. This the Apostle expressly teaches in the latter part of the foregoing chapter, where after enumerating many miraculous gifts, he advises Christians to covet or desire the best of them, but then adds, "But yet I show unto you a more excellent way," namely, to seek the influence of the Spirit of God, working charity or divine love in the heart. Surely the Scriptures, when speaking of the future glorious state of the church as being such an excellent state, give us no reason to conclude that the Spirit of God will be poured out then in any other way than in the most excellent way.

And doubtless the most excellent way of the Spirit, is for the most excellent state of the church.

The future state of the church being so much more perfect than in previous times, does not tend to prove that then there shall be miraculous gifts, but rather the contrary. For the Apostle himself, in the text and context, speaks of these extraordinary gifts ceasing and vanishing away to give place for a kind of fruits or influences of the Spirit that are more perfect. If you do but read the text in connection with the two following verses, you will see that the reason implied why prophecy and tongues fail, and charity remains, is this, that the imperfect gives way to the perfect, and the less excellent to the more excellent; and the more excellent, he declares, is charity or love. Prophecy and miracles argue the imperfection of the state of the church, rather than its perfection. For they are means designed by God as a stay or support, or as a leading-string, if I may so say, to the church in its infancy, rather than as means adapted to it in its full growth; and as such the Apostle seems to speak of them. When the Christian church first began, after the ascension of Christ, it was in its infancy, and then it needed miracles, &c., to establish it; but being once established, and the canon of the Scriptures being completed, they ceased, which, according to the Apostle's arguing, shows their imperfection, and how much inferior they are to that fruit or influence of the Holy Spirit which is seen in divine love. Why, then, should we expect that they should be restored again, when the church is in its most perfect state? All these miraculous gifts the Apostle seems to call "childish things," in comparison with the nobler fruit of Christian love. They are adapted to the childish state of the church, while holy love is more to be expected in its full grown and manly state; and in themselves they are childish, in comparison with that holy love which will so abound in the church when it comes to its perfect stature in Christ Jesus.

Nor is the gloriousness of the future times of the church any argument for the continuance, in those times, of the miraculous gifts of the Spirit. For surely the state of the church then will not be more glorious than the heavenly state; and yet the Apostle teaches that in the heavenly state all these gifts shall be at an end, and the influence of the Spirit in producing divine love only shall remain. Nor does it appear that there shall be any need of miraculous gifts in order to the bringing about of the future glorious times of the church; for God is able to bring them about without the instrumentality of these gifts. If the Spirit of God be poured out in only his gracious influences in converting souls, and in kindling divine love in them in such measure as he may and will, this will be enough, without new revelations or miracles, to produce all the effects that need to be produced in order to the bringing in of the glorious times of which we are speaking; as we may all be convinced by the little we have seen in the late outpouring of the Spirit in this and the neighboring towns. If we needed any new rule to go by, and the common influences of the Spirit together with the word of God were insufficient, then there might be some necessity for restoring miracles. But there is no need whatever of new Scriptures being given, or of any additions being made to those we have, for they are in themselves a perfect rule for our faith and practice; and as there is no need of a new canon of Scripture, so there is no need of those miraculous gifts, the great object of which was, either to confirm the Scriptures, or to make up for the want of them when as yet they had not been given by the inspiring Spirit.

2. *The subject we have been considering should make persons exceedingly cautious how they give heed to anything that may look like a new revelation, or that may claim to be any extraordinary gift of the Spirit.*—Sometimes a person may have an impression in his mind as to something that he thinks immediately revealed to him that is to come to pass concerning himself or some of his relatives or friends; or as to something that is to come to pass that before was hid from him, and if it had not been revealed, would remain still a secret; or perhaps he thinks it has been revealed to him what is the spiritual state of some other person, or of his own soul, in some other way than by the Scriptural marks and evidences of grace in the heart. Sometimes persons imagine that they have an immediate direction from heaven to go and do this, or that, or the other thing, by impressions immediately made on their minds, or in some other way than by learning from Scripture or

reason that it is their duty. And sometimes they fancy that God immediately reveals to them by a dream what the future shall be. But all these things, if they were from God's Spirit, would be of the nature of those extraordinary gifts of the Spirit which the Apostle says do cease and are done away, and which having long since failed there is no reason to suppose that God will restore again. And if they are not from God's Spirit, they are but gross delusions. And once more,

3. *The subject teaches how greatly we should value those influences and fruits of the Spirit which are evidences of true grace in the soul, and which are all summarily included in charity, or divine love.*—This is the end and design of the Apostle in the text and context, to teach us to value this charity or love, by showing that it never fails, though all the miraculous gifts of the Spirit do fail and come to an end. This grace is the most excellent fruit of the Spirit, without which the most extraordinary and miraculous gifts are nothing. This is the great *end* to which they are but the *means;* and which is, of course, more excellent than all these means. Let us all therefore earnestly seek this blessed fruit of the Spirit,

and let us seek that it may abound in our souls; that the love of God may more and more be shed abroad in our hearts; and that we may love the Lord Jesus Christ in sincerity, and love one another as Christ hath loved us. Thus we shall possess the richest of all treasures, and the highest and most excellent of all graces. Having within us that love which is immortal in its nature, we shall have the surest evidence that our immortality will be blessed, and that our hope of eternal life is that good hope which shall never disappoint us. Love cherished in the soul on earth, will be to us the foretaste of, and the preparation for that world which is a world of love, and where the Spirit of love reigns and blesses forever.

LECTURE XVI.

HEAVEN, A WORLD OF CHARITY, OR LOVE.

'Charity never faileth. But whether there be prophecies, they shall fail; whether there be tongues, they shall cease; whether there be knowledge, it shall vanish away. For we know in part, and we prophesy in part. But when that which is perfect is come, then that which is in part shall be done away."—1 Cor. xiii. 8, 9, 10.

From the first of these verses, I have already drawn the doctrine, that that great fruit of the Spirit in which the Holy Ghost shall not only for a season, but everlastingly be communicated to the church of Christ, is charity or divine love. And now I would consider the same verse in connection with the two that follow it, and upon the three verses would make two observations.

First, That it is mentioned as one great excellence of charity, that it shall remain when all other fruits of the Spirit have failed. And,

Second, That this will come to pass in the perfect state of the church, when that which is in part shall be done away, and that which is perfect is come.

There is a two-fold *imperfect*, and so a two-fold *perfect* state of the Christian church. The church in its beginning, or in its first age, before it was strongly established in the world, and settled in its New Testament state, and before the canon of Scripture was completed, was in an imperfect state—a state, as it were, of childhood, in comparison with what it was to be in its elder and later ages when it should have reached its state of manhood, or of comparative earthly perfection. And so, again, this comparatively perfect church of Christ, so long as it remains in its militant state, that is, down to the end of time, will still be in an imperfect, and as it were in a childish state in comparison with what it will be in its heavenly state, in which latter it is comparatively in its state of manhood or perfection.

And so there is a two-fold failing of these miraculous gifts of the Spirit here mentioned. One was at the end of the first or infant age of the church, when the canon of Scripture was completed, and so there was to be no need of such gifts for the church in its latter ages, when it should have put away childish things, and come to a state of manhood before the end of the world, and when the Spirit of God should most gloriously be poured out and manifested in that love or charity, which is its greatest and everlasting fruit. And the other will be, when all the common fruits of the Spirit cease with respect to particular persons at death, and with respect to the whole church at the end of the world, while charity shall still remain in heaven, and there the Spirit of God shall be poured forth and manifested in perfect love in every heart to all eternity.

The Apostle, in the context, seems to have respect to both these states of the church, but especially to the latter. For though the glorious state of the church in its latter age on earth, will be perfect in comparison with its former state, yet its state in heaven is that state of the church to which the expressions of the Apostle seem most agreeable, when he says, " when that which is perfect is come, &c.," and " now we see through a glass darkly, but then face to face; now I know in part, but then shall I know even as also I am known." The doctrine, then, that I would draw from the text, is, that

HEAVEN IS A WORLD OF CHARITY, OR LOVE.

The Apostle speaks, in the text, of a state of the church when it is perfect in heaven, and therefore a state in which the Holy Spirit shall be more perfectly and abundantly given to the church than it is now on earth. But the way in which it shall be given when it is so abundantly poured forth, will be in that great fruit of the Spirit, holy and divine love in the hearts of all the blessed inhabitants of that world. So that the heavenly state of the church, is a state that is distinguished from its earthly state, as it is that state which God has designed especially for such a communication of his Holy Spirit, and in which it shall be given perfectly, whereas in the present state of the church it is given with great imperfection. And it is also a state in which this holy love or charity shall be, as it were, the only gift or fruit of the Spirit, as being the most perfect and glorious of all, and which being brought to perfection renders all other gifts that God was wont to bestow on his church on earth, needless. And that we may the better see how heaven is thus a world of holy love, I would consider *first*, the great cause and fountain of love that is in heaven; *second*, the objects of love that it contains; *third*, the subjects of that love; *fourth*, its principle, or the love itself; *fifth*, the excellent circumstances in which it is there exercised and expressed and enjoyed; and *sixth*, the happy effects and fruits of all this. And,

I. *The* CAUSE *and* FOUNTAIN *of love in heaven.* Here I remark that the God of love himself dwells in heaven. Heaven is the palace or presence-chamber of the high and holy One, whose name is love, and who is both the cause and source of all holy love. God, considered with respect to his essence, is everywhere: he fills both heaven and earth. But yet he is said, in some respects, to be more especially in some places than in others. He was said of old to dwell in the land of Israel, above all other lands; and in Jerusalem, above all other cities of that land; and in the temple, above all other buildings in the city; and in the holy of holies, above all other apartments of the temple; and on the mercy-seat over the ark of the covenant, above all other places in the holy of holies. But heaven is his dwelling-place above all other places in the universe; and all those places in which he was said to dwell of old, were but types of this. Heaven is a part of creation that God has built for this end, to be the place of his glorious presence, and it is his abode forever; and here will he dwell, and gloriously manifest himself to all eternity.

And this renders heaven a world of love; for God is the fountain of love, as the sun is the fountain of light. And therefore the glorious presence of God in heaven, fills heaven with love, as the sun placed in the midst of the visible heavens in a clear day, fills the world with light. The Apostle tells us that "God is love;" and therefore, seeing he is an infinite being, it follows that he is an infinite fountain of love. Seeing he is an all-sufficient being, it follows that he is a full, and overflowing, and inexhaustible fountain of love. And in that he is an unchangeable and eternal being, he is an unchangeable and eternal fountain of love.

There, even in heaven, dwells the God from whom every stream of holy love, yea, every drop that is, or ever was, proceeds. There dwells God the Father, God the Son, and God the Spirit, united as one, in infinitely dear, and incomprehensible, and mutual, and eternal love. There dwells God the Father, who is the father of mercies, and so the father of love, who so loved the world as to give his only-begotten Son to die for it. There dwells Christ, the Lamb of God, the prince of peace and of love, who so loved the world that he shed his blood, and poured out his soul unto death for men. There dwells the great Mediator, through whom all the divine love is expressed toward men, and by whom the fruits of that love have been purchased, and through whom they are communicated, and through whom love is imparted to the hearts of all God's people. There dwells Christ in both his natures, the human and the divine, sitting on the same throne with the Father. And there dwells the Holy Spirit, the spirit of divine love, in whom the very essence of God, as it were, flows out and is breathed forth in love, and by whose immediate influence all holy love is shed abroad in the hearts of all the saints on earth and in heaven. There, in heaven, this infinite fountain of love—this eternal three in one—is set open without any obstacle to hinder access to it, as it flows forever. There this glorious God is manifested and shines forth, in full glory, in beams of love. And there this glorious fountain forever flows forth in streams, yea, in rivers of love and delight, and these rivers swell, as it were, to an ocean of love, in which the souls of the ransomed may bathe with the sweetest enjoyment, and their hearts, as it were, be deluged with love! Again, I would consider heaven, with regard,

II. *To the* OBJECTS *of love that it contains.* And here I would observe three things.

1. *There are none but lovely objects in heaven.*—No odious, or unlovely, or polluted person or thing is to be seen there. There is nothing there that is wicked or unholy. "There shall in no wise enter into it anything that defileth, neither whatsoever worketh abomination," Rev. xxi. 27. And there is nothing that is deformed with any natural or moral deformity; but everything is beauteous to behold, and amiable, and excellent in itself. The God that dwells and gloriously manifests himself there, is infinitely lovely; gloriously lovely as a heavenly Father, as a divine Redeemer and as a holy sanctifier.

All the persons that belong to the blessed society of heaven are lovely. The Father of the family is lovely, and so are all his chil dren; the head of the body lovely, and so are all the members. Among the angels there are none that are unlovely; for they are all holy; and no evil angels are suffered to infest heaven as they do this world, but they are kept forever at a distance by that great gulf which is between them and the glorious world of love. And among all the company of the saints there are no unlovely persons. There are no false professors or hypocrites there; none that pretend to be saints, and yet are of an unchristian and hateful spirit or behavior, as is often the case in this world; none whose gold has not been purified from its dross; none who are not lovely in themselves and to others. There is no one object there to give offence, or at any time to give-occasion for any passion or emotion of hatred or dislike, but every object there shall forever draw forth love.

And not only shall all objects in heaven be lovely, but

2. *They shall be perfectly lovely.*—There are many things in this world that in the general are lovely, but yet are not perfectly free from that which is the contrary. There are spots on the sun; and so there are many men that are most amiable and worthy to be loved, who

yet are not without some things that are disagreeable and unlovely. Often there is in good men some defect of temper, or character, or conduct, that mars the excellence of what otherwise would seem most amiable; and even the very best of men are, on earth, imperfect. But it is not so in heaven. There shall be no pollution, or deformity, or unamiable defect of any kind, seen in any person or thing; but every one shall be perfectly pure, and perfectly lovely in heaven. That blessed world shall be perfectly bright, without any darkness; perfectly fair, without any spot; perfectly clear, without any cloud. No moral or natural defect shall ever enter there; and there nothing be seen that is sinful, or weak, or foolish; nothing, the nature or aspect of which is coarse or displeasing, or that can offend the most refined taste, or the most delicate eye. No string shall there vibrate out of tune, to cause any jar in the harmony of the music of heaven; and no note be such as to make discord in the anthems of saints and angels.

The great God who so fully manifests himself there, is perfect with an absolute and infinite perfection. The Son of God, who is the brightness of the Father's glory, appears there in the fulness of his glory, without that garb of outward meanness in which he appeared in this world. The Holy Ghost shall there be poured forth with perfect richness and sweetness, as a pure river of the water of life, clear as crystal, proceeding out of the throne of God and the Lamb. And every member of that holy and blessed society, shall be without any stain of sin, or imperfection, or weakness, or imprudence, or blemish of any kind. The whole church, ransomed and purified, shall there be presented to Christ, as a bride, clothed in fine linen, clean and white, without spot or wrinkle, or any such thing. Wherever the inhabitants of that blessed world shall turn their eyes, they shall see nothing but dignity, and beauty, and glory. The most stately cities on earth, however magnificent their buildings, yet have their foundations in the dust, and their streets dirty and defiled, and made to be trodden under foot; but the very streets of this heavenly city are of pure gold, like unto transparent glass, and its foundations are of precious stones, and its gates are pearls. And all these are but faint emblems of the purity and perfectness of those that dwell therein. And in heaven,

3. *Shall be all those objects that the saints have set their hearts upon, and which they have loved above all things while in this world.*—There they will find those things that appeared most lovely to them while they dwelt on earth; the things that met the approbation of their judgments, and captivated their affections, and drew away their souls from the most dear and pleasant of earthly objects. There they will find those things that were their delight here below, and on which they rejoiced to meditate, and with the sweet contemplation of which their minds were often entertained; and there, too, the things which they chose for their portion, and which were so dear to them that they were ready for the sake of them to undergo the severest sufferings, and to forsake even father, and mother, and kindred, and friends, and wife, and children, and life itself. All the truly great and good, all the pure and holy and excellent from this world, and it may be from every part of the universe, are constantly tending toward heaven. As the streams tend to the ocean, so all these are tending to the great ocean of infinite purity and bliss. The progress of time does but bear them on to its

blessedness; and us, if we are holy, to be united to them there. Every gem which death rudely tears away from us here, is a glorious jewel forever shining there; every Christian friend that goes before us from this world, is a ransomed spirit waiting to welcome us in heaven. There will be the infant of days that we have lost below, through grace to be found above; there the Christian father, and mother, and wife, and child, and friend, with whom we shall renew the holy fellowship of the saints, which was interrupted by death here, but shall be commenced again in the upper sanctuary, and then shall never end. There we shall have company with the patriarchs and fathers and saints of the Old and New Testaments, and those of whom the world was not worthy, with whom on earth we were only conversant by faith. And there, above all, we shall enjoy and dwell with God the Father, whom we have loved with all our hearts on earth, and with Jesus Christ our beloved Saviour, who has always been to us the chief among ten thousands and altogether lovely, and with the Holy Ghost our Sanctifier, and guide, and comforter; and shall be filled with all the fulness of the Godhead forever!

And such being the objects of love in heaven, I pass,

III. *To its subjects.* And these are the hearts in which it dwells. In every heart in heaven, love dwells and reigns. The heart of God is the original seat or subject of love. Divine love is in him, not as in a subject that receives it from another, but as in its original seat, where it is of itself. Love is in God, as light is in the sun, which does not shine by a reflected light as the moon and planets do, but by its own light, and as the great fountain of light. And from God, love flows out toward all the inhabitants of heaven. It flows out, in the first place, necessarily and infinitely, toward his only begotten Son, being poured forth, without mixture, as to an object that is infinite, and so fully adequate to all the fulness of a love that is infinite. And this infinite love is infinitely exercised toward him. Not only does the fountain send forth streams to this object, but the very fountain itself wholly and altogether goes out toward him. And the Son of God is not only the infinite object of love, but he is also an infinite subject of it. He is not only the beloved of the Father, but he infinitely loves him. The infinite essential love of God, is, as it were, an infinite and eternal mutual holy energy between the Father and the Son: a pure and holy act, whereby the Deity becomes, as it were, one infinite and unchangeable emotion of love proceeding from both the Father and the Son. This divine love has its seat in the Deity, as it is exercised within the Deity, or in God toward himself.

But this love is not confined to such exercises as these. It flows out in innumerable streams toward all the created inhabitants of heaven, to all the saints and angels there. The love of God the Father flows out toward Christ the head, and to all the members, through him in whom they were beloved before the foundation of the world, and in whom the Father's love was expressed toward them in time by his death and sufferings, as it now is fully manifested in heaven. And the saints and angels are secondarily the subjects of holy love, not as those in whom it is as in an original seat, as light is in the sun, but as it is in the planets that shine only by reflected light. And the light of their love is reflected in the first place, and chiefly, back to its great source. As God has given the saints and angels, love, so their love is chiefly exercised towards God, its fountain, as is most reasonable. They all love God with a supreme love. There is no enemy of God in heaven; but all, as his children, love him as their father. They are all united, with one mind, to breathe forth their whole souls in love to God their eternal Father, and to Jesus Christ their common Redeemer, and head, and friend.

Christ loves all his saints in heaven. His love flows out to his whole church there, and to every individual member of it. And they all, with one heart and one soul, unite in love to their common Redeemer. Every heart is wedded to this holy and spiritual husband, and all rejoice in him, while the angels join them in their love. And the angels and saints all love each other. All the members of the glorious society of heaven are sincerely united. There is not a single secret or open enemy among them all. Not a heart is there that is not full of love, and not a solitary inhabitant that is not beloved by all the others. And as all are lovely, so all see each other's loveliness with full complacence and delight. Every soul goes out in love to every other; and among all the blessed inhabitants, love is mutual, and full, and eternal. I pass next, to speak, as proposed,

IV. *Of the principle of love in heaven.* And by this I mean the love itself that fills and blesses the heavenly world, and which may be noticed both as to its nature and degree. And,

1. *As to its nature.*—In its nature, this love is altogether holy and divine. Most of the love that there is in this world, is of an unhallowed nature. But the love that has place in heaven, is not carnal but spiritual. It does not proceed from corrupt principles or selfish motives, nor is it directed to mean and vile purposes and ends. As opposed to all this, it is a pure flame, directed by holy motives, and aiming at no ends inconsistent with God's glory and the happiness of the universe. The saints in heaven love God for his own sake, and each other for God's sake, and for the sake of the relation that they have to him, and the image of God that is upon them. All their love is pure and holy. We may notice this love, also,

2. *As to its degree.*—And in degree it is perfect. The love that dwells in the heart of God is perfect, with an absolutely infinite and

divine perfection. The love of angels and saints to God and Christ, is perfect in its kind, or with such a perfection as is proper to their nature. It is perfect with a sinless perfection, and perfect in that it is commensurate to the capacities of their nature. So it is said in the text, that when that which is perfect is come, that which is in part shall be done away. Their love shall be without any remains of any contrary principle, having no pride or selfishness to interrupt it or hinder its exercises. Their hearts shall be full of love. That which was in the heart on earth as but a grain of mustard seed, shall be as a great tree in heaven. The soul that in this world had only a little spark of divine love in it, in heaven shall be as it were turned into a bright and ardent flame, like the sun in its fullest brightness when it has no spot upon it.

In heaven there shall be no remaining enmity, or distaste, or coldness, or deadness of heart towards God and Christ. Not the least remainder of any principle of envy shall exist to be exercised toward angels or other beings who are superior in glory; nor shall there be aught like contempt or slighting of those who are inferiors. Those that have a lower station in glory than others, suffer no diminution of their own happiness by seeing others above them in glory. On the contrary, all the members of that blessed society rejoice in each other's happiness, for the love of benevolence is perfect in them all. Every one has not only a sincere, but a perfect good-will to every other. Sincere and strong love is greatly gratified and delighted in the prosperity of the beloved object; and if the love be perfect, the greater the prosperity of the beloved is, the more is the lover pleased and delighted; for the prosperity of the beloved, is, as it were, the food of love, and therefore the greater that prosperity, the more richly is love feasted. The love of benevolence is delighted in beholding the prosperity of another, as the love of complacence is, in beholding the beauty or perfection of another. So that the superior prosperity of those that are higher in glory, is so far from being a hindrance to the degree of love felt toward them, that it is an addition to it, or a part of it.

There is undoubtedly an inconceivably pure, sweet, and fervent love between the saints in glory; and that love is in proportion to the perfection and amiableness of the objects beloved, and therefore it must necessarily cause delight in them when they see that the happiness and glory of others are in proportion to their amiableness, and so in proportion to their love to them. Those that are highest in glory, are those that are highest in holiness, and therefore are those that are most beloved by all the saints; for they most love those that are most holy, and so they will all rejoice in their being the most happy. And it will not be a grief to any of the saints to see those that are higher than themselves in holiness and likeness to God, more loved also than themselves, for all shall have as much love as they desire, and as great manifestations of love as they can bear; and so all shall be fully satisfied; and when there is perfect satisfaction, there can be no reason for envy. And there will be no temptation for any to envy those that are above them in glory on account of the latter being lifted up with pride, for there will be no pride in heaven. We are not to conceive that those who are more holy and happy than others in heaven, will be elated and lifted up in their spirit above others, for those who are above others in holiness, will be superior to them in humility. The saints that are highest in glory, will be the lowest in humbleness of mind, for their superior humility is part of their superior holiness. Though all are perfectly free from pride, yet as some will have greater degrees of divine knowledge than others, and larger capacities to see more of the divine perfections, so they will see more of their own comparative littleness and nothingness, and therefore will be lowest and most abased in humility.

And besides, the inferior in glory will have no temptation to envy those that are higher than themselves, for those that are highest will not only be more loved by the lower for their higher holiness, but they will also have more of the spirit of love to others, and so will love those that are below them more than if their own capacity and elevation were less. They that are highest in degree in glory, will be of the highest capacity; and so having the greatest knowledge, will see most of God's loveliness, and consequently will have love to God and love to the saints most abounding in their hearts. And on this account those that are lower in glory will not envy those that are above them, because they will be most beloved by those that are highest in glory. And the superior in glory will be so far from slighting those that are inferior, that they will have most abundant love to them—greater degrees of love in proportion to their superior knowledge and happiness. The higher any are in glory, the more they are like Christ in this respect, so that the love of the higher to the lower will be greater than the love of the equals of the latter to them. And what puts it beyond all doubt that seeing the superior happiness of others will not be a damp to the happiness of the inferior, is this, that their superior happiness consists in their greater humility, and in their greater love to them, and to God, and to Christ, than the inferior, will have in themselves. Such will be the sweet and perfect harmony among the heavenly saints, and such the perfect love reigning in every heart toward every other, without limit, or alloy, or interruption; and no envy, or malice, or revenge, or contempt, or selfishness shall ever enter there, but all such feelings shall be kept as far away, as sin is from holiness, and as hell is from heaven! Let us next consider,

V. *The excellent circumstances in which*

love shall be exercised and expressed, and enjoyed in heaven. And

1. *Love in heaven is always mutual.*—It is always met with answerable returns of love; with returns that are proportioned to its exercise. Such returns, love always seeks; and just in proportion as any person is beloved, in the same proportion is his love desired and prized. And in heaven this desire of love, or this fondness for being loved, will never fail of being satisfied. No inhabitants of that blessed world will ever be grieved with the thought that they are slighted by those that they love, or that their love is not fully and fondly returned.

As the saints will love God with an inconceivable ardency of heart, and to the utmost of their capacity, so they will know that he has loved them from all eternity, and still loves them, and will continue to love them forever. And God will then gloriously manifest himself to them, and they shall know that all that happiness and glory which they are possessed of, are the fruits of his love. And with the same ardor and fervency will the saints love the Lord Jesus Christ; and their love will be accepted; and they shall know that he has loved them with a faithful, yea, even with a dying love. They shall then be more sensible than now they are, what great love it manifested in Christ that he should lay down his life for them; and then will Christ open to their view the great fountain of love in his heart for them, beyond all that they ever saw before. Hereby the love of the saints to God and Christ, is seen to be reciprocated, and that declaration fulfilled, "I love them that love me;" and though the love of God to them cannot properly be called the return of love, because he loved them first, yet the sight of his love, will, on that very account, the more fill them with joy, and admiration, and love to him.

The love of the saints, one to another, will always be mutual and reciprocated, though we cannot suppose that every one will, in all respects, be equally beloved. Some of the saints are more beloved of God than others, even on earth. The angel told Daniel that he was "a man greatly beloved" (Dan. ix. 23); and Luke is called "the beloved physician" (Col. iv. 14); and John, "the disciple whom Jesus loved" (John xix. 26). And so, doubtless, those that have been most eminent in fidelity and holiness, and that are highest in glory, are most beloved by Christ in heaven: and doubtless those saints that are most beloved of Christ, and that are nearest to him in glory, are most beloved by all the other saints. Thus we may conclude that such saints as the Apostle Paul, and the Apostle John, are more beloved by the saints in heaven than other saints of lower rank. They are more beloved by lower saints than those of equal rank with themselves. But then there are answerable returns of love in these cases; for as such are more beloved by all other saints, so they are fuller of love to other saints. The heart of Christ, the great head of all the saints, is more full of love than the heart of any saint can be. He loves all the saints, far more than any of them love each other. But the more any saint is loved of him, the more is that saint like him, in this respect, that the fuller his heart is of love.

2. *The joy of heavenly love shall never be interrupted or damped by jealousy.*—Heavenly lovers will have no doubt of the love of each other. They shall have no fear that the declarations and professions of love are hypocritical; but shall be perfectly satisfied of the sincerity

and strength of each other's affection, as much as if there were a window in every breast, so that everything in the heart could be seen. There shall be no such thing as flattery or dissimulation in heaven, but there perfect sincerity shall reign through all, and in all. Every one will be just what he seems to be, and will really have all the love that he seems to have. It will not be as in this world, where comparatively few things are what they seem to be, and where professions are often made lightly, and without meaning; but there every expression of love shall come from the bottom of the heart, and all that is professed shall be really and truly felt.

The saints shall know that God loves them, and they shall never doubt the greatness of his love, and they shall have no doubt of the love of all their fellow-inhabitants in heaven. And they shall not be jealous of the constancy of each other's love. They shall have no suspicion that the love which others have felt toward them is abated, or in any degree withdrawn from themselves for the sake of some rival, or by reason of anything in themselves which they suspect is disagreeable to others, or through any inconstancy in their own hearts or the hearts of others. Nor will they be in the least afraid that the love of any will ever be abated toward them. There shall be no such thing as inconstancy and unfaithfulness in heaven, to molest and disturb the friendship of that blessed society. The saints shall have no fear that the love of God will ever abate towards them, or that Christ will not continue always to love them with unabated tenderness and affection. And they shall have no jealousy one of another, but shall know that by divine grace the mutual love that exists between them, shall never decay or change.

3. *There shall be nothing within themselves, to clog or hinder the saints in heaven, in the exercises and expressions of love.*—In this world the saints find much to hinder them in this respect. They have a great deal of dulness and heaviness. They carry about with them a heavy-moulded body—a clod of earth—a mass of flesh and blood that is not fitted to be the organ for a soul inflamed with high exercises of divine love; but which is found a great clog and hindrance to the spirit, so that they cannot express their love to God as they would, and cannot be so active and lively in it as they desire. Often they fain would fly,

but they are held down as with a dead weight upon their wings. Fain would they be active, and mount up as a flame of fire, but they find themselves, as it were, hampered and chained down, so that they cannot do as their love inclines them to do. Love disposes them to burst forth in praise, but their tongues are not obedient; they want words to express the ardency of their souls, and cannot order their speech by reason of darkness, Job xxxvii. 19; and often for want of expressions, they are forced to content themselves with groanings that cannot be uttered, Rom. viii. 26.

But in heaven they shall have no such hindrance. There they will have no dulness and unwieldiness, and no corruption of heart to war against divine love, and hinder its expressions; and there no earthly body shall clog with its heaviness the heavenly flame. The saints in heaven shall have no difficulty in expressing all their love. Their souls being on fire with holy love, shall not be like a fire pent up, but like a flame uncovered and at liberty. Their spirits being winged with love, shall have no weight upon them to hinder their flight. There shall be no want of strength or activity, nor any want of words wherewith to praise the object of their affection. Nothing shall hinder them from communing with God, and praising and serving him just as their love inclines them to do. Love naturally desires to express itself, and in heaven the love of the saints shall be at full liberty to express itself as it desires, whether it be towards God, or to created beings.

4. *In heaven love will be expressed with perfect decency and wisdom.*—Many in this world that are sincere in their hearts, and have indeed a principle of true love to God and their neighbor, yet have not discretion to guide them in the manner and circumstances of expressing it. Their intentions, and so their speeches, are good, but often not suitably timed, or discreetly ordered as to circumstances, but are attended with an indiscreetness that greatly obscures the loveliness of grace in the eyes of others. But in heaven, the amiableness and excellence of their love shall not be obscured by any such means. There shall be no indecent, or unwise, or dissonant speeches or actions—no foolish and sentimental fondness—no needless officiousness—no low or sinful propensities of passion—and no such thing as affections clouding or

deluding reason, or going before or against it. But wisdom and discretion shall be as perfect in the saints as love is, and every expression of their love shall be attended with the most amiable and perfect decency, and discretion, and wisdom.

5. *There shall be nothing external in heaven, to keep its inhabitants at a distance from each other, or to hinder their most perfect enjoyment of each other's love.*—There shall be no wall of separation in heaven to keep the saints asunder, nor shall they be hindered from the full and complete enjoyment of each other's love by distance of habitation; for they shall all be together, as one family, in their heavenly Father's house. Nor shall there be any want of full acquaintance to hinder the greatest possible intimacy; and much less shall there be any misunderstanding between them, or misinterpreting things that are said or done by each other. There shall be no disunion through difference of temper, or manners, or circumstances, or from various opinions, or interests, or feelings, or alliances, but all shall be united in the same interests, and all alike allied to the same Saviour, and all employed

in the same business, serving and glorifying the same God.

6. *In heaven all shall be united together in very near and dear relations.*—Love always seeks a near relation to the one who is beloved; and in heaven they shall all be nearly allied and related to each other. All shall be nearly related to God the supreme object of their love, for they shall all be his children. And all shall be nearly related to Christ, for he shall be the head of the whole society, and the husband of the whole church of saints, all of whom together shall constitute his spouse. And they shall all be related to each other as brethren, for all will be but one society, or rather but one family, and all members of the household of God. And more than this,

7. *In heaven all shall have property and ownership in each other.*—Love seeks to have the beloved its own; and divine love rejoices in saying, "My beloved is mine, and I am his." And in heaven all shall not only be related one to another, but they shall be each other's, and belong to each other. The saints shall be God's. He brings them home to himself in glory, as that part of the creation that he has chosen for his peculiar treasure. And

on the other hand, God shall be theirs, made over to them in an everlasting covenant in this world, and now they shall be forever in full possession of him as their portion. And so the saints shall be Christ's, for he has bought them with a price; and he shall be theirs, for he that gave himself for them, will have given himself to them; and in the bonds of mutual and everlasting love, Christ and the saints will have given themselves to each other. And as God and Christ shall be the saints', so the angels shall be their angels, as is intimated in Matt. xviii. 10; and the saints shall be one another's, for the Apostle speaks (2. Cor. viii. 5) of the saints in his days, as first giving themselves to the Lord, and then to one another by the will of God; and if this is done on earth, it will be more perfectly done in heaven.

8. *In heaven they shall enjoy each other's love in perfect and uninterrupted prosperity.*— What often on earth alloys the pleasure and sweetness of worldly friendship, is, that though persons live in love, yet they live in poverty, or meet with great difficulties and sore afflictions, whereby they are grieved for themselves and for one another. For though in such cases, love and friendship in some respects

lighten the burden to be borne, yet in other respects they rather add to its weight, because those that love each other become, by their very love, sharers in each other's afflictions, so that each has not only his own trials to bear, but those also of his afflicted friends. But there shall be no adversity in heaven, to give occasion for a pitiful grief of spirit, or to molest or disturb those who are heavenly friends, in the enjoyment of each other's friendship. But they shall enjoy one another's love in the greatest prosperity, and in glorious riches and comfort, and in the highest honor and dignity, reigning together in the heavenly kingdom—inheriting all things, sitting on thrones, all wearing crowns of life, and being made kings and priests unto God forever.

Christ and his disciples while on earth were often together in affliction and trial, and they kept up and manifested the strongest love and friendship to each other under great and sore sufferings. And now in heaven they enjoy each other's love in immortal glory, all sorrow and sighing having forever fled away. Both Christ and his saints were acquainted with much sorrow and grief in this world, though Christ had the greatest share, being peculiarly a "man of sorrows." But in heaven they shall sit together in heavenly places, where sorrow and grief shall never more be known. And so all the saints will enjoy each other's love in heaven, in a glory and prosperity in comparison with which the wealth and thrones of the greatest earthly princes, are but as sordid poverty and destitution. So that as they love one another, they have not only their own but each other's prosperity to rejoice in, and are by love made partakers of each others' blessedness and glory. Such is the love of every saint to every other saint, that it makes the glory which he sees other saints enjoy, as it were, his own. He so rejoices that they enjoy such glory, that it is in some respects to him as if he himself enjoyed it in his own personal experience.

9. *In heaven all things shall conspire to promote their love, and give advantage for mutual enjoyment.*—There shall be none there to tempt any to dislike or hatred; no busybodies, or malicious adversaries, to make misrepresentations, or create misunderstandings, or spread abroad any evil reports, but every being and every thing shall conspire to promote love, and the full enjoyment of love. Heaven

itself, the place of habitation, is a garden of pleasures, a heavenly paradise, fitted in all respects for an abode of heavenly love; a place where they may have sweet society and perfect enjoyment of each other's love. None are unsocial or distant from each other. The petty distinctions of this world do not draw lines in the society of heaven, but all meet in the equality of holiness and of holy love.

All things in heaven do, also, remarkably show forth the beauty and loveliness of God and Christ, and have the brightness and sweetness of divine love upon them. The very light that shines in and fills that world, is the light of love, for it is the shining of the glory of the Lamb of God, that most wonderful influence of lamb-like meekness and love that fills the heavenly Jerusalem with light. "The city had no need of the sun, neither of the moon to shine in it; for the glory of God did lighten it, and the Lamb is the light thereof," Rev. xxi. 23. The glory that is about him that reigns in heaven, is so radiant and sweet that it is compared (Rev. iv. 3) to "a rainbow round about the throne, in sight like unto an emerald;" and it is the rainbow that is so often used in the Old Testament, as the fit token of God's love and grace manifested in his covenant. The light of the New Jerusalem, which is the light of God's glory, is said to be like a jasper stone, clear as crystal (Rev. xxi. 11), thus signifying the greatest preciousness and beauty; and as to its continuance, it is said there is no night there, but only an endless and glorious day. This suggests, once more, that,

10. *The inhabitants of heaven shall know that they shall forever be continued in the perfect enjoyment of each other's love.*—They shall know that God and Christ shall be forever with them as their God and portion, and that his love shall be continued and fully manifested forever, and that all their beloved fellow-saints shall forever live with them in glory, and shall forever keep up the same love in their hearts which they now have. And they shall know that they themselves shall ever live to love God, and love the saints, and to enjoy their love in all its fulness and sweetness forever. They shall be in no fear of any end to this happiness, or of any abatement from its fulness and blessedness, or that they shall ever be weary of its exercises and expressions, or cloyed with its enjoyments, or

that the beloved objects shall ever grow old, or disagreeable, so that their love shall at last die away. All in heaven shall flourish in immortal youth and freshness. Age will not there diminish any one's beauty or vigor; and there love shall abide in every one's heart, as a living spring perpetually springing up in the soul, or as a flame that never dies away. And the holy pleasure of this love shall be as a river that is forever flowing, clear and full, and increasing continually. The heavenly paradise of love shall always be kept as in a perpetual spring, without autumn or winter, where no frosts shall blight, or leaves decay and fall, but where every plant shall be in perpetual freshness and bloom, and fragrance, and beauty, always springing forth, and always blossoming, and always bearing fruit. The leaf of the righteous shall not wither, Ps. i. 3. And in the midst of the streets of heaven, and on either side of the river, grows the tree of life, which bears twelve manner of fruits, and yields her fruit every month, Rev. xxii. 2. Everything in the heavenly world shall contribute to the joy of the saints, and every joy of heaven shall be eternal. No night shall settle down with its darkness upon the brightness of their everlasting day.

Having thus noticed many of the blessed circumstances with which love in heaven is exercised, and expressed, and enjoyed, I proceed as proposed to speak, lastly,

VI. *Of the blessed effects and fruits of this love, as exercised and enjoyed in these circumstances.*—And of the many blessed fruits of it, I would at this time mention but two.

1. *The most excellent and perfect behavior of all the inhabitants of heaven toward God and each other.*—Charity or divine love is the sum of all good principles, and therefore the fountain whence proceed all amiable and excellent actions. And as in heaven this love will be perfect, to the perfect exclusion of all sin consisting in enmity against God and fellow-creatures, so the fruit of it will be a most perfect behavior toward all. Hence life in heaven will be without the least sinful failure or error. None shall ever come short, or turn aside from the way of holiness in the least degree, but every feeling and action shall be perfect in itself and in all its circumstances. Every part of their behavior shall be holy and

divine in matter, and form, and spirit, and end.

We know not particularly how the saints in heaven shall be employed; but in general we know that they are employed in praising and serving God; and this they will do perfectly, being influenced by such a love as we have been considering. And we have reason to think that they are so employed as in some way to be subservient under God, to each other's happiness, for they are represented in the Scriptures as united together in one society which, it would seem, can be for no other purpose but mutual subserviency and happiness. And they are thus mutually subservient by a most excellent and perfectly amiable behavior one towards another, as a fruit of their perfect love one to another. And even if they are not confined to this society, but if any or all of them are at times sent on errands of duty or mercy to distant worlds, or employed, as some suppose them to be, as ministering spirits to friends in this world, they are still led by the influence of love to conduct, in all their behavior, in such a manner as is well pleasing to God, and thus conducive to their own and others' happiness. The other fruit of love as exercised in such circumstances, is,

2. *Perfect tranquillity and joy in heaven.*—Charity, or holy and humble Christian love, is a principle of wonderful power to give ineffable quietness and tranquillity to the soul. It banishes all disturbance, and sweetly composes and brings rest to the spirit, and makes all divinely calm and sweet and happy. In that soul where divine love reigns and is in lively exercise, nothing can cause a storm, or even gather threatening clouds.

There are many principles contrary to love, that make this world like a tempestuous sea. Selfishness, and envy, and revenge, and jealousy, and kindred passions keep life on earth in a constant tumult, and make it a scene of confusion and uproar, where no quiet rest is to be enjoyed except in renouncing this world and looking to another. But O! what rest is there in that world which the God of peace and love fills with his own gracious presence, and in which the Lamb of God lives and reigns, filling it with the brightest and sweetest beams of his love; where there is nothing to disturb or offend, and no being or object to be seen that is not surrounded with perfect amiableness and sweetness ; where the saints shall find and enjoy all that they love, and so be perfectly satisfied ; where there is no enemy and no enmity, but perfect love in every heart and to every being ; where there is perfect harmony among all the inhabitants, no one envying another, but every one rejoicing in the happiness of every other; where all their love is humble, and holy, and perfectly Christian, without the least carnality or impurity ; where love is always mutual and reciprocated to the full ; where there is no hypocrisy or dissembling, but perfect simplicity and sincerity ; where there is no treachery, or unfaithfulness, or inconstancy, or jealousy in any form; where there is no clog or hindrance to the exercises or expressions of love, no imprudence or indecency in expressing it, and no influence of folly or indiscretion in any word or deed ; where there is no separation wall, and no misunderstanding or strangeness, but full acquaintance and perfect intimacy in all ; where there is no division through different opinions or interests, but where all in that glorious and loving society shall be most nearly and divinely related, and each shall belong to every other, and all shall enjoy each other in perfect prosperity and riches, and honor, without any sickness, or grief, or persecution, or sorrow, or any enemy to molest them, or any busybody to create jealousy or misunderstanding, or mar the perfect, and holy, and blessed peace that reigns in heaven! And all this in the garden of God—in the paradise of love, where everything is filled with love, and everything conspires to promote and kindle it, and keep up its flame, and nothing ever interrupts it, but everything has been fitted by an all-wise God for its full enjoyment under the greatest advantages forever! And all, too, where the beauty of the beloved objects shall never fade, and love shall never grow weary or decay, but the soul shall more and more rejoice in love forever!

O! what tranquillity will there be in such a world as this! And who can express the fulness and blessedness of this peace! What a calm is this! How sweet, and holy, and joyous! What a haven of rest to enter, after having passed through the storms and tempests of this world, in which pride, and selfishness, and envy, and malice, and scorn, and contempt, and contention, and vice are as waves of a restless ocean, always rolling, and often dashed about in violence and fury! What a Canaan of rest to come to, after going through this waste and howling wilderness full of snares, and pitfalls, and poisonous serpents, where no rest could be found!

And O! what joy will there be, springing up in the hearts of the saints, after they have passed through their wearisome pilgrimage, to be brought to such a paradise as this! Here is joy unspeakable indeed, and full of glory—joy that is humble, holy, enrapturing, and divine in its perfection! Love is always a sweet principle; and especially divine love. This, even on earth, is a spring of sweetness; but in heaven, it shall become a stream, a river, an ocean! All shall stand about the God of glory, who is the great fountain of love, opening, as it were, their very souls to be filled with those effusions of love that are poured forth from his fulness, just as the flowers on the earth, in the bright and joyous days of spring, open their bosoms to the sun to be filled with his light and warmth, and to flourish in beauty and fragrancy under his cheering rays.

Every saint in heaven is as a flower in that garden of God, and holy love is the fragrance and sweet odor that they all send forth, and with which they fill the bowers of that paradise above. Every soul, there, is as a note in some concert of delightful music, that sweetly harmonizes with every other note, and all together blend in the most rapturous strains in praising God and the Lamb forever. And so all help each other, to their utmost, to express the love of the whole society to its glorious father and head, and to pour back love into the great fountain of love whence they are supplied and filled with love, and blessedness, and glory. And thus they will love, and reign in love, and in that godlike joy that is its blessed fruit, such as eye hath not seen, nor ear heard, nor hath ever entered into the heart of man in this world to conceive; and thus in the full sunlight of the throne, enraptured with joys that are forever increasing and yet forever full, they shall live and reign with God and Christ forever and ever!

In the application of this subject, I remark,

1. *If heaven be such a world as has been described, then we may see a reason why contention and strife tend to darken our evidence of fitness for its possession.*—Experience teaches that this is the effect of contention.

When principles of malignity and ill-will prevail among God's people, as they sometimes do through the remaining corruption of their hearts, and they get into a contentious spirit or are engaged in any strife whether public or private, and their spirits are filled with opposition to their neighbors in any matter whatever, their former evidences for heaven seem to become dim, or die away, and they are in darkness about their spiritual state, and do not find that comfortable and satisfying hope that they used to enjoy.

And so when converted persons get into ill frames in their families, the consequence commonly if not universally, is, that they live without much of a comfortable sense of heavenly things, or any lively hope of heaven. They do not enjoy much of that spiritual calm and sweetness that those do who live in love and peace. They have not that help from God, and that communion with him, and that near intercourse with heaven in prayer, that others have. The Apostle seems to speak of contention in families as having this influence. His language is (1 Pet. iii. 7), " Likewise ye husbands dwell with them" (your wives), "according to knowledge, giving honor unto the wife as unto the weaker vessel, and as being heirs together of the grace of life, that your prayers be not hindered." Here he intimates that discord in families tends to hinder Christians in their prayers. And what Christian, that has made the sad experiment, has not done it to his sorrow, and in his own experience does not bear witness to the truth of the Apostle's intimation.

Why it is so, that contention has this effect of hindering spiritual exercises and comforts and hopes, and of destroying the sweet hope of that which is heavenly, we may learn from the doctrine we have considered. For heaven being a world of love, it follows that when we have the least exercise of love, and the most of a contrary spirit, then we have the least of heaven, and are farthest from it in the frame of our mind. Then we have the least of the exercise of that wherein consists a conformity to heaven, and a preparation for it, and what tends to it; and so, necessarily, we must have least evidence of our title to heaven, and be farthest from the comfort which such evidence affords. We may see, again, from this subject,

2. *How happy those are who are entitled to*

heaven.—There are some persons living on earth, to whom the happiness of the heavenly world belongs as much, yea much more than any man's earthly estate belongs to himself. They have a part and interest in this world of love, and have a proper right and title to it, for they are of the number of those of whom it is written (Rev. xxii. 14), " Blessed are they that do his commandments, that they may have right to the tree of life, and may enter in through the gates into the city." And doubtless there are such persons here, amongst us. And O! how happy are all such, entitled as they are to an interest in such a world as heaven! Surely they are the blessed of the earth, and the fulness of their blessedness, no language can describe, no words express. But here some may be ready to say, " Without doubt they are happy persons that have a title to such a blessed world, and are soon to enter on the eternal possession of its joys. But who are these persons? How shall they be known, and by what marks may they be distinguished?" In answer to such an inquiry, I would mention three things that belong to their character:—

First, They are those that have had the

principle or seed of the same love that reigns in heaven, implanted in their hearts, in this world, in the work of regeneration.—They are not those who have no other principles in their hearts than natural principles, or such as they have by their first birth, for "that which is born of the flesh is flesh." But they are those who have been the subjects of the new birth, or who have been born of the Spirit. A glorious work of the Spirit of God has been wrought in their hearts, renewing them by bringing down from heaven, as it were, some of the light and some of the holy, pure flame that is in that world of love, and giving it place in them. Their hearts are a soil in which this heavenly seed has been sown, and in which it abides and grows. And so they are changed; and from being earthly, have become heavenly in their dispositions. The love of the world is mortified and the love of God implanted. Their hearts are drawn to God and Christ, and for their sakes flow out to the saints in humble and spiritual love. "Being born, not of corruptible seed, but of incorruptible," 1 Pet. i. 23, "Which were born not of blood, nor of the will of the flesh, nor of the will of man, but of God," John i. 13.

Second, They are those who have freely chosen the happiness that flows from the exercise and enjoyment of such love as is in heaven, above all other conceivable happiness.— They see and understand so much of this as to know that it is the best good. They do not merely yield that it is so from rational arguments that may be offered for it, and by which they are convinced that it is so, but they know it is so from what little they have tasted of it. It is the happiness of love, and the beginning of a life of such love, holy, humble, divine and heavenly love. Love to God, and love to Christ, and love to saints for God and Christ's sake, and the enjoyment of the fruits of God's love in holy communion with God, and Christ, and with holy persons, this is what they have a relish for; and such is their renewed nature that such happiness suits their disposition and appetite and wishes above all other things; and not only above all things that they have, but above all that they can conceive it possible that they could have. The world does not afford anything like it. They have chosen this before all things else, and chosen it freely. Their souls go out after it more than after everything else, and their hearts are more eager in pursuit of it. They have chosen it not merely because they have met with sorrow, and are in such low and afflicted circumstances that they do not expect much from the world, but because their hearts were so captivated by this good that they chose it for its own sake before all worldly good, even if they could have ever so much of the latter, and enjoy it ever so long.

Third, They are those who from the love that is in them, are in heart and life, in principle and practice, struggling after holiness.— Holy love makes them long for holiness. It is a principle that thirsts after growth. It is in imperfection, and in a state of infancy in this world, and it desires growth. It has much to struggle with. In the heart in this world there are many opposite principles and influences; and it struggles after greater oneness, and more liberty, and more free exercise, and better fruit. The great strife and struggle of the new man, is after holiness. His heart struggles after it, for he has an interest in heaven, and therefore he struggles with that sin that would keep him from it. He is full of ardent desires, and breathings, and longings, and strivings to be holy. And his hands struggle as well as his heart. He strives in his practice. His life is a life of sincere and earnest endeavor to be universally and increasingly holy. He feels that he is not holy enough, but far from it; and he desires to be nearer perfection, and more like those who are in heaven. And this is one reason why he longs to be in heaven, that he may be perfectly holy. And the great principle which leads him thus to struggle, is love. It is not only fear; but it is love to God, and love to Christ, and love to holiness. Love is a holy fire within him, and like any other flame which is in a degree pent up, it will and does struggle for liberty; and this its struggling, is the struggle for holiness.

3. *What has been said on this subject may well awaken and alarm the impenitent.*—And,

First, By putting them in mind of their misery, in that they have no portion or right in this world of love.—You have heard what has been said of heaven, what kind of glory and blessedness is there, and how happy the saints and angels are in that world of perfect love. But consider that none of this belongs to you. When you hear of such things, you hear of that in which you have no interest. No such person as you, a wicked hater of God and Christ, and one that is under the power of a spirit of enmity against all that is good, shall ever enter there. Such as you are, never belong to the faithful Israel of God, and shall never enter their heavenly rest. It may be said to you, as Peter said to Simon (Acts viii. 21), "Thou hast neither part nor lot in this matter, for thy heart is not right in the sight of God;" and as Nehemiah said to Sanballat and his associates (Neh. ii. 20), "You have no portion, nor right, nor memorial in Jerusalem." If such a soul as yours should be admitted into heaven, that world of love, how nauseous would it be to those blest spirits whose souls are as a flame of love; and how would it discompose that loving and blessed society, and put everything in confusion! It would make heaven no longer heaven, if such souls should be admitted there. It would change it from a world of love to a world of hatred, and pride, and envy, and malice, and revenge, as this world is! But this shall never be; and the only alternative is, that such as you shall be shut out with "dogs, and sorcerers, and whoremongers, and murderers, and idolaters, and whosoever loveth and maketh a lie," Rev. xxii. 15; that is, with all that is vile, and unclean, and unholy. And this subject may well awaken and alarm the impenitent.

Secondly, By showing them that they are in danger of hell, which is a world of hatred.— There are three worlds. One is this, which is an intermediate world—a world in which good and evil are so mixed together as to be a sure sign that this world is not to continue forever. Another is heaven, a world of love, without any hatred. And the other is hell, a world of hatred, where there is no love, which is the world to which all of you who are in a Christless state properly belong. This last is the world where God manifests his displeasure and wrath, as in heaven he manifests his love. Everything in hell is hateful. There is not one solitary object there, that is not odious and detestable, horrid and hateful. There is no person or thing to be seen there, that is amiable or lovely; nothing that is pure, or holy, or pleasant, but everything abominable and odious. There are no beings there but devils, and damned spirits that are like devils. Hell is, as it were, a vast den of poisonous, hissing serpents; the old serpent, who is the devil and Satan, and with him all his hateful brood.

In that dark world there are none but those whom God hates with a perfect and everlasting hatred. He exercises no love, and extends no mercy to any one object there, but pours out upon them horrors without mixture. All things in the wide universe that are hateful shall be gathered together in hell, as in a vast receptacle provided on purpose that the universe which God has made may be cleansed of its filthiness by casting it all into this great sink of wickedness and woe. It is a world prepared on purpose for the expression of God's wrath. He has made hell for this; and he has no other use for it but there to testify forever his hatred of sin and sinners, where there is no token of love or mercy. There is nothing there but what shows forth the divine indignation and wrath. Every object shows forth wrath. It is a world all overflowed with a deluge of wrath, as it were, with a deluge of liquid fire, so as to be called a lake of fire and brimstone, and the second death.

There are none in hell but what have been haters of God, and so have procured his wrath and hatred on themselves; and there they shall continue to hate him forever. No love to God will ever be felt in hell; but every one there perfectly hates him, and so will continue to hate him; and without any restraint will express their hatred to him, blaspheming and raging against him, while they gnaw their tongues for pain. And though they all join together in their enmity and opposition to God, yet there is no union or friendliness among themselves: they agree in nothing but hatred, and the expression of hatred. They hate God, and Christ, and angels, and saints in heaven, and not only so, but they hate one another, like a company of serpents or vipers, not only spitting out venom against God, but at one another, biting and stinging and tormenting each other.

The devils in hell will hate damned souls. They hated them while in this world, and therefore it was, that with such subtilty and indefatigable temptations they sought their ruin. They thirsted for the blood of their souls, because they hated them; they longed to get them in their power to torment them; they watched them as a roaring lion does his prey; because they hated them, therefore they flew upon their souls, like hell-hounds, as soon as ever they were parted from their bodies, full of eagerness to torment them. And now they have them in their power, they will spend eternity in tormenting them with the utmost strength and cruelty that devils are capable of. They are, as it were, continually and eternally tearing these poor damned souls that are in their hands. And these latter will not only be hated and tormented by devils, but they will have no love or pity one towards another, but will be like devils one to another, and will to their utmost torment each other, being like brands in the fire, each of which helps to burn the others.

In hell all those principles will reign and rage that are contrary to love, without any restraining grace to keep them within bounds. Here will be unrestrained pride, and malice, and envy, and revenge, and contention in all its fury and without end, never knowing peace. The miserable inhabitants will bite and devour one another, as well as be enemies to God and Christ and holy beings. Those who in their wickedness on earth were companions together, and had a sort of carnal friendship one for another, will here have no appearance of fellowship; but perfect and continual and undisguised hatred will exist between them. As on earth they promoted each other's sin, so now in hell they will promote each other's punishment. On earth they were the instruments of undoing each other's souls: there they were occupied in blowing up the fires of each other's lusts, and now they will blow forever the fires of each other's torments. They ruined one another in sinning, setting bad examples to each other, poisoning each other by wicked talk, and now they will be as much engaged in tormenting, as once they were in tempting and corrupting each other.

And there their hatred, and envy, and all evil passions will be a torment to themselves. God and Christ whom they will hate most, and toward whom their souls will be as full of hatred as an oven is ever full of fire, will be infinitely above their reach, dwelling in infinite blessedness and glory which they cannot diminish. And they will but torment themselves by their fruitless envy of the saints and angels in heaven, whom they cannot come nigh to or injure. And they shall have no pity from them or from any one, for hell is looked on only with hatred, and with no pity or compassion. And thus they will be left to spend their eternity together.

Now consider, all ye that are out of Christ, and that were never born again, and that never had any blessed renovation of your hearts by the Holy Spirit implanting divine love in them, and leading you to choose the happiness that consists in holy love as your best and sweetest good, and to spend your life in struggling after holiness,—consider your danger, and what is before you. For this is the world to which ye are condemned; and so the world to which you belong through the sentence of the law; and the world that every day and hour you are in danger of having your abode everlastingly fixed in; and the world to which, if you repent not, you will soon go, instead of going to that blessed world of love of which you have now heard. Consider, O! consider, that it is indeed thus with you. These things are not cunningly-devised fables, but the great and dreadful realities of God's word, and things that, in a little while, you will know with everlasting certainty are true. How then can you rest in such a state as you are in, and go about so carelessly from day to day, and so heedless and negligent of your precious, immortal souls? Consider seriously these things, and be wise for yourself, before it is too late; before your feet stumble on the dark mountains, and you fall into the world of wrath and hatred, where there is weeping, and wailing, and gnashing of teeth, with spiteful malice and rage against God, and Christ, and one another, and with horror and anguish of spirit forever. Flee to the stronghold while ye are prisoners of hope, before the door of hope is closed, and the agonies of the second death shall begin their work, and your eternal doom is sealed!

4. *Let the consideration of what has been said of heaven, stir up all earnestly to seek after it.*—If heaven be such a blessed world, then let it be our chosen country, and the inheritance that we look for and seek. Let us turn our course this way, and press on to its possession. It is not impossible but that this glorious world may be obtained by us. It is offered to us. Though it be so excellent and blessed a country, yet God stands ready to give us an inheritance there, if it be but the country that we desire, and will choose, and diligently seek. God gives us our choice. We may have our inheritance wherever we

choose it, and may obtain heaven if we will but seek it by patient continuance in well-doing. We are all of us, as it were, set here in this world as in a vast wilderness, with diverse countries about it, and with several ways or paths leading to these different countries, and we are left to our choice what course we will take. If we heartily choose heaven, and set our hearts entirely on that blessed Canaan —that land of love, and if we choose and love the path that leads to it, we may walk in that path, and if we continue to walk in it, it will lead us to heaven at least.

Let what we have heard of the land of love, stir us all up to turn our faces toward it, and bend our course thitherward. Is not what we have heard of the happy state of that country, and the many delights that are in it, enough to make us thirst after it, and to cause us with the greatest earnestness and steadfastness of resolution, to press towards it, and spend our whole lives in travelling in the way that leads thither? What joyful news might it well be to us when we hear of such a world of perfect peace and holy love, and to hear that it is possible, yea, that there is full opportunity for us to come to it, and spend an eternity in its joys! Is not what we have heard of that blessed world, enough to make us weary of this world of pride, and malice, and contention, and perpetual jarring and jangling, a world of confusion, a wilderness of hissing serpents, a tempestuous ocean where there is no quiet rest, where all are for themselves, and selfishness reigns and governs, and all are striving to exalt themselves regardless of what becomes of others, and all are eager after worldly good which is the great object of desire and contention, and where men are continually annoying, and calumniating, and reproaching, and otherwise injuring and abusing one another—a world full of injustice, and oppression, and cruelty,—a world where there is so much treachery, and falsehood, and fickleness, and hypocrisy, and suffering, and death—where there is so little confidence in mankind, and every good man has so many failings, and has so much to render him unlovely and uncomfortable, and where there is so much of sorrow, and guilt, and sin in every form?

Truly this is an evil world, and so it is like to be. It is in vain for us to expect that it will be any other than a world of sin, a world of pride, and enmity, and strife, and so a restless world. And though the times may hereafter be mended, yet these things will always be more or less found in the world so long as it stands. Who, then, would content himself with a portion in such a world? What man acting wisely and considerately, would concern himself much about laying up in store in such a world as this, and would not rather neglect the world, and let it go to them that would take it, and apply all his heart and strength to lay up treasure in heaven, and to press on to that world of love? What will it signify for us to hoard up great possessions in this world, and how can the thought of having our portion here be pleasing to us, when there is an interest offered us in such a glorious world as heaven is, and especially when if we have our portion here, we must, when the world has passed away, have our eternal portion in hell, that world of hatred, and of the endless wrath of God, where only devils and damned spirits dwell.

We all naturally desire rest and quietness, and if we would obtain it, let us seek that world of peace and love of which we have now heard, where a sweet and blessed rest remaineth for God's people. If we get an interest, in that world, then when we have done with this, we shall leave all our cares, and troubles, and fatigues, and perplexities, and disturbances forever. We shall rest from these storms that are raging here, and from every toil and labor, in the paradise of God. You that are poor, and think yourselves despised by your neighbors and little cared for among men, do not much concern yourselves for this. Do not care much for the friendship of the world; but seek heaven, where there is no such thing as contempt, and where none are despised, but all are highly esteemed and honored, and dearly beloved by all. You that think you have met with many abuses, and much ill-treatment from others, care not for it. Do not hate them for it, but set your heart on heaven, that world of love, and press toward that better country where all is kindness and holy affection. And here for direction how to seek heaven.

First, Let not your heart go after the things of this world, as your chief good. Indulge not yourself in the possession of earthly things, as though they were to satisfy your soul. This is the reverse of seeking heaven;

it is to go in a way contrary to that which leads to the world of love. If you would seek heaven, your affections must be taken off from the pleasures of the world. You must not allow yourself in sensuality, or worldliness, or the pursuit of the enjoyments or honors of the world, or occupy your thoughts or time in heaping up the dust of the earth. You must mortify the desires of vain glory, and become poor in spirit and lowly in heart.

Second, You must, in your meditations and holy exercises, be much engaged in conversing with heavenly persons, and objects, and enjoyments. You cannot constantly be seeking heaven, without having your thoughts much there. Turn, then, the stream of your thoughts and affections towards that world of love, and towards the God of love that dwells there, and toward the saints and angels that are at Christ's right hand. Let your thoughts, also, be much on the objects and enjoyments of the world of love. Commune much with God and Christ in prayer, and think often of all that is in heaven, of the friends who are there, and the praises and worship there, and of all that will make up the blessedness of that world of love. "Let your conversation be in heaven."

Third, Be content to pass through all difficulties in the way to heaven. Though the path is before you, and you may walk in it if you desire, yet it is a way that is ascending, and filled with many difficulties and obstacles. That glorious city of light and love is, as it were, on the top of a high hill or mountain, and there is no way to it but by upward and arduous steps. But though the ascent be difficult, and the way full of trials, still it is worth your while to meet them all for the sake of coming and dwelling in such a glorious city at last. Be willing, then, to undergo the labor, and meet the toil, and overcome the difficulty. What is it all in comparison with the sweet rest that is at your journey's end? Be willing to cross the natural inclination of flesh and blood, which is downward, and press onward and upward to the prize. At every step it will be easier and easier to ascend; and the higher your ascent, the more will you be cheered by the glorious prospect before you, and by a nearer view of that heavenly city where in a little while you shall forever be at rest.

Fourth, In all your way let your eye be fixed on Jesus, who has gone to heaven as your forerunner. Look to him. Behold his glory in heaven, that a sight of it may stir you up the more earnestly to desire to be there. Look to him in his example. Consider how by patient continuance in well-doing, and by patient endurance of great suffering, he went before you to heaven. Look to him as your mediator, and trust in the atonement which he has made, entering into the holiest of all in the upper temple. Look to him as your intercessor, who forever pleads for you before the throne of God. Look to him as your strength, that by his Spirit he may enable you to press on, and overcome every difficulty of the way. Trust in his promises of heaven to those that love and follow him, which he has confirmed by entering into heaven as the head, and representative, and Saviour of his people. And,

Fifth, If you would be in the way to the world of love, see that you live a life of love; of love to God, and love to men. All of us hope to have part in the world of love hereafter, and therefore we should cherish the spirit of love, and live a life of holy love here on earth. This is the way to be like the inhabitants of heaven, who are now confirmed in love forever. Only in this way can you be like them in excellence and loveliness, and like them, too, in happiness, and rest, and joy. By living in love in this world you may be like them, too, in sweet and holy peace, and thus have, on earth, the foretastes of heavenly pleasures and delights. Thus, also, you may have a sense of the glory of heavenly things, as of God, and Christ, and holiness; and your heart be disposed and opened by holy love to God, and by the spirit of peace and love to men, to a sense of the excellence and sweetness of all that is to be found in heaven. Thus shall the windows of heaven be, as it were, opened, so that its glorious light shall shine in upon your soul. Thus you may have the evidence of your fitness for that blessed world, and that you are actually on the way to its possession. And being thus made meet, through grace, for the inheritance of the saints in light, when a few more days shall have passed away, you shall be with them in their blessedness forever. Happy, thrice happy those, who shall thus be found faithful to the end, and then shall be welcomed to the joy of their Lord! There they shall hunger no more, neither thirst any more; neither shall the sun light on them, nor any heat, for the Lamb which is in the midst of the throne, shall feed them, and lead them to fountains of living waters, and God shall wipe away all tears from their eyes!

THE END.

www.ingramcontent.com/pod-product-compliance
Lightning Source LLC
Chambersburg PA
CBHW031944290426
44108CB00011B/668